Praise for *View*

"*View from the Top* is the best advice from the top advisors. Written by world-class HR chiefs, academics, consultants, and recruiters, this book is the most comprehensive body of work out there today. Every chapter is chock full of ideas and wisdom that remind us that the only way to win is through people. The HR game is the talent game."

—PETER FASOLO, PH.D., EXECUTIVE VICE PRESIDENT AND CHRO, JOHNSON & JOHNSON

"My experience has taught me that people are unique and so too are organizations. There is no one-size-fits-all for HR, but there are HCM approaches that best enable your company's strategies. This book contains great insights from many of the top thinkers and leaders in HR—there is something in here for every business and HR leader looking to enhance the people side of their business impact."

—DERMOT O'BRIEN, CORPORATE VICE PRESIDENT AND CHIEF HUMAN RESOURCES
    OFFICER, ADP

"It's easy to get caught up in the narrative that we see in business magazines—that HR doesn't have the skills or structure to contribute positively to today's organizations. *View from the Top* shatters that narrative with multiple tangible examples of HR creating tremendous shareholder and social value. From Mara Swan's challenge to rethink the leaky leadership pipeline of women, to SunTrust's exciting insight about the power of execution to drive high performance, to Ed Lawler's vision of CHROs as 'chief organizational effectiveness officers,' *View from the Top* gives current and future HR and business leaders plenty of proven models to adopt within their own organizations."

—MELANIE L. STEINBACH, CHRO, MILLIKEN & COMPANY

"This is a distinctive and unusual book. It is distinctive because it features both organizational and human capital models and because it integrates these models to show how they collectively drive value creation. It is unusual because the models it offers are grounded in both research and practice, which in turn is the result of drawing on the contributions of leading human resource management researchers and chief human resource officers of leading companies. For these reasons, the book merits and will no doubt achieve a wide reading audience. It is quite likely to become the leading volume of its type."

—DAVID LEWIN, NEIL H. JACOBY PROFESSOR OF MANAGEMENT, HUMAN RESOURCES AND
    ORGANIZATIONAL BEHAVIOR, UCLA ANDERSON SCHOOL OF MANAGEMENT

View from the Top

**Edited by Patrick M. Wright, Dave Ulrich,
Richard L. Antoine and Elizabeth "Libby" Sartain**

View
from the
Top

Leveraging Human and
Organization Capital to Create Value

Society for Human Resource Management
Alexandria, VA | shrm.org

Society for Human Resource Management, India Office
Mumbai, India | shrmindia.org

Society for Human Resource Management
Haidian District Beijing, China | shrm.org/cn

Society for Human Resource Management, Middle East and Africa Office
Dubai, UAE | shrm.org/pages/mena.aspx

The Society for Human Resource Management (SHRM) is the world's largest HR professional society, representing 285,000 members in more than 165 countries. For nearly seven decades, the Society has been the leading provider of resources serving the needs of HR professionals and advancing the practice of human resource management. SHRM has more than 575 affiliated chapters within the United States and subsidiary offices in China, India and United Arab Emirates. Visit us at shrm.org.

Interior and Cover Design: Shirley E.M. Raybuck

Library of Congress Cataloging-in-Publication Data
[on file]

16-0226

Part VII:

Foreword

Henry G. "Hank" Jackson

At the Society for Human Resource Management (SHRM), the world's largest HR professional association, we are fortunate to hear from hundreds of individuals committed to the practice of HR—from students to those who lead HR strategy in the largest corporations around the world. Their challenges and triumphs inspire our work every day. In my role, I am also able to connect with other CEOs and business leaders about their perspectives on HR and what's needed in business today. Looking over the HR horizon, I see a growing, dynamic profession whose value to organizations has made us the business leaders.

Ever-evolving business trends have propelled the HR function to the forefront of business strategy. Technological developments, globalization and increasing diversity are but a few of the multiple and sometimes competing trends that are transforming the workforce and the workplace. Moreover, the speed of this change is all but forcing organizations to be highly adaptable and competitive. The key to meeting this challenge is having an engaged, productive and talented team, *making human capital the differentiator in business today*.

It's a pivotal moment in the history of the HR profession when most business leaders now understand what we have known all along: Great HR makes great organizations. At SHRM, we are urging our members to seize this unique opportunity and develop themselves to meet and exceed the higher demands of HR today—and certainly tomorrow.

In the pages that follow, leading HR executives and thinkers join us in this rallying call. *View from the Top* lays out not only *why* HR must focus on delivering the greatest value to organizations but *how* we can do so. It is a blueprint for HR professionals to assume their rightful place in business leadership and impact the bottom line of their organizations.

We are living in what I call the Decade of Human Capital—a time when effective human resource management has become the most critical contributor to the strategic direction of organizations. As Patrick, Dave, Richard and Libby conclude: "Opportunity knocks," and HR must answer. In *View from the Top*, we now have the definitive guide to this process.

Henry G. "Hank" Jackson is president and CEO of SHRM.

Introduction: Human Capital, Organizational Capability, and Competitive Success

Patrick M. Wright, Dave Ulrich,
Richard L. Antoine, and Elizabeth "Libby" Sartain

The past decade has seen an upsurge in interest in how companies manage their human capital competitively. One does not have to look far to find papers, podcasts, white papers, or books arguing for the criticality of a firm's people as part of any firm's competitive success. Since McKinsey's *War for Talent,* followed by Jack Welch's *Winning* book, the centrality of a firm's talent in competitive advantage has become accepted, if not assumed. Given this state, one wonders what is left to say about the topic that has not already been said.

In spite of this increasing interest, easy answers seem to elude those searching for them. The purpose of this book is not to provide easy answers, but to present readers with ideas, frameworks, and examples of how firms can leverage their human capital to create value for shareholders, customers, and even the human capital themselves, employees.

Each year the Center for Executive Succession at the Darla Moore School of Business, University of South Carolina, conducts the HR@Moore Survey of Chief HR Officers, surveying almost 600 chief human resource officers (CHROs) at *Fortune* 500 and private-equity owned firms. Every year the question "What are the top two to three deliverables that the CEO expects of HR?" produces "talent" as the overwhelmingly most popular response, usually with upward of 90 percent of respondents mentioning it. Because the CHRO leads the HR function, that individual must ensure that the proper processes exist to deliver against that requirement. How he or she does so is the topic of this book.

The term "talent" has as many meanings as there are people asking for it. At one level, talent refers to any of the firm's human capital that are critical to the firm's success. This may be research and development scientists working on developing the breakthrough drug that will position a firm for the next 10 years, the front-line employee delivering service in the moment to a customer to make certain that the customer returns tomorrow, or the administrative assistant who ensures the efficiency and organization of his or her executive leader. At another level, talent refers to the high-potential managers and executives who will one day become the C-suite executives with responsibility for managing in a competitive environment we cannot begin to predict right now. Finally, talent may refer to the current business leaders tasked with navigating the current competitive landscape and making the decisions regarding how to position the firm. Thus, rather than confuse readers by using the term "talent," we have chosen to focus on human capital. In essence, we believe that successful firms leverage more than just their talent. The most successful firms manage their entire workforces, or their pool of human capital, better than their competitors.

Whatever the specific group of focus, what has become increasingly clear is that treating talent as individuals misses the greater potential that comes from viewing talent as a group that, when working collectively, underlies a firm's capability. Individuals seldom maximally contribute to a firm as individuals. Rather, when working alongside others with whom they share attitudes, beliefs, and values, they become part of a synergistic system having the potential to achieve things the sum of the individuals alone never could. Enter the concept of organizational capability, which is embodied in a firm's culture. Culture serves as the mechanism through which a number of individuals can more cohesively and smoothly coordinate their behaviors in ways that create the organizational capabilities on which firms compete.

Thus, firms must seek to attract, select, develop, motivate, and retain individuals, each of whom possesses the autonomous will to choose to join and contribute, or to free ride and ultimately leave. This means that part of the challenge in managing human capital takes place at the level of the individuals. Individuals take employment tests. Individuals have their performance evaluated. Individuals receive paychecks. Individual executives such as CEOs or CHROs must be replaced by other individuals who the firm hopes perform as well or better than the previous role occupant. Consequently, organizations must design and deliver HR systems that build the human capital of the firm through decisions made with regard to individuals. Organizations do not think; people do.

But organizations shape how people think and act. Individuals work within the larger social system of the firm, surrounded by peers, working for superiors, and often communicating across multiple organizational boundaries. Their skills may be accentuated when surrounded by others with aligned skills, beliefs, and values. On the other hand, even an individual with tremendously superior skills may underperform when surrounded by others whose skills, beliefs, and values do not align. This creates a second challenge for firms to simultaneously manage the social system and to recognize the need to view the collective human capital pool. By focusing on building strong cultures firms can best align the collective behavior of diverse individuals toward the achievement of the company's objectives. Just like talent, or human capital, can be defined, assessed, and developed, so can an organization's culture.

This book provides this multilevel approach to exploring how firms can create value through their human capital. Some of the essays focus on individuals such as CHROs or CEOs, whereas others take a more collective approach, such as the entire workforce or the HR function.

Outline of the Book

We begin with a set of essays regarding the changing requirement of the HR function. Dave Ulrich of the University of Michigan discusses the need for HR functions to have a new perspective in terms of the problems that HR solves, with a focus on the outcomes that HR contributes to firm success and on calling for HR to invest in building its own capability to be able to do so successfully. Ed Lawler of the University of Southern California then contrasts the traditional HR role with that of an executive team member and calls for HR to step out of the former and into the latter. Finally, Jim Duffy, CHRO at Ally, traces some of the trends that have caused HR to evolve and calls for four responses that can better position HR to positively contribute to firm success.

Given the changing nature of the HR function, certainly the CHRO role has changed as well, and the next section examines the new CHRO role. Marcia J. Avedon, CHRO at Ingersoll Rand, begins this section with a multilevel examination of the impact of CHROs. She notes that they tend to focus on the individual, team, and organizational levels of impact, but that in the future they will need to also address their impact on societies. Dick Antoine, former CHRO at Procter & Gamble, follows this with a model of the eight competencies needed to function effectively in the CHRO role. Finally, Wayne Brockbank of the University of Michigan provides a provocative questioning of the usual priorities of CHROs, arguing that these result only in good results. He calls for a new set of priorities that can better lead to *great* results.

The book then moves away from HR and toward the larger organization by exploring the new levers for competitive success. Ken Carrig, CHRO of SunTrust, Scott Snell of the University of Virginia, and Aki Onozuka-Evans of AOSIS Consulting argue for the critical need for firms to effectively execute their strategies and provide a model for facilitating it. Elizabeth "Libby" Sartain, former CHRO at Southwest Airlines and Yahoo, then explores the importance of culture and how it can be effectively managed. Mike D'Ambrose, CHRO at Archer Daniels Midland, questions the basic "control"-oriented paradigm firms use to manage their workforces and shows how an alternative—trusting people—can lead to competitive success. Finally, Eva Sage-Gavin, former CHRO at Gap, describes how building social capital, particularly through impacting societies, will be the foundation of future capability.

Having presented models of the new levers, the next section provides real organizational examples of how these levers have been implemented. Matt Schuyler, CHRO of Hilton, begins with an exploration of how Hilton created value by building a great environment, great careers, great rewards, and a higher purpose. Judy Zagorski, CHRO at BASF, describes the change driven at BASF that enabled it to grow financially and to be recognized as a "Best Company to Work For." Finally, Gina Qiao, CHRO at Lenovo, also describes a change process, but with a particular focus on taking a traditional Chinese company and transforming it to become a true multinational one.

The focus then turns to talent. Rich Floersch, CHRO at McDonald's, shares his perspective and experience on the relatively greater importance of talent over strategy. Former Accenture CHRO Jill B. Smart and Debra

Exstrom of Accenture discuss the necessity of effectively managing the supply chain of talent, and describe how Accenture built its talent supply chain. Mara Swan, CHRO at ManpowerGroup, highlights how leaky pipelines of female talent can cause firms to miss tremendous talent opportunities. Joe Ruocco, former CHRO at Goodyear, describes how the company transformed its approach to talent management to drive financial success. Finally, Rob Ployhart and Anthony Nyberg of the University of South Carolina review rigorous empirical data that show the links between talent and organizational performance.

Having explored talent at a firm level, the next section more narrowly focuses on managing talent in the C-suite. Sue Suver, CHRO at Delphi Automotive, begins by describing the risks inherent in CEO succession, and provides strategies for mitigating those risks. Patrick Wright, Donald Schepker, Anthony Nyberg, and Mike Ulrich of the University of South Carolina report the results of the HR@Moore Survey of CHROs regarding the assessment practices used to gain information on CEO successor candidates. Finally, Michelle "Shelly" Carlin, former CHRO at Motorola Solutions, argues against the idea of best practices in executive compensation as advocated by a number of proxy advisory firms, and instead suggests that incentive design be based on the unique situations in which each firm finds itself.

Finally, as CHROs play a central role in all the issues previously discussed, it seems fitting to examine what prepares them to succeed. Mirian Graddick-Weir, CHRO of Merck, weaves CHRO survey data with her own experience and insight to challenge CHROs to be more proactive and effective in developing their own successors. Debra J. Cohen, formerly of the Society for Human Resource Management (SHRM), then describes the competencies central to HR and suggests that courage has emerged as the most important one for CHROs. Finally, Jim Bagley of Russell Reynolds reports his firm's research on what makes for a successful CHRO.

Summary

This book consists of a current, comprehensive, and coherent set of perspectives on how firms create value through their human capital which includes both individual talent and organizational capabilities It combines academic research with practitioner insights to provide a set of tools, frameworks, and perspectives that can lead to innovative strategies for managing people in ways that create value for employees, customers, and investors. We hope that the content you discover here will lead to success for you and your organization.

PART 1

NEW DEMANDS FOR HR

Chapter 1.
HR PODcast: Perspective, Outcomes, and Determinants

Dave Ulrich

Podcasts broadcast insights on a wide range of topics. I propose an HR PODcast focused on how HR leaders can respond to increased expectations. The bar has been raised on HR: *The Conference Board CEO Challenge 2014* survey found that human capital issues are the number one challenge around the globe.[1] The leadership profile of successful CEOs matches the leadership profile of effective CHROs.[2] HR issues are increasingly a part of firm valuation by thoughtful investors.[3] Estimates are that about one-third of the issues discussed at board level are related to HR (for example, succession planning, talent review, executive compensation, governance, strategy execution, ethics, and culture). In brief, HR leaders now have more opportunity than ever to influence business success. HR professionals no longer need to get "a seat at the table" but to demonstrate real value when they are there. To deliver this value, I propose a forward-thinking Perspective, Outcomes, and Determinants (PODcast) for senior HR leaders.

Perspective: What Challenges Does HR Solve?

I begin most discussions with senior HR professionals with a version of the question, "What are the greatest challenges you face in your job to-day?" The answer to this question not only gives insight into the predisposition of the respondent but lays out an evolution of the HR profession. There are generally four types of responses that capture perspective on the challenges HR faces.

- Phase 1 emphasizes administrative efficiency focusing on the operational efficiency of HR practices (for example, cost per employee hire).
- Phase 2 highlights functional excellence in which HR's challenge is to manage people, performance, information, or work. In this phase, HR focuses on innovation and integration of HR services with an emphasis on HR best practices and new ideas.
- Phase 3 features strategic HR work in which the HR practices align with business strategy. Depending on the organization's strategic goals (for example, innovation, customer service, or geographic expansion), HR practices can be used to deliver those strategies.
- Phase 4 shifts to an outside-in focus in that HR practices align with customers, investors, and other external community stakeholders. Outside-in HR is based on the premise that the business of HR *is the business*. Outside-in logic goes beyond the current state of the HR profession, in which the focus is on connecting strategy to HR. We now believe that business strategy, often seen as a mirror in which HR practices are reflected, should be regarded as a window through which HR professionals observe, interpret, and translate external conditions and stakeholder expectations into internal actions.

FIGURE 1.1. EVOLUTION OF HR WORK IN WAVES

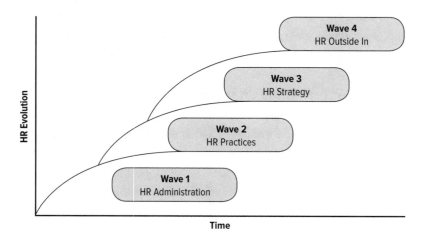

Perspective means that HR professionals have evolved their thinking about how HR delivers value (captured in Figure 1.1). As HR has shifted from administrative to functional, to strategy, and to outside-in thinking, the perspective has evolved to one of value created through serving key external stakeholders and responding to business conditions of change. With their business focus, HR professionals can accurately converse about customers, products, operations, and financials, but also help create the right type of organization that sustains market value.

Outcomes: What Unique Value Does HR Contribute to Business Results?

With an outside-in perspective, HR professionals offer unique information, insights, and recommendations to deliver competitive advantage. In formal and informal business discussions, each staff group brings its own insights to drive business results: Finance talks about economic performance with information about revenues, costs, and financial returns; marketing discusses customers with recommendations on targeting key customers, customer response (for example, net promoter score), and customer connection; operations makes recommendations about systems, quality, and supply chain. When HR professionals partner in these strategy discussions, we propose that they provide insight, information, and recommendations on talent (people, workforce, human capital), capability (culture, processes, key success factors, systems), and leadership.

Talent

At the risk of grossly oversimplifying, let me suggest that there is actually a deceptively simple formula for talent that makes people more productive: Talent = Competence x Commitment x Contribution. All three elements of this equation need to be considered and integrated to fully manage talent.

Competence means that individuals have the knowledge, skills, and values required for today's and tomorrow's jobs. One company clarified competence as *right skills, right place, right job, right time.* For example, an emerging trend in the workforce planning domain of competence improvement is to identify key positions and match people to positions. Competence should start outside-in by turning customer expectations into the talent requirements for the future.

Committed or engaged employees work hard and do what they are asked to do, but may be doing the wrong things. By contrast, committed employees with an outside-in focus direct their attention to work and activities that will deliver value to customers, investors, and communities. Committed employees have an employee value proposition that balances what employees give to the firm with what they get back. Dozens of engagement studies have shown that more committed employees are more productive.

Contribution refers less to behavioral engagement and more to emotional connection to the organization. When employees find meaning (sometimes called well-being or growth mindset), they become personally connected to the values of the organization. Their engagement comes from within and endures over time.

In business conversations, HR professionals focused on talent outcomes can raise questions such as:

- To what extent do our employees have the knowledge and skills required to deliver on our expectations for customers, investors, and communities?
- To what extent do we have an employee value proposition that increases commitment and engagement of our employees to the right goals?
- To what extent do our employees find meaning and purpose from their work so that they are self-motivated to accomplish work?

Capability

In the last 15 to 20 years, the HR profession has been shaped by remarkable work captured in the "war for talent."[4] Many HR professionals have built systems for bringing people into the organization (sourcing, having a value proposition), moving them through the organization (development, performance management, engagement), and removing them from the organization (outsourcing).[5]

But in today's business, HR professionals need to establish organizations that leverage individual talent through collective actions. Talent is not enough. The whole organization should be greater than the separate parts. United states are stronger than individual states. Teams outperform individuals. Individuals are champions, but teams win championships. The following simple statistics show the importance of teamwork over talent:

- In hockey, the leading scorer is on the team that wins the Stanley Cup 22 percent of the time.
- In soccer, the winner of the Golden Boot (leading scorer) is on the team that wins with World Cup 20 percent of the time.
- In basketball, the player who scores the most points is on the team that wins the NBA finals 15 percent of the time.
- In movies, the Best Picture winner also has the leading actor (25 percent of the time) and actress (15 percent of the time).

Let me propose a three-step process (summarized in Table 1.1) for HR professionals to bring discipline to moving from the war for talent to creating victory through organization.[6]

First, organizational capabilities represent what the organization is known for, what it is good at doing, and how it allocates resources to win in its market. Organizations should be defined less by their structure and more by their ability to establish the capabilities required to win—that is, to serve customers in ways that competitors cannot readily copy. Organizational capabilities might include the ability to respond to or serve customers, drive efficiency, manage change, collaborate both inside and outside, innovate on products and on the business model, access information, and establish the right culture. HR professionals can facilitate capability audits to determine if the organization has prioritized the right capabilities to win.[7]

Second, culture represents the pattern of how people think and act in the organization. Although organizations can have many capabilities, culture is likely to be the key for future success. The right culture takes what the organization should be known for by major customers and uses this external identity to shape internal thought and action. HR professionals can audit the extent to which an organization has the right culture.

Third, management actions can be identified and implemented to create and sustain the desired culture. My colleagues and I have clas-

TABLE 1.1. THREE DIMENSIONS OF COMPETITIVE ORGANIZATION: CAPABILITY, CULTURE, MANAGEMENT ACTION

Summary Logic	Key Question and Focus	Previous Research
Capability ⬇	What is the organization good at doing and what should it be known for? Competitive differentiators.	Resources Strategic capabilities Core competencies
Culture ⬇	How do we shape the right patterns that will enable us to win? How the organization works: Event, pattern, identity.	Competing values Organization types Organization health
Management action 1: Intellectual agenda	Create a clear message about the desired culture to share inside and outside.	Shared mindset Values
Management action 2: Behavioral agenda	Turn culture identity into employee actions.	Climate
Management action 3: Process agenda	Create, shape, and reinforce culture through management practices.	Systems • 7s • STAR • High-performing work system Organization Processes

sified these actions into intellectual, behavioral, and process agendas. Intellectual agendas ensure that managers create a shared culture inside and outside the organization. Behavioral agendas show the extent to which all employees behave consistently with the desired culture, and process agendas institutionalize the culture through management practices.

In business dialogues, HR professionals can be the architects (defining the logic and blueprint) and anthropologists (interpreting the right pattern) of capability by raising the following questions:

Audits That Can Be Done	Analogue with Individual
Capability audit: • What do we have to be known for and good at to win? This should be tightly linked to strategy. • Measure the extent to which priorities are shared about capabilities required to win.	What is my personality? We each have a personality that can be dissected into five core personality traits based on what comes naturally to us.
Cultural audit: • Do we have the right patterns for thinking and behaving? • Measure the clarity and accuracy of the culture.	What habits define my lifestyle and identity? We each have habits or routines that determine who we are.
Unity audit: • Do we have a shared culture? • Do we make recognize implicit our assumptions? • Measure unity of culture and clarity of assumptions.	What are my thought patterns (schema)?
Behavioral audit: • Do employee behaviors link to the culture? • Measure behavior alignment and change.	What are my daily actions? (calendar test)
Process or system audit: • Do we have processes that reinforce and embed the culture? • Measure process alignment and change.	How do my emotions shape my experience and sustain my desired routines?

- To what extent have we defined our culture from the outside in, making sure that our external firm brand becomes the basis for our internal ways of thinking and acting?
- To what extent have we created a disciplined process of evaluating and transforming our culture?

Leadership

Ultimately, leaders bring together both individuals and organizations to solve customer problems. But there is a difference between leaders and leadership. The term "leaders" refers to individuals who are able to effectively guide the behavior of others. "Leadership" refers to an organization's capacity to build future leaders. An individual leader matters, but an organization's collective leadership matters more over time. Looking forward, HR professionals will not only need to help individual leaders be more effective through coaching, 360-degree feedback, and individual development plans, but they will also need to build leadership depth.

The outcomes of effective leadership include employee engagement and organizational goal achievement, as well as shareholder (debt or equity) confidence. I have proposed a leadership capital ratings index (like the Moody's creditworthiness index) that could be used to define effective leadership.[8] This index would have two dimensions, or domains: individual and organizational. Individual refers to the personal qualities (competencies, traits, characteristics) of the key leaders in the organization. Organization refers to the systems (often called human capital) that these leaders create to manage leadership throughout the organization and the application of organizational systems to specific business conditions. Using these two domains, previous leadership and human capital work may be synthesized into a leadership capital index that investors and others can use to inform their valuation decisions and HR professionals to enhance their impact.

Five leadership factors define the individual domain of a leadership ratings index that covers half of leadership capital.

1. *Personal proficiency.* To what extent does the leadership demonstrate the personal qualities required of an effective leader?
2. *Strategist.* To what extent does the leadership articulate a point of view about the future and strategic positioning?
3. *Executor.* To what extent does the leadership make things happen and deliver as promised?
4. *People manager.* To what extent does the leadership build competence, commitment, and contribution of the organization's people today and tomorrow?
5. *Leadership differentiator.* To what extent does leadership behave consistently with customer expectations?

Leadership capital includes not only personal or individual leadership traits but also investments made to build future leaders within the organization. To build future leaders, leaders create organizational cultures and invest in HR practices (often called human capital) in five domains:

1. *Culture capability:* To what extent has the leadership created a customer-focused cultural capability that is shared throughout the organization?
2. *Talent:* To what extent has the leadership invested in practices that manage the flow of talent into, through, and out of the organization?
3. *Performance accountability:* To what extent has the leadership created performance management practices (for example, compensation) that reinforce the right behaviors?
4. *Information:* To what extent has the leadership managed information flow to gain information asymmetries (which means that an organization has unique information that competitors may not have)?
5. *Work:* To what extent has the leadership created organizational and work practices that deal with the increasing pace of change in today's business settings?

By using a leadership capital index, the requirements of effective leaders could be defined and clarified from the outside in.

In business settings, HR professionals may prod a discussion of the right leadership with questions such as:

- To what extent do we recognize the importance of collective leadership in reaching our goals?
- To what extent do we create a leadership brand that defines how leaders inside our company better serve external stakeholders?
- To what extent do we regularly assess our leadership capability to discover areas of strengths and weakness?
- To what extent do we seriously invest in developing future leaders who will respond to future business requirements?

Determinants: How Can HR Invest in HR?

HR for HR means that HR professionals apply to their own function the knowledge and tools they apply to their organizations. This means building the right HR organization by making sure that the HR department aligns with the business organization. It also means designing the right HR practices to offer business solutions. And it means investing in the HR professionals to ensure that they respond to future opportunities.

The governance of the HR function should match how the business is governed. All organizational design choices can be arrayed into a centralized (efficient) versus decentralized (effective) grid. Highly centralized governance describes single businesses with a strong corporate agenda; highly decentralized governance describes holding companies with autonomous and independent operating units; diversified allied governance attempts to manage both through multidivisional firms governed through matrices of shared decision-making. The HR organization should match the business structure. Centralized businesses require functionally driven specialists (staffing, training, compensation, organization development). Decentralized businesses dedicate these functional specialists to each business. Diversified-allied organizations share knowledge through centers of expertise and embedded HR generalists.

HR practices should provide integrated solutions of individual HR practices focused on business results. For example, a firm seeking to compete through innovation will align staffing, training, compensation, organizational design, and communication practices to foster innovation. However, a firm competing through efficiency, service, or global growth would use these similar HR practices in a different way depending on the business's strategic focus. With an outside-in perspective, these HR practices should also reflect expectations of customers, investors, and communities. HR should not build practices only to be the "employer of choice" but rather to be the employer of choice *of employees customers would choose.* Instead of training occurring just for individuals inside the organization, customers could participate in the design, delivery, and attendance in the training activities.

HR professionals also need to up their game to deliver value in today's business settings. This means that HR professionals need to build relationships of trust with business leaders by being credible activists.

They also take strong positions to build business success. These HR professionals must both know the business and be able to strategically position the business. They must master the processes of individual and institutional change. They must be knowledgeable in the science and art of HR. And they must use information to inform decision-making. When they master this knowledge, skill, and ability, they can deliver the talent, leadership, and capability a business requires to compete in a changing world.

Conclusion

My POD (Perspective, Outcomes, Determinants) for HR is a positive affirmation of why and how HR will continue to deliver value. With an outside-in perspective, HR delivers clear talent, capability, and leadership outcomes by determined HR professionals with the right competencies.

The future is quite positive when HR leaders respond to the opportunities of this PODcast for HR.

Endnotes

1. *The Conference Board CEO Challenge 2014: People and Performance.* The Conference Board. http://www.ceochallenge.org.
2. Dave Ulrich and Ellie Filler. 2014. CEOs and CHROs: Crucial Allies and Potential Successors. Korn Ferry Institute. Also to be published in *Leader to Leader.*
3. Dave Ulrich. 2015. *Leadership Capital Index: Realizing the Market Value of Leadership.* Oakland, CA: Berrett-Koehler; and Laurie Bassi, David Creelman, and Andrew Lambert. *The Smarter Annual Report.* Prepared by Creelman Lambert and McBassi & Company. 2014.
4. Ed Michaels, Helen Handfield-Jones, and Beth Axelrod. 2001. *The War for Talent.* Boston, MA: Harvard Business School Press.
5. Justin Allen and Dave Ulrich. 2013. *Talent Accelerator: Secrets for Driving Business Growth in Asia.* Singapore: RBL Group and Ministry of Manpower.
6. Ulrich. 2015. *Leadership Capital Index.*
7. Dave Ulrich and Norm Smallwood. 2004. Capitalizing on Capabilities. *Harvard Business Review.* 119-128.
8. Ulrich. 2015. *Leadership Capital Index.*

Chapter 2.
Executive Team Member Needed

Edward E. Lawler III

First, the obvious: The world of business has changed dramatically since the "personnel" department became the HR department in the 1970s. Second, also obvious, is that change has not stopped. In fact it is occurring at an increasingly rapid rate that is likely to continue. Among the major drivers of change are the continued globalization of business, how the information technology revolution affected us with respect to big data, analytics, and communications, and the continued political upheavals that change the global landscape of business.

To survive, organizations have had to keep pace with the changes that have occurred. In the future they will have to keep up with an increasingly rapid rate of change to survive. Organizations will need to change the way they are structured and managed, the kind of talent they have, and how they deal with that talent. The decisions organizations make in these areas will profoundly affect their effectiveness and survival (Worley, Williams, and Lawler, 2014). This raises the key question: How do organizations need to be structured, staffed, and managed to be able to have the level of agility that will allow them to effectively respond to the rapidly changing environments that they will face?

An organization's talent and its effectiveness is key to its ability to successfully adapt to the changing environments it faces. Not changing the behavior of individuals and organizations is a nonstarter. Because of the importance of the talent, the structure and nature of the HR function and its leadership deserve special attention. They warrant examination with respect to their ability to support strategic change and organizational effectiveness. Organizations also need an individual who is a member of the senior management team who can contribute HR expertise to business strategy and organizational design decisions.

HR and Change

There is a considerable amount of evidence that despite many calls for change, HR has changed little over the last 30 or 40 years (Lawler and Boudreau, 2015). It is no longer the "personnel department"; instead it is typically called the human resource department and is headed by a chief human resource officer (CHRO). However, the name change does not mean that the function has changed. It continues to spend most of its time doing administrative work and has not become a major player in developing business strategies or implementing strategy or organizational designs and capability changes. There is also little change in the frequency with which the head of HR reports directly to the CEO; it remains slightly less than 60 percent of major U.S. corporations (Lawler and Boudreau, 2015). Apparently, HR does not often have "a seat at the table" even though, in many cases, it is "responsible" for principal corporate assets and can potentially help organizations respond more effectively to the rapidly changing and increasingly challenging business environments that they face.

There are a number of reasons why HR has not changed. Perhaps the most important is the demanding character of the administrative work HR does. To cite just one example, accurate pay checks need to go out on a timely basis and be correct, and when this does not happen, it becomes a number one priority. An additional reason is HR's reputation in many organizations as a largely transactional unit that does not relate to business objectives. Its reputation has influenced its ability to attract the best and the brightest talent. Overall, HR has had great difficulty moving on from its personnel administration days, in part because it still does many of the same things it did when it was the personnel department, despite the change of its name.

Should HR Be a Business Partner?

The term "business partner" is frequently used to identify what HR should be, but it is a poor fit for what HR should be in an organization. In a world in which talent is the key asset of many corporations and change is continuous, organizations need to constantly develop new strategies and re-design themselves. What organizations need is not a function that acts as a partner and has a "seat at the table," but one that helps design, influence, and implement an organization's business strategy. In other words, organizations need a business unit that has expertise in talent management and in a number of other organizational issues that are fundamental to the development of business strategy and its implementation. These other areas include organizational change, organizational design, and corporate board relations.

Central to creating the right kind of business unit is having an executive with the right knowledge of strategic organizational effectiveness at the senior level of management. This individual needs to be sure that discussions about business strategy are informed and guided by knowledge concerning organizational design, organizational development, and talent management.

To return to the earlier point about HR being at the table, it is clear that today "being at the table" is no longer enough. The person representing HR at the senior executive table needs to have more than just a seat at the table; he or she needs to be part of *setting* the table. The executive needs to bring to the table information about the existing talent in the organization, knowledge concerning the marketplace for talent, knowledge of how the organization should be designed to support different business strategies, what business strategies are feasible given the existing condition of the organization, what talent can be obtained in the market, and so on. In other words, HR professionals need to be able to point out the positives and negatives of different strategies from a human capital point of view. They need to be able to help their peers understand how human capital management and organizational design can influence the marketing, sales, finance, production, and research functions in corporations.

It is one thing to make the case that talent and organizational design issues should be front and center when strategic management decision-making takes place; it is quite another to create organizational designs and structures that support this decision process and support the implementation of the decisions made. Because most HR departments are focused on administration and operations, they are poorly positioned to develop and implement strategy-driven business decisions. As popular press magazine and newspaper articles have pointed out for decades, HR is designed and operates in a bureaucratic manner that does little to positively influence major business results and strategy implementation (see Table 2.1 for examples of criticism). A CEO I once worked with commented about his HR department, "The BPU (business prevention unit) tells you all the reasons why you can't do things and rarely suggests changes or practices that will help implement new strategies and changes." Although not explicitly stated, one reason is because most traditional HR functions do not have the capability to develop and contribute to new business strategies or to change efforts that are strategy driven.

TABLE 2.1. CRITICISM OF HR—A SAMPLING

- Skinner, Wickham. (1981). "Big Hat, No Cattle: Managing Human Resources." *Harvard Business Review*.
- Stewart, Thomas. (1996). "Taking on the Last Bureaucracy." *Fortune*.
    - » "Why not blow the sucker up? Improvements are for wimps. I mean abolish it. Deep-six it."
- Hammonds, Keith. (2005). "Why We Hate HR." *Fast Company*.
- Charan, Ram. (2014). "It's Time to Split HR." *Harvard Business Review*.

What Should Organizations Do?

It is obvious that talent management needs to have an administrative component to it. As a result of constant legal changes and societal demands concerning how human capital is treated by an organization, skilled administration and quick responses to talent management issues are important. Further, it is clear that organizations need to quickly take advantage of the new technology that exists so they can speed up the bureaucratic processes that they must go through. This also allows them to have better and more accurate data about what is happening to the employees in an organization and how they are being treated.

Making better use of information technology is not all that HR needs to do and can do to become an effective contributor to organizational performance. My research shows that the more time HR spends on strategy, the more effective it is, and the same is true with respect to change management (Lawler and Boudreau, 2015). Finally, the more HR integrates human capital strategy with business strat-

FIGURE 2.1. BUSINESS PARTNER

FIGURE 2.2. STRATEGIC CONTRIBUTOR

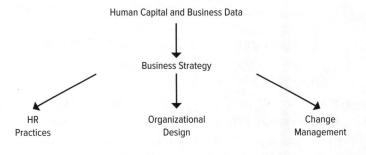

egy, the more effective HR is, and the more effective the organization is overall. This point brings us back to the earlier discussion of HR as a strategic contributor versus a business partner. As shown in Figure 2.1, the focus of a business partner is to help with the operation of an organization. What a business partner does not do, however, is influence the development of business strategy. For this to take place, someone with deep expertise in talent, organizational design, and change needs to participate at the executive level and add value when the business strategy is developed and implemented (see Figure 2.2). The chief organizational design question is whether this person should have only HR reporting to him or her or have a broader set of direct reports. A related question is: What type of background and expertise should this person have?

FIGURE 2.3. ORGANIZATION EFFECTIVENESS

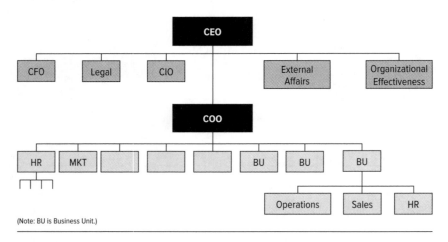

(Note: BU is Business Unit.)

Organizational Effectiveness Design

Figure 2.3 shows an approach to organizational design that positions HR, the HR function, and the CHRO as a key operating member of the organization but not part of the top management team. HR reports to the chief operating officer (COO), not to the CEO. Reporting to the CEO is the organizational effectiveness unit. The chief organizational effectiveness officer (COEO) functions at the executive level and is responsible for the development of the businesses strategy, talent management, sustainability, organizational development, organizational design, change management, and social responsibility. This position is expected to examine the management team's decision-making process and to relate to the CHRO on issues of talent management and other HR areas. Some CHROs currently do provide strategic organizational effectiveness expertise even though they are not identified as the COEO. Still, it may be worth identifying them as the COEO to establish the role in the executive team.

One way to think about the organizational effectiveness approach is that the CHRO has a dotted-line reporting relationship to the COEO, but a solid-line reporting relationship to the COO. This approach is designed to ensure that strategic organization and human capital information is considered when the top management team operates and makes key decisions. When a COO is absent in an organizational structure, the CHRO's reporting relationship should be to the COEO or the CEO.

Separating HR from organizational effectiveness has some parallels with respect to other business functions. Finance and accounting are separate, as are sales and marketing. Like traditional HR and organizational effectiveness, the first is transactional and the second is strategic.

It is one thing to create the position of COEO, but it is quite another to find individuals with the skills and knowledge that are needed to perform it well. Ideally, the person holding the job should have expertise in HR, organizational design, and business strategy and has spent significant time in a line management job. Individuals like this are rare, so on-the-job training may be required.

Conclusion

Overall, it is clearly time for change in what the HR function does and how it is organized and positioned within large organizations. The business world has changed in ways that make the traditional HR function model obsolete. There is a single new model that fits most corporations. Companies are likely to develop their own particular models because of the diversity that exists in the business world and the issues that human resource management should deal with vary so much. Some companies are already doing this. For example, they have adopted a version of the organizational effectiveness approach that is represented in Figure 2.3. Others have added more reporting relations to the CHRO, including sustainability and social responsibility.

Perhaps the best conclusion at this time is that the traditional HR model of a largely administrative unit does not provide the HR information and knowledge executive teams need to create and operate effective organizations. To be a major player in the effectiveness of organizations, HR executives need to develop new areas of expertise and provide strategic leadership in organizational effectiveness. If HR and its executives continue to do business as usual, organizations will look elsewhere for the support they need to effectively manage themselves and their talent.

References

Lawler, E. E., and Boudreau, J. W. (2015). *Global Trends in Human Resource Management: A Twenty-Year Analysis.* Palo Alto, CA: Stanford University Press.

Worley, C. G., Williams, T., and Lawler, E. E. (2014). *The Agility Factor: Building Adaptable Organizations for Superior Performance.* San Francisco, CA: Jossey-Bass.

Chapter 3.
The HR Leadership Paradox

James Duffy

This year marks the 42nd in which I have been involved in and with the "business of business" and the people who make it interesting, as either a student or a practitioner. The evolution of my work life, and, in parallel, that of what we now refer to as "human resources," has seen the metamorphosis from "personnel" to "employee relations" to "human resources." The first 30 years of my career coincided with tremendous expansion of our understanding of organizations, the people who lead them, and how the business of talent acquisition and cultivation significantly affects performance. The work that was done by the field's most notable academic colleagues and consulting partners was—and still is—nothing short of revolutionary.

And then, 10 to 15 years ago, everywhere I looked, the efficacy of this work was being questioned or challenged. To this day it is difficult to find a trade journal, symposium, or keynote that does not pose the question (in one form or another), "*How does HR get a seat at the table?*"

Thus began what to me is the age of "great whine." As a group, we in human resources are a pretty self-absorbed lot, dwelling on the "why can't we?/why don't they?/when will they?" questions about being in the mix when it comes to developing business strategy, which, of course, then becomes the fodder for conferences, research projects, books, and articles.

How do we as HR practitioners move beyond this "great whine" and the perception that we do not currently have a seat at the table? In my opinion, this evolution will require understanding how we got here in the first place and then identifying how best to move forward. In this chapter, I intend to explore some of the major evolutionary trends that have molded the current landscape of HR, and then ultimately provide some suggestions for how we can both navigate and change the landscape in the future.

What Happened: Four Trends That Shaped HR

Where along the road, as we traveled from the 1970s to the 1990s, did the perception of our work change?

A disclaimer before I go on: I am not relying on any empirical evidence to support my thesis. What follows is essentially a recounting of what I have experienced personally throughout the decades of my career—or at least my perception of those experiences upon reflection—and in the particular industries in which I have worked.

None of these observations are fully defined, but they serve to draw attention to what I feel are the most obvious influences that have affected the nature of human resources work over the past several decades: the decline of manufacturing industries, a lack of HR investment among the service industries, the challenge of the multigenerational and constantly changing workforce, and macro changes brought about by globalization and the ever-changing legislative and political environment.

These represent the "what." The "how"—in terms of how these changes have led to our so-called leadership paradox—comes later.

Practitioners of a certain age can identify (to one degree or another) with most of the above phenomena, and we all can likely expound on or add to the list. The point is that virtually every change to our environment, whether externally driven or internally developed, has some effect on how we do our work. The entire employment life cycle has been reinvented several times over.

How we design jobs, how we source talent, how we develop and reward talent, how we define our employment brands, how we deal with our regulators—all of it continues to change, and it is increasingly difficult to keep pace with these changes. I can think of no other area of business practice whose work is as dramatically and frequently altered as HR by the forces I have described, and therefore, they are not assessed as critically.

The Decline of Manufacturing Industries

I joined the field as an HR practitioner in the mid-1970s in the manufacturing industry, just as human-capital-intensive manufacturing industries such as steel, auto, and heavy machines began to decline. As I would learn, this decline would have a profound impact on the infrastructure of human resources as a function.

But let me back up even further for a moment. Personnel work, as the field was initially called, developed rapidly during World War I and initially focused on tools and techniques for staffing and selection.

This type of work continued, with a focus on managing large groups of people in large organizations throughout the period of great industrialization. Specialties such as labor relations, industrial engineering, and so forth—all of which were propelled by labor activism and progressive legislation (for example, the Railway Labor Act, Taft-Hartley Act)—placed personnel practitioners in positions of great influence and authority.

By the time I joined the field, organization development, change management, succession planning, and the other elements of strategic leadership development were growing in importance, but they were primarily "technical specialties" reserved for the industrial scientists among us; they certainly were not priorities to the operating personnel managers who were busy dealing with the manufacturing-related issues viewed as core to the business. In fact, as recently as 2000, it was rare to find a senior personnel executive who had not started his or her career in some labor-relations capacity versus these other HR disciplines.

In the late 1970s and early 1980s, I worked at a name-brand firm, widely known for progressive and frequently benchmarked HR work. The company had two distinctly separate career tracks: The first involved employee relations (operating HR positions), and the second involved organization and manpower (O&M). The functions ultimately intersected at the top of the HR pyramid; however, it was very rare (in fact, I cannot recall an example) for people to move across the walls of the two siloes. What I can recall is hearing a story about the senior-most operating HR executive, who had decades of tenure, saying at a large gathering of HR staff, "I can tell you that I have not once been awakened at 3:00 a.m. for an O&M problem, but have often been raised from a sound sleep with a labor relations issue."

I do not recall the issue of "having a seat at the table" being a topic of discussion or concern during this period. It was not until the manufacturing industry hit its decline—and hence there was less emphasis on labor relations (or very little, in the case of the growing services industries)—that HR's strategic contributions began to be called into question.

Service Industries' Lack of HR Investment

The next observation I will make, based on my first-hand experience, is that service industries were slow to invest in contemporary HR processes.

The experience of closing plants dulls the senses and tamps down the passion for work, so in the mid-1980s I moved from the world of manufacturing into the world of financial services. What I quickly discovered was that there was little in the way of HR infrastructure, and limited investment in the hiring and developing of HR thought leaders (at least to the degree that one would observe in manufacturing). The emphasis was almost exclusively on recruiting individuals with a master's in business administration.

Clearly, the financial services industry employed some of the best and brightest minds you could find, but my contemporaries and I had the distinct feeling that we could mine so much more value were the industry to invest in organizational development and people management. The back offices, which are the equivalent of operating environments, were—of necessity—more focused on employee relations versus leadership development or business strategy, and hence this reality offered more evidence of the need for HR to be a value-adding resource. This remained the case through the late 1980s, but even today some industries tend to be more evolved than others with regard to human capital management.

Multigenerational, Changing Workforce

Another challenge that needs to be understood as central to the story is the inexorable change in the nature of the workforce from Baby Boomers to Millennials.

The needs and expectations of each succeeding generation have done more to transform the world of HR work than any other outside influence. The "employment contract" has changed dramatically throughout my tenure in the field. Everything from employment security to the nature of workers' formal relationships with the firm (for example, contractor, consultant, interim versus full-time employee) is different.

We as HR practitioners have had to challenge ourselves to rethink each element of our people-management foundation, from selection to development, to compensation, to how and where work can be done. Insourcing, outsourcing, virtual teams, flexible scheduling, remote workers, and on and on. And for the personnel we support, that has meant frequent disruptions and changes to their operating models.

Think also about the pace at which technology has evolved and intruded on the workplace: 24/7 communication; instant availability of information; vast amounts of data being collected and reported; the disintermediation of classic structures through the use of crowdsourcing, real-time online access, networks, and so forth. The pace of change now easily outpaces our ability to react to it. For example, LinkedIn has created a virtual candidate pool and put every organization's key talent in play.

Macro Changes Due to Globalization and Legislative/Political Influences

Accompanying all of the foregoing have been many macro changes brought on by globalization and other legislative and political influences. The shifts in the global economy, the related impact on the competitive landscape, and the resultant response by the business community have been enormous and transformational. Change management, agility, speed, and process reengineering—each has given birth to processes and practices that have proven to be accelerants to the revolution(s) in the workplace.

Furthermore, the legislative and political environment has played a part throughout. Seminal labor legislation like the Sherman Antitrust Act, the Occupational Safety and Health Act, and the Fair Labor Standards Act has affected what kind of work we do and how we do it. While each piece of legislation is important in the development of worker protections—from defining unfair labor practices, promoting worker safety, and setting wage standards—each has also brought rules and oversight that have required expertise and technical know-how, which ultimately became the purview of HR. The Dodd-Frank Wall Street Reform and Consumer Protection Act and the Patient Protection and Affordable Care Act have had a particularly significant impact on the function. And beyond legislation, activist investors have also had an impact on the nature of HR work.

In both cases there are now many more rules-based processes, which heretofore were the purview of management's judgment and discretion. For example, "say on pay," which is a provision of Dodd-Frank, allows shareholders to vote on proxy ballots for the proposed compensation of certain elements of executive pay.

The role of HR has been materially affected by these changes to corporate governance. The chief human resource officer (CHRO) is central to advising the CEO and board of directors, as well as to creating reward systems and processes that conform to the rules, while at the same time supporting the strategic mission of the organization. There is inherent risk in all of this, which HR must manage.

What Should We Do? Four Responses

In terms of how we address this so-called paradox, some of my thoughts are layups, and others are far more difficult and complex.

Drive Change

In most cases, each of the changes I have described has had an accompanying implication to the workforce, in whole or in part, and HR has had to communicate the change(s) and resultant impact(s) as well as implement them.

Change is often disruptive, frequently by design. As a rule, people do not relish disruption. Managers chafe, employees are wary and cautious, and leaders become concerned about negative impacts on business plans.

What has developed over the years, I have observed, is a level of frustration and weariness, which manifests in criticism of the HR function—a type of "shoot the messenger" mindset. We hear it in the use of terms and phrases like "bureaucratic," "HR has too many policies and rules," "corporate cops," and "too much control." I am pretty sure that this notion requires little amplification for those who work in HR.

The work we do in this regard is necessary and essential to the well-being of any institution, and therefore needs to be done well and flaw-lessly. It should not, however, be the benchmark that defines our work.

We often hear our leaders say something along the lines of, "I love my HR generalist, but hate HR." What really is being said is, "I find all of the changes and administration to be really annoying." This mentality, I believe, seeps into our own narrative as HR professionals and ultimately starts to fuel the notion of "seat at the table."

Eschew Administration/Embrace Value

There are other influences that reinforce the notion that HR is not influ-ential in setting business strategy. There is much less consistency with regard to whom the CHRO reports than, say, the chief financial officer (CFO). Without exception, CFOs report to CEOs. Too often CHROs report to either a chief administrative officer (CAO) or other staff function. By definition, such structures imply that HR has a less central and critical role in managing the business. In some cases it is a historical artifact, and in some cases not.

I have been privileged to work with many sitting CHROs. Some were peers, some were direct reports, and some I reported to. Without excep-tion they have represented the best of what a senior business executive should be: thoughtful, knowledgeable, business-savvy, creative, and strong. In every case, they have been active and often central partici-pants in strategy development and business planning. These business professionals could be interchangeable with most line executives with-out skipping a beat. (I do not mean to imply that all CHROs or HR organi-zations represent the ideal any more than all chief information officers or CFOs. But I do mean that the HR-excellence critical mass is on par with other business functions. No debate.)

There needs to be standards of excellence, which are understood and adhered to across the HR landscape. Consistently rewarding per-formance and behavior reflective of meaningful contributions to the business is the minimum. Promoting those who are models of success is essential. Our search partners need to understand and appreciate the standards, educate their clients, and influence candidate selection accordingly. This includes the notion of a CHRO reporting solely to the CEO. We as candidates should accept nothing less.

Change the Conversation

We as HR practitioners can help ourselves immeasurably by changing the narrative. First, let's stop asking the question, "How do I get a seat at the table?"

Have you ever heard that refrain from a counterpart in a different function? Probably not.

Reinforcing the perception of inadequacy perpetuates the myth. Doing our jobs well as business professionals—including sharing thoughts and views and challenging others—is the normal course.

Develop a Construct

Finally, and most importantly, we need to develop a construct—applicable across the universe of HR—that incorporates everything, including standards of performance, a definition of our role in corporate governance (that is, our relationship with boards of directors), a common language based on business terminology, development frameworks, common tools, and others.

In other words, we need to develop the same type of architecture that already exists in the main for many other business practice areas, such as finance and technology. Much work has been done on this front—for example, Boudreau and Randstad's HC Bridge—and more work is underway. But what we need is an approach to knitting the pieces of the quilt together, and a forum for doing so. I think this dialogue has begun, but we need to ensure that it continues.

And, in the end, while we in HR often say we need a seat at the table, I think what we really mean is that we need a bigger table. Part 1:

PART II

NEW PERSPECTIVES FOR THE CHRO

Chapter 4.

The Four Levels of Impact of the Chief Human Resource Officer: HR 4.0

Marcia J. Avedon

Most organizations today have competency models and job descriptions that explain the requirements, skills, and knowledge needed for HR leadership positions. While competency models are useful for the hiring and development of people in the field, they are not sufficient to provide a framework for the potential impact of HR leaders and the HR discipline. This chapter provides a framework for HR leaders to consider the additional value that can be created by HR—beyond individuals, teams, and organizations—to the larger profession, community, and society at large: I think of it as four levels of impact.

It is important to explore the four levels of impact for a number of reasons. First, for those aspiring to be senior HR officers and for incumbent chief human resource officers (CHROs), this model may expand their development and provide direction and meaning to their HR organizations. Also, for CEOs, line leaders, and even boards of directors, it may broaden the expectations and engagement of the CHRO and the HR function to more critical opportunities. Last, I believe the field of human resources has the opportunity to make an even greater impact on the human experience at work, and even on major social and economic issues.

The Origin of the Four Levels of Impact Model

Several years ago, in one of my first board meetings at the Center for Creative Leadership (CCL), a leader presented a simple framework organizing the CCL offerings to show impact at four levels: individual, team, organization, and society (see Figure 4.1). It occurred to me that this model also articulated the potential we have as CHROs to broaden our impact beyond the organizational level.

FIGURE 4.1. CENTER FOR CREATIVE LEADERSHIP, LEVELS OF IMPACT

In my first few years as a CHRO, I had focused my time and that of my HR leaders on the first three levels of impact. While I recognized that HR functions needed a framework to focus how they deliver value, in a typical manner I channeled our energy almost exclusively on impact within our organization. Figure 4.2 shows a model I used to integrate, organize, and focus the work of the HR function. This framework was helpful in aligning the activities and goals of hundreds of HR professionals across the globe, but it was missing one important perspective—the connection to the external world. Although this model ensured a balance of strategic and operational contributions, and allowed the HR function to deliver value for employees, teams, and Ingersoll Rand (Levels 1-3), it did not speak to the potential for a larger impact on society or in the communities in which we live and work.

Following my discovery of the CCL "four levels of impact" model, I was inspired by the tremendous opportunity we have to add value beyond our organizations. At Ingersoll Rand, where I lead global human resources, communications, and corporate affairs, we have begun to broaden our understanding and focus on how we can positively affect the

FIGURE 4.2. AVEDON'S HR IMPACT MODEL

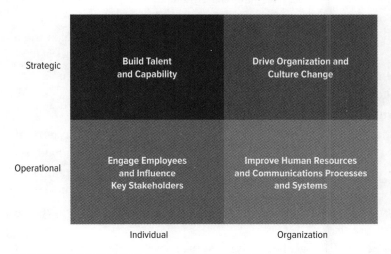

Contributions to Company

	Individual	Organization
Strategic	Build Talent and Capability	Drive Organization and Culture Change
Operational	Engage Employees and Influence Key Stakeholders	Improve Human Resources and Communications Processes and Systems

world around us. The book *HR from the Outside In* focuses on HR working from the customer and shareholder value creation back into the HR solutions provided.[1] At Ingersoll Rand, over the past couple of years we have been applying this "outside-in" approach to our HR strategy, accelerating our movement to Level 4 impact.

This chapter provides a model that encourages HR leaders to work beyond the boundaries of their particular organizations to positively change the communities and social strata in which their organizations reside. As CHROs and the HR function achieve impact across all four levels, collectively, the HR field can make a broader impact in the world.

The Four Levels of Impact

This section presents each of the levels of impact for HR leaders and examines the intersection between competencies and impact with specific CHRO examples. Each level of impact can become even more valuable if an HR leader understands how each level can enhance higher levels.

Level 1: Individual Impact

It is intuitive that an HR leader must have strong interpersonal skills and be able to influence and coach others in a highly effective manner, but impact at the individual level goes well beyond interpersonal savvy. It is the cumulative results of these interpersonal skills on others that matters most. For example, does the CHRO coach the CEO and other executives in a way that actually improves individual performance and helps them achieve their goals? Does the CHRO have both the courage and the skill to provide meaningful feedback that an executive can hear and act on? Does the CHRO make talent decisions, or encourage others to do so, in a way that results in stronger leadership?

In addition to an executive's personal behaviors, it is important for the CHRO to ensure that the processes focused on individuals reinforce the right outcomes. For example, do the reward systems sufficiently differentiate pay for top performers? Do the selection systems result in the most qualified people being chosen without interference of bias or politics?

While Level 1 impact is necessary to the success of the CHRO, it is not too different from the success profile required for other roles in the field of HR in terms of coaching and developing talent, providing feedback, and enhancing individual performance. The major difference is the complexity and scope of the positions and processes that the CHRO must oversee and influence. Clearly, having impact at the individual level is core for any HR professional, but the consequences are much greater for the CHRO, given his or her sphere of influence.

Level 2: Team Impact

The CHRO has the opportunity to heighten team effectiveness and results in many ways. The CHRO leads an HR leadership team, sits on the executive leadership team of the corporation, and typically participates in meetings with the board of directors. The CHRO also has impact by forming, facilitating, or participating on teams for critical new opportunities such as an acquisition or a strategic initiative. These teams may be cross-functional, cross-geography, or even across organizations. How deliberately and intentionally the CHRO works to improve team performance is key to his or her impact at this level.

Whether or not the CHRO has a formal role on a team, he or she can influence the success formula. For example, in a diversified industrial company such as Ingersoll Rand, there are numerous strategic business units (SBUs), each with a president and a leadership team. Part of my role is to assess and improve the effectiveness of the SBU leadership teams. My impact can be a function of facilitating changes in the composition of the team by adding particular skills or balancing leadership styles, helping clarify and align goals, or improving interpersonal dynamics through formal interventions. I may also advise on stakeholder communications or recommend changes to team processes such as decision-making. The impact of this work should be evident over time in metrics from financial results, to customer satisfaction, to the retention and engagement of talent.

In recent years, in an effort to move to "business partners," I have seen HR leaders focus primarily on the official content of the meeting such as the financial results or operating performance, while missing some of the subtle but consequential team dynamics that can either impede or accelerate team performance. The CHRO is in a unique position to report back to the team or to the team leader observations about the team's effectiveness and to recommend changes to improve performance. Some of the more difficult types of issues to address at the team level include managing conflict, handling poor performance, addressing misaligned goals, or managing derailing behaviors.

The CHRO must diagnose and address these opportunities, as well as potential inhibitors to performance, to have impact at the team level. The CHRO should plan time periodically for the team to work on team norms and expectations and evaluate what is working and not working. Often, it is valuable to use an outside facilitator since the CHRO is part of the team dynamic as a key member. In this case, the CHRO might help plan the event to ensure it focuses on the greatest areas of opportunity.

Executive teams have certain routines that can assist with positive team effectiveness. For example, many organizations have a formal goal deployment process to ensure the executive leadership team agrees on the most critical goals and initiatives for the year and formally shares them throughout the organization. Such a process facilitates alignment and reduces ambiguity and conflict. Another crucial process is around problem-solving. How does the team address areas that are problems or are falling short of expectations? How constructive and rigorous is the process? The CHRO can play an essential role in establishing such routines or in improving execution to enhance team performance.

Level 3: Organizational Impact

CHROs are in an unparalleled position to affect the organization as a whole—from culture change, to strategic capabilities, to employment brand and leadership effectiveness and sustainability. The CHRO has the opportunity to profoundly influence the organization's effectiveness in the eyes of employees, customers, and shareholders.

As an example of organizational impact, in 2013 Ingersoll Rand crafted a spin-off of its residential and commercial security business into a new publicly traded company, Allegion. As CHRO, I led much of the work on the spin-off, including CEO and officer selections, organizational design, and transition plans to make the new entity self-sufficient. Ensuring Allegion had the talent, capabilities, and processes to perform successfully outside of Ingersoll Rand is Level 3 impact. This is especially evident in that the measures of success were at the organizational level, including shareholder value, financial measures such as growth and income, and HR metrics such as talent retention.

Concurrent with the spin-off, my team and I worked with the executive leadership team to determine the new organizational design for Ingersoll Rand following a refreshed corporate strategy. This work involved not only creating a new formal organizational structure and making talent selections but also revising the operating cadence in terms of the content and participation in leadership meetings. The impact from this work was significant in terms of the objectives achieved, including greater customer focus to accelerate growth, reduction in general and administrative costs following the spin-off, greater agility and responsiveness to market changes, and record levels of key talent retention and employee engagement.

Another example of organizational impact is developing strategic capabilities across the company. At Ingersoll Rand we have multiyear initiatives that require development of talent, processes, and learning to achieve a differentiated level of performance versus the competition. These critical few capabilities are at the organizational level (versus competencies, which are at the individual level) and deliver value in terms of human development and company performance. For example, to support our growth strategy we have developed a strategic capability of product management, including the talent to perform these jobs and the skills and tools required, as well as standard work and processes for product management activities such as pricing, new product development, and launching new offerings.

To achieve organizational impact, the CHRO should work with the executive leadership team on the strategy of the organization and identify the most critical strategic capabilities required for success. Then, he or she must implement and continuously improve these capabilities to deliver the required impact.

Level 4: Community, Professional, and Societal Impact

Often, Level 4 impact evolves from work done initially at another level of the model. For example, in developing entry-level talent strategies, most companies identify colleges or universities to partner with for recruiting purposes. The most advanced HR functions and CHROs realize that these are not just transactional relationships to fill positions or to place students in jobs. University relations can be a combination of community relations, research and development partnerships, workforce development, and philanthropic opportunities. The annual hiring of graduates should be a part of a larger set of relationships and impact on the community and society. Also, university relations can provide opportunities for leaders to teach and better prepare the next generation of workers. The question is whether CHROs and other HR leaders are orchestrating and integrating these activities to provide this greater value both to the organization, in terms of talent, capabilities and brand/reputation, and to the community and larger profession, in terms of relevance, outcomes, and value.

Not long ago I attended a meeting of the HR Policy Association, where we discussed the growing concerns about income inequality in the U.S. and the connection to the need for greater skill development. A CHRO from Wegmans shared an example of how the company made a significant positive impact on high school dropout rates in its headquarters location of Rochester, New York, through part-time employment opportunities, mentoring, and a college scholarship program. This may have originally been a typical co-op program, but Wegmans realized that in addition to filling jobs and creating a talent pool, it could have a broader impact on the community as well as on workforce development. The company also recognized the customer loyalty and brand value of this work.

The CHRO can reach Level 4 impact by aligning the goals of the organization with what matters most to the surrounding communities and social sphere. Several years ago, Ingersoll Rand partnered with the Girl Scouts of the USA to create an energy efficiency "badge" program for girls in grades four through six, promoting energy conservation and also encouraging careers in science, technology, engineering, and mathematics (STEM). The program was tested with troops in 20 of our U.S. manufacturing markets, and we found that a majority of the girls who earned a badge were inspired to conserve energy at home, were willing to advocate for energy efficiency with others, and were more likely to consider careers in engineering. The program is now a national leadership program for Girl Scout Juniors, and has also been refined and implemented with older students at community and technical colleges.

This program illustrates the power of Level 4 impact. Not only did it help our company, but it helped address larger societal challenges in multiple ways. Ingersoll Rand was able to advance its vision of a more sustainable world by educating and involving young students in energy conservation. In addition, our efforts are helping address macro issues around the availability of skilled talent for growing STEM job needs as well as around the underrepresentation of women in STEM fields, building a stronger national talent pipeline.

Moreover, Level 4 impact has the ability to grow exponentially with the full power of the HR field behind it. In this particular example, if more companies focused their efforts on STEM programming and early workforce development, the HR field could achieve an even greater collective impact on education, innovation, and even national competitiveness.

Impact at All Levels: HR 4.0

The HR field began with a focus on the first level of individual impact—personnel management. Over time, HR evolved to also encompass team dynamics and effectiveness. Today, we are in the HR 3.0 era, where human resources is primarily focused on having broader strategic impact on organizations as a whole. That is a worthy goal, but in addition, it is important to explore how, from the position of the CHRO, we can affect many aspects of society, including critical social and economic issues like workforce development.

While Level 4 impact is the ultimate aspiration, all four levels of impact are necessary and important, and each level builds on the prior level. For example, team effectiveness is reliant on individual performance; organizational success is dependent on highly effective executive and project teams; and typically, having an impact in the larger community depends on the strength of an organization's capabilities, brand, and reputation. The CHRO must maintain a focus across all four levels to achieve the strongest impact.

Adopting this model and working outside the boundaries of the organization can provide additional purpose and meaning to the work of the CHRO and the HR team. Furthermore, if the CHRO collaborates with other HR leaders outside of the organization, the ability to drive lasting change in the world around us becomes exponentially greater. Our collective impact could change the future of health care, immigration, workforce development, income inequality, diversity and inclusion, or sustainability. It is possible that this higher order, HR 4.0, may become the next paradigm or identity for our discipline.

Endnote

[1.] Dave Ulrich, Jon Younger, Wayne Brockbank, and Mike Ulrich, *HR from the Outside In: Six Competencies for the Future of Human Resources* (New York: McGraw Hill, 2012).

Chapter 5.
8 C Model for Effective HR Leaders

Richard L. Antoine

We are all too familiar with the complaint from business leaders and employees in organizations that the top HR leader is "just a plans and benefits person" or, even worse, "clueless." However, there are many HR leaders who "get it" and are "valued business partners."

So what characteristics define and distinguish those HR leaders who are effective and valued from those who are not? This chapter presents a model that defines the key skills and attributes of effective HR leaders. This model is based on my experience as the CHRO of Procter & Gamble (P&G) for over a decade and as the president of the National Academy of Human Resources for the past six years. In both of those roles I have had the privilege to work with and observe many talented HR leaders who are true business partners. Based on these interactions and observations,

FIGURE 5.1. 8 C MODEL FOR EFFECTIVE HR LEADERS

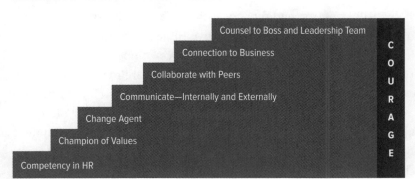

43

I have developed a model that seeks to capture the common character-istics of effective HR leaders. The "8 Cs of Effective HR Leaders" model is shown in Figure 5.1 for reference. In the succeeding paragraphs I will try to provide clarification, understanding, and examples of these various characteristics.

The 8 C model is constructed with the foundational characteristics at the bottom. It then progresses upward through skills of increasing impor-tance and complexity. And it concludes with the most distinguishing char-acteristic of all for effective HR leaders—COURAGE. But more on that last characteristic later.

Competency in HR

The first characteristic of effective HR leaders is certainly the most ob-vious. They must be highly competent in the skills and technologies of human resources. Like any other function, HR has methodologies and ap-proaches that enable people and organizations to be effective and to meet the requirements of the law. The list of those competencies is long, but several are critical to the effective HR leader:

- Strategy deployment and implementation.
- Organizational design.
- Executive compensation.
- Talent development.
- Change management.
- Coaching.

Most HR leaders spend most of their careers in HR exposed to these and other HR competencies. The effective HR leader must be knowledge-able about the broad range of human resource competencies and be ex-pert in a few of them. The six I have listed above are the most critical in my opinion and require some level of expertise and preferably experience.

There is a tendency in some organizations to bring in an HR leader from outside of the function. I in fact was one of those. I spent my first 25 years with P&G in the supply chain before assuming the CHRO role. As such, I believe I am qualified to say that this is not a preferable or even always effective way of staffing the top HR role. Most HR competencies are new to someone coming into HR from outside of HR. Therefore, the inexperienced HR leader is certain to struggle as he or she learns these skills. If bringing in someone from outside HR is the organizational choice, the new CHRO must rely on and learn from the talented subject matter experts within his or her HR organization. I did just that, and owe each of those individuals a debt of gratitude. I also supplemented that learning of HR competencies by joining a couple of senior HR peer groups. In my case, Organization Resource Counselors (ORC) and Personnel Roundtable (PRT) were particularly valuable. I was able to learn from talented and experienced CHROs who put up with my uninformed questions and naive views. Even if you come into the top HR leader role with considerable experience in human resources, joining peer groups is almost always a beneficial idea.

Champion of Values

An effective HR leader must be the champion of the values of the company or organization. Virtually every company that I have seen or visited or read about has a series of values that are posted on the website or hanging on the walls of various rooms in the company offices. Most of these values statements have a familiar ring. The list is neither long nor hard to understand. At P&G the values were:

- Leadership.
- Ownership.
- Integrity.
- Passion for winning.
- Trust.

Whatever the values, the challenge is to make these values fundamental to how the company operates and how people within the company behave. The HR leader must own the incorporation of these values into the very fabric of the company. He or she must be a visible champion of these values through word and deed. The "words" start with the training of all people in the organization on the meaning and application of these values. Since the values are usually pretty straightforward, the meaning is also usually straightforward. For example, most people know what integrity means. The application, the "deed," however, is where the real meaning of these values and the importance of these values are demonstrated in the organization. If an employee, especially a senior one, has an undeclared conflict of interest, then this situation becomes a matter that violates the integrity value of the organization. The more senior the person who is involved in an ethics violation, the more important it is to deal with that breach of trust clearly and decisively. The rest of the organization is looking to see whether those values are merely words on the wall or are in fact the way that the organization operates—everyone, all the time.

It is certainly obvious but must be stated that the HR leader must be exemplary in living all of these values. The HR leader must hold himself or herself to the absolute highest standards. Otherwise there is no way to enforce these values in the culture of the organization. I have often wondered where the HR leaders were in Enron and WorldCom and Tyco many years ago when severe ethics violations brought down those companies. Were they unaware of the excesses? Were they themselves not living up to those values? Were they fearful to stand up for those values? I do not know the answer, but the outcome was devastating for thousands of employees in those organizations.

Being a champion of the values also means that an effective HR leader must help and defend those people in the organization "with small roles and small voices." People low in the organization sometimes feel that they are subject to or witness ethics violations that are inconsistent with the company's stated values. But when they raise these issues, they worry that no one will protect them from the more powerful boss. At the other end of the organizational scale, I have also seen senior managers who were reluctant to bring up values violations. Again, who can help these people bring their issues to the light of day when they are being drowned out by more vocal, and sometimes bullying, colleagues? In both situations it is the role of the HR leader to make sure that ethics violations receive a fair and open hearing.

Change Agent

The third critical competency for effective HR leaders is that of change agent. Businesses and organizations share one thing in common with the laws of physics and energy: They can either get better or worse. Stability, while seemingly desirable, just does not happen for more than a brief period of time. The list of companies that have not been able to adapt to the changing world around them is many times greater than those organizations that have succeeded over time. Indeed, the *Fortune* 100 list of the largest companies in the world from 60 years ago has only 40 companies remaining in business as stand-alone entities. The failure rate of smaller companies is even higher.

Therefore, being able to learn, adapt, and change is vital to the long-term success of businesses and organizations. And it is certainly the responsibility of the HR leader to be at the forefront of those changes. To be effective at leading change, the HR leader must know the key changes needed and must have a "model" for implementing change in an organization. To document and have clarity within the organization about the changes needed, it is helpful to use a "from this/to that" list, for example, on decision-making: "We will go from a centralized corporate decision-making model to a decentralized decision-making approach." Obviously more detail is needed on just this one behavioral and organizational change, but a "from this/to that" list is simple and effective. Regarding models, there are many useful and helpful organizational change approaches. Each consulting company seems to have its favorite, and one can find dozens if not hundreds of approaches on the Internet. I am partial to the Kotter model of organizational change. We used it successfully for many years at P&G. There are only eight steps, but change is hard enough without making the change process itself too complicated. Most importantly, pick a change model that you are comfortable with and that can clearly explain to the people who have to make the change in your business or organization.

Communication: Internally and Externally

The effective HR leader must also have excellent communication skills, both internally and externally. And those skills must be both verbal and written. The range of topics and audiences is quite impressive from plans and benefits that affect all employees, to communication of the corporate strategy to employees, to compensation discussions with the board, and to interviews with and articles in external publications. The CHRO, often with help from the corporate public relations leader, who was invaluable to me, must be adept at communicating clearly and persuasively with a broad range of constituents.

One of the best examples of the breath and complexity of HR communications occurred in 2006 when IBM made vast changes to its employee retirement plans, converting them to a defined contribution plan. Randy MacDonald, the CHRO of IBM at the time, had to sell the IBM board on the merits of the change. Then he had to lead many town hall sessions and prepare written documents that went to all employees explaining the change and a new financial counseling program. And, finally, he also briefed members of Congress. Randy is an example of the kind of effective and distinguished HR leader that served as a role model for all of us.

Today, the methods of communications have dramatically expanded. Not too long ago, the communication choices were face to face, one to many in a room full of people, via e-mail, or via a website. Social media has added new opportunities that many people in the organization prefer to other methods of communication. Previously, the hardest part of communicating important changes and initiatives was make the message clear and persuasive. Now, the HR leader has to decide on the most effective combination of delivery vehicles.

Collaboration with Peers

The best HR leaders collaborate frequently and effectively with peers. The HR leader must be in constant touch with the business leaders and other functional leaders. He or she must be aware of talent, organizational design, performance management, or other issues affecting the business or functional area. Then the HR leader can work in partnership with the business or functional leader to develop approaches and solutions that solve any problems.

Business or functional leaders face significant challenges to deliver their profit forecast, their budget, and their goals (for example, cash flow, productivity). They are continually sorting through scenarios and potential solutions. If the issue is market position, or pricing or branding, the HR leader is not central to the solution. But many other issues necessarily involve aspects of human resources. If decision-making lags market speed, if the organization is too "fat," if the incentive system rewards the wrong behaviors, or if the organization lacks the proper skills or talent, then the HR leader must be actively involved to help. "Help" looks like practical business-relevant solutions accompanied by a change plan. While there is a no "instant pudding recipe," solutions that take many months or years to implement are not viewed as helpful by your business peers.

Connection to Business

Of course, collaboration requires that the HR leader be connected to the business and that he or she have credibility with the business leaders. Credibility in turn comes from understanding the real business situation and issues that the business leaders face every day. Effective HR leaders must become students of the business. They must understand the business model, the metrics of success, the levers that lead to success, and certainly the business terminology. Here are just a few questions to test your understanding of the business:

- What is the business strategy?
- How does the business make money?
- Who are the key competitors?
- Who are the key customers?
- What drives business success—innovation, capital utilization, customer connectivity, service excellence, or low-cost structure?
- What are the business metrics—profit, margin, cash flow productivity, or share?

Effective HR leaders either have this information because of their prior experiences or they seek it out from the business or functional leaders. They must spend time with the finance organization to understand the return on investment calculation, the risk analysis model used to assess business investments in various countries, and the terminology used to report the organization's business results. With the sales leader, the CHRO needs to understand what drives customer receptivity and customer preferred status. There is a bulleted list of key questions above that you can and should ask each business and functional leader to make sure that you truly understand the business. When you collaborate, it must be from a position of connecting with the various leaders because they know that you understand the challenges and issues they face.

Besides a sound business grasp, business or functional leaders will value their HR counterparts if HR can help them develop solutions to real business challenges. This in turn requires yet another model or process in the arsenal of the effective HR leader—a problem-solving model. Again there are many models that range in effectiveness from "a shot in the dark" to "a reasonable chance of delivering the desired outcome." My favorite problem-solving model for complex organizational situations is the model developed by Dave Hannah more than two decades ago. It is a holistic way of looking at the current situation, the desired outcome, and then all the systems and processes that can affect the potential solution. For example, what are the talent implications of the desired change? Does this require a new organizational design? Are the information systems sufficient to support the desired change? How must decisions be made to match the pace of the business? Do the reward systems incent the right behaviors and right people? Whichever model you use must address these and other considerations. The HR leader who can collaborate with the business or functional leader on the development of clear, actionable, and effective solutions is a highly sought-after individual. Such HR leaders do not just have a seat at the table; they help set the table.

Counsel to Boss and Leadership Team

Understanding the business is also a key requirement for the seventh C— counsel to the boss and leadership team. For the CHRO, the main customer is the CEO. The relationship between CEO and CHRO is one of the most important to the company. The CEO is the unquestioned leader, sets the strategy and direction for the company, has the biggest impact on the culture, and is accountable for delivering the results of the organization. It is a big, complex, demanding, and lonely job. The CEO needs someone he or she can rely on for impartial advice, someone whose only objective is to make the CEO and the organization better. The CHRO must fill this role. The various business leaders and some of the functional leaders have a different relationship with the CEO. They are held accountable for delivering results and are judged on their performance. Besides the obvious pay consequences, many of these people are seeking to succeed or even replace the

CEO—or become CEO of another organization. As human beings, what do you think are the odds that they will be totally candid and forthright with the CEO about the CEO's performance? By contrast, the CHRO is trained in performance assessment and evaluation, and he or she is not viewed as a successor. I would like to think this is not due to a lack of talent. I believe it is because the CHRO has a unique role in the organization to provide clear, honest, and helpful feedback to the CEO. As my boss often said, "The CHRO has to tell the emperor he has no clothes . . . because no one else will."

So providing feedback and counsel to the CEO is an important aspect of the job. The best feedback occurs in real time when specific examples can be used. But there is also a need for periodic (that is, annual) performance feedback to assess the "body of work" of the CEO. Again the CHRO should be involved in this process along with the lead director of the board. The CHRO initiates the process by gathering 360-degree input from subordinates, managers another level down, and the CEO's assistant. To obtain credible information, you have to promise confidentiality and nonattribution. In this feedback we focused on identifying those skills and capabilities that were helping the CEO at P&G drive outstanding business and organizational results. By focusing on these critical skills and capabilities, the CEO learned or reaffirmed what he could leverage to deliver even better results going forward. We also sought out information on "the one thing" that the CEO could do to further improve his performance. Long lists of improvement items are virtually useless. No one has the time or even the human capability to change behaviors across a broad range of activities. One or two improvement areas that are backed by solid development plans can lead to significant and positive change. Once I assembled, digested, and summarized the 360-degree input, I shared it with the lead director of the board. The lead director added the board input and then provided feedback on the entirety of the performance summary to the CEO. In a separate conversation with the CEO, I provided more detail and nonattributable examples from the organization to improve understanding. The process is actually similar to performance management feedback for anyone else in the organization. One unique feature is eliciting input from outside people—the board members. Of course these are experienced and talented people whose input is important to the CEO and highly valued.

While I did not conduct the performance reviews of other C-suite members, the HR leader winds up being a counselor and advisor to many of these people. If HR leaders have some business credibility with their C-suite peers and if they are trusted, they are often sought out for advice on performance and career development. The tricky part in this role is handling information flow between the C-suite leader, the HR leader, and the CEO. The C-suite leaders are often seeking perspective on how the boss views their performance. They are occasionally sharing information on their careers, perhaps including expressions of interest from outside companies. How much of this information should the CHRO share with the CEO? There is no good roadmap for how the CHRO should handle this. Judgment is important. Trust is the most valued commodity.

Courage!

The final C and the one that is the most critical to distinguishing the capable HR leader from a highly effective one is courage. The CHRO is often in the middle of many complex and difficult situations. As mentioned previously, the ability to analyze and assess these complex situations is paramount. The ability to develop applicable solutions is also important. But often the implementation of those solutions requires a large dose of personal courage. The courage to "do the right thing" amid potential negative consequences often separates the highly respected leader from the pretender. Quite literally, the CHRO has to be willing to put his or her job on the line. Doing that is neither trivial nor easy. But occasionally it is necessary.

CHROs need to be prepared to thoughtfully and honestly respond to questions that come at them from a variety of sources. For example, I was in talent review sessions with the CEO of P&G when a board member asked if I agreed with the CEO's assessment of an individual. Because of the time we spent with each other trying to determine the correct assessment, I was almost always able to say "yes, I agree." But occasionally, we disagreed, and I shared my own opinion with the board. It did not matter whether I was right or wrong. The board expected my candid evaluation.

With the CEO, you have to be willing to tell him or her that the last meeting with a top subordinate did not go exactly the way the CEO viewed the meeting. I seldom had to use that Hertz commercial term of "not exactly" when the CEO told me about the glowing meeting he had with one of his direct reports. But occasionally I did have to share that the individual was in my office later seeking career advice rather than thinking he or she just had the best meeting ever with the boss.

One of the work processes the CEO and I initiated at P&G was to sit down immediately after each board meeting and top leadership team meeting to debrief. We exchanged candid views on what we saw happening or not happening in those meetings. Given that CEOs are focused on leading meetings, they appreciate hearing a second opinion of how the meeting went and of participants' reactions. If all you do is affirm that the CEO handled everything brilliantly and that everyone was totally on board, you have failed to meet your obligation to the boss to be a trusted counselor.

A final area of courage comes when the CHRO must recommend that another member of the leadership team needs to leave because of ethical violations. This is extraordinarily difficult because these are your peers with whom you have shared experiences for perhaps many years. But if they violate the fundamental ethics of the company, they must receive the same treatment as anyone else in the organization—neither better or worse. In my experience there was not anything harder than having to recommend separation of a top team member to the CEO and then having to talk to one of my colleagues (and friends) about the need to leave.

There are other instances and situations when courage is needed in the top HR job. I wish I could say that it is only required rarely. It is not. This is the quality that distinguishes effective and great HR leaders from those who are not. The same thing can be said of effective and great CEOs. In that respect we have a lot in common.

Conclusion

It is a convenient coincidence that the final wrap-up starts with yet another "C." The CHRO role is critical to the success of any organization, whether a for-profit company or a nonprofit. Effective CHROs make major contributions to their organization that show up in the bottom line, in the achievement of the organization's mission, and in the talent reputation of that entity. Being an effective HR leader requires a set of skills, capabilities, and attributes that are difficult to acquire but essential for success.

The 8 Cs for Effective HR Leaders is intended to provide a series of steps that HR leaders must take to be great business leaders as viewed by their bosses, peers, and organizations.

Chapter 6.

7 Common CHRO Priorities that Create Good but Not Great Performance

Wayne Brockbank

A fundamental attribute of effective executives is their ability to set clear priorities and to establish actions by which to achieve those priorities. They understand the importance of focus. They do not allow important priorities to stand in the way of the *most* important priorities. This ability builds on the concept of Pareto analysis that Jim Collins popularized as "good is the enemy of great."[1] The challenge is that chief human resource officers (CHROs) sometimes set *good* priorities that become obstacles to *great* priorities. Good priorities create value, but they create value that is inferior to the great priorities. As a result, CHROs who focus on the good at the expense of the great thereby marginalize their contributions to their firms' competitive advantage.

Good priorities may become emphasized over great priorities for three reasons. First, good priorities are often easier to achieve than great ones. There is more risk in seeking great priorities, which, by definition, are more difficult to achieve and are, therefore, scarcer. Second, good priorities are often embedded in existing habit patterns, which have been ingrained through successfully repeated actions. A common question is, "We have always done it this way, so why change?" The existing habit patterns become part of the comfort zone. Third, great priorities are almost always less certain. The path to achieve them is less known, and their outcomes are less predictable.

On the other hand, great priorities are the roads "less traveled" and may be more capable of affecting business results than the good priorities that are easy, stable, and predictable. Through years of personal experience with dozens of CHROs and hundreds of senior HR executives, and 25 years of conducting the Human Resource Competency Study[1] at the University of Michigan and the RBL Group, my colleagues and I have identified seven good agendas on which CHROs frequently focus that can displace the most important—the great—priorities.

In this chapter, I will describe each of the seven good but not great priorities and their limitations. I will then provide the alternative great agenda and rationale behind designating the great agenda as such. Finally, I will provide initial suggestions on how to successfully embed the great agendas into your personal priorities.

You will quickly note that I have worded the seven good but not great priorities to be somewhat provocative. My rationale for so doing is that in many cases, CHROs are more comfortable with the good priorities that receive greater focus than the great priorities for the reasons given above.

Good but Not *Great* Priority #1:
Focus on Serving Internal Customers

In the history of HR, CHROs have focused on serving internal customers, including the CEO, other leaders, and employees in general. Given that most HR processes have direct influence on internal customers, this focus is understandable. They focus on building their employees' technical and cultural capabilities, commitment, and motivation that will create results.

The problem is of course that the capability, commitment, and motivation of employees have value only if they create results that meet the requirements of the marketplace. The law of supply and demand dictates that nothing a firm does on the inside has economic value unless it creates value on the outside. Thus, the starting point of all HR logic should be line-of-sight to the customers' wallets.

Every business function should be accountable for that line of sight. For example, we say that product development does a good job if it creates products that result in customers taking money out of their wallets and putting the money in our company's wallet. This is true for every function: marketing, manufacturing, service, accounting, and IT. If we hold HR to the same standard to which we hold every other department, then we expect HR to create the human and organizational capabilities that meet the requirement of the external marketplace. Thus, effective

CHROs understand and focus on the external customer. If they fail to do so, the good contributions they make by focusing on internal customers may stand in the way of their focusing on the central requirement of external customers. This is supported by our research, which shows that companies whose HR professionals understand and focus on internal knowledge will have inferior performance when compared to companies whose HR professionals understand and focus on knowledge of external customers and competitors.

What to do to be *great*:

1. Study and understand the competitive market environment with focus on customers, competitors, and capital markets, and expect that your key HR executives do the same.
2. Ensure that all HR practices are designed and delivered to create the human and organizational capabilities that meet the requirements of external customers.

Good but Not *Great* Priority #2: Focus on Talent

Over the past decade or so, the talent paradigm has gained considerable momentum. Dozens of books have appeared. Talent management consulting practices have proliferated. Many HR departments have established talent management functions. Obviously, having the right people in the right place at the right time is important. In the 1990s, this phrase was a popular definition of HR's purpose.

Every year in dozens of forums around the world, I ask groups of senior HR executives, "How much time and effort does your HR department spend trying to hire really good people?" They uniformly respond, "Quite a lot." I continue, "And how good of a job do you do?" They again uniformly respond, "Reasonably good." I continue, "Now, all of you leave the room and have your exact counterparts from your most aggressive competitor take your seat in the room. Now I ask your competitor the same two questions. How do they respond?" The executives confirm, "Our competitors will respond just as we did." Then I ask, "So who is right, you or your competitors?" They respond, "We are both right." With that response, they confirm what labor economists have known for many years—over time, major competitors will have roughly the same raw talent.

The critical issue is not the individual talent that you have; competitive advantage resides in what you do with the talent once you have it. Competitive advantage resides in making the organization whole greater than the sum of the talent parts. It is this integrating and leveraging function of organization that creates sustained competitive advantage. This is why organizations exist in the first place. Thus, a focus on talent is a good agenda, but it is inferior to the great agenda of building and sustaining superior organizations.

What to do to be *great*:

1. Do you balance your focus on individual talent and organizational capability with recognition that much of competitive advantage is at the organization level?
2. Do you ensure that your HR department effectively acquires, develops, and retains individual talent?
3. Do you ensure that your HR department creates and sustains the optimal organization through cultural management, work process design, information architecture, organization structure, and systems thinking?

Good but Not *Great* Priority #3:
Focus on Measuring HR

Another developing HR agenda is HR analytics. Two categories of HR analytics may be distinguished: efficiency measures—such as cost per hire, training hours, and ratio of salaries to competitors' salaries—and effectiveness predictive analytics—such as leadership practices that influence employee engagement, impact of training on levels of innovation, and relationship between competency models and individual performance. These are laudable and useful—good—metrics to track the progress of HR.

However, the application of measurement expertise to the business instead of to HR will result in greater impact on business results. As the framers of performance management logic and process, HR should be able to design three categories of robust business metrics: output results, organizational capabilities, and behaviors. Obviously, measuring output results of profitability, market share, revenue growth, and repeat business is essential. As lead indicators of output results, organizational capabilities should be tracked and measured. Measurements of organizational capabilities depend, of course, on the specific organizational capability under consideration. For example, for innovation, the metric might be percent of sales from products that are less than three years old; for service the metric might be customer satisfaction. However, even more essential are behavioral metrics. Just as output results are the lag indicators of the effectiveness of organizational capabilities, organizational capabilities are lag indicators of employee behaviors. The behavioral measurement that should be addressed is, "How do our people need to think and behave differently in the future rather than they have in the past, so that we get better results in the future than we have had in the past?" For a variety of reasons, most competency models fail to address this most important lead-indicating metric. Because of their significance and because most companies fail to establish and use strategically focused lead behavioral indicators, this final type of metric is a source of potential competitive advantage. The combination of these three great business metrics will drive more enhanced business results than good HR-focused metrics.

What to do to be *great*:

1. Develop a clear set of output metrics.
2. Develop a clear set of metrics that represent the operationalization of your company's most valued organizational capabilities.
3. Develop measurements that indicate the extent to which employees are exhibiting the behaviors that will result in high-performance organizational capabilities and superior organizational output results.

Good but Not *Great* Priority #4:
Focus on Applying Best Practices

Membership has grown substantially in the major HR associations from around the world, including the Society for Human Resource Management, or SHRM (U.S.); the Chartered Institute of Personnel and Development, or CIPD (U.K.); the National Human Resource Development Network, or

NHRDN (India); the Australian Human Resources Institute, or AHRI (Australia); and the European Association for People Management, or EAPM (Europe); among others. A proliferation of books, journals, and magazines with an HR best-practice focus has also intensified. A major reason for this growth is the desire of HR professionals to be current about HR best practices from around their respective regions and around the world. Understanding and applying the opportunities and options for HR innovation is a good thing.

Three factors limit the benefit of focusing on best practices. First, by definition, copying what others are already doing will limit your contribution to competitive parity. Second, there is a fine line between legitimate best practices and "flavor of the month," which is frequently attributed to HR. Third and most important is that the focus on best practices may detract from a disciplined line of sight to building the specific culture and organizational capabilities that your firm requires to achieve superior business results. Rather, CHROs should ensure that their collective HR practices focus on a few but critical business issues.

Suppose that one HR executive returns from an HR conference and announces, "I have just returned from my favorite annual HR conference, and I saw this wonderful HR practice from ABC Company. It was a powerful presentation, and I am really enthusiastic about what I saw. This is something that we should consider doing." Compare this to a different HR executive who works for an oil company and says, "I just returned from annual meetings of the Society of Petroleum Engineers. I learned about the major trends that are occurring in our industry. Therefore, these are some of things we should consider doing in HR." The former starts with a good focus on HR best practices; the latter focuses on the great strategic requirements of the business. The most valuable HR best practice is to avoid all other HR best practices except for the best practice that aligns all HR practices with discipline and diligence to a few but critical business issues.

What to do to be *great*?

1. Have a clear definition of how your company creates unique value for customers and shareholders.
2. Ensure that the firm's strategic priorities are clearly defined and ordered.

3. Ensure that your collective HR practices are aligned with line of sight to the few but critical business issues.

Good but Not *Great* Priority #5:
Focus on Communicating HR's Policies and Priorities

HR is the repository of much good information. HR information systems contain information about employees, their performances, their demographics, their capabilities, and their developmental requirements. As part of the HR communication agenda, HR information systems also communicate HR policies and practices such as performance management, talent initiatives, developmental options, promotional criteria, and employee survey results. HR may also take the communications agenda a step further by helping orchestrate and communicate speeches and priorities of the firm's leadership. These are all good information agendas. However, these good information agendas may inadvertently detract focus from HR's involvement in great information agendas.

In the 2012 offering of our research, we found that HR's role in designing the comprehensive flow of business information had more impact on business results than any other HR agenda or activity. Furthermore, we found that this is one area in which HR professionals around the world tend to have the weakest knowledge and skill. The intersection of a practice that is generally not done well but that adds great value when it is done well is a noticeable source of potential competitive advantage.

What does it mean for HR to have a central role in designing the flow of information? Our research shows that six phases of information management may be differentiated: identify and access centrally important external information with a focus on customers and competitors, bring that information into the firm, glean competitive insights from the information through rigorous analysis and discussion, facilitate the optimal dissemination of information for full use in decision-making, and reduce the flow of good but less valuable information. Our research shows that HR departments in a small number of high-performing firms are involved in these activities. In these few firms, HR adds great value by helping their firms move in sync with the ever-changing requirements of the competitive marketplace.

What to do to be *great*:

1. Ensure your personal familiarity with the marketplace information that is most crucial for your firm's capacity to have information advantage over your competitors.
2. Understand the logic and processes through which the entire flow of information may be optimally managed.
3. Undertake initiatives to reduce the flow of less valuable information that can get in the way of the most important information.

Good but Not *Great* Priority # 6:
Focus on Building Credible Relationships in the C-suite

For years, senior HR executives have worked to establish their personal credibility that allow them membership in and access to the C-suite. We are seeing CHROs increasingly invited into the halls of corporate influence. This is a good trend for many reasons. It helps focus senior line leaders' attention on people and organizational issues. It provides representation of the pulse of the internal organization into executive decision-making. It helps legitimize the role of HR in resolving inevitable interpersonal and interdepartmental misunderstanding and conflict. These are good results from CHROs' efforts to build strong relationships in the C-suite.

However, we have noticed a limitation on this focus. It is frequently the case that CHROs who successfully transition into the C-suite become so focused on C-suite dynamics that they allow their attention to be diverted from their HR department focus. This diversion may be self-imposed for ego or other reasons or may be imposed by a CEO who needs a trusted confidant. When this happens, it appears that such CHROs assume that their role in the C-suite will have more impact on business results than the efforts of the collective HR activities.

In the 2012 round of our research, we found that establishing personal credibility is the competency that every level of HR professionals exhibits at a higher level than any other HR competency. The problem is that the personal credibility competency has less impact on business results than any other area of HR involvement. One might argue that this is the price of entry into having influence through other HR agendas.

Such may be the case, but we have no statistics to support this conjecture. Rather, we do have statistics that clearly show the great alternative. When CHROs ensure the integration of their HR department activities with a focus on market-based business results, their impact on business results soars.

What to do to be *great*:

1. Certainly CHROs must build strong relationships with other members of the C-suite.
2. But CHROs must concurrently recognize that their primary value to their firms is in the design and delivery of HR practices that are strategically focused and are delivered by a unified and integrated HR department.

Good but Not *Great* Priority #7:
Focus on Crafting the HR Organization Structure

For much of the last decade and a half, crafting the ideal HR organization has been an ongoing focus of many CHROs and their departments. We frequently ask in dozens of senior HR forums, "What are the top three HR strategies for his year?" One of the common responses is, "Getting the right structure for HR." In the search for the right structure, HR departments seek the optimal combination of many dimensions: centralization, decentralization, shared services, service centers, centers of expertise, business partners, headquarters, embedded HR, outsourcing, insourcing, specialists, generalists, process designers, process deliverers, menu of choices, front-line drivers, and back office support. The good news is that our research concludes that HR departments around the world are effective at designing their organizational structures. The less good news is that having the ideal organizational structure has less influence on HR's contribution to business results that almost anything else that HR does. And as the debate continues, HR's intellectual focus and energy are pulled away from the business and toward building its own structure. The adage that structure is not strategy is sometimes forgotten.

Our research also shows the clear and obvious resolution of this issue. The structure of HR processes and practices that directly affect the business should exactly reflect and support the structure of the business.

This agenda may be divided into two steps. First, the transactional HR work needs to be identified, and the time and money spent on them should be reduced through six ways: centralize into a shared service function, automate, outsource, eliminate, move the work to line leaders, or move it to employees themselves. Second, understand the corporate structure, and craft the HR structure to reflect the corporate configuration.

Four corporate portfolio configurations may be distinguished. Each has different implications for HR structure:

- *Holding company.* In a holding company structure, centralized or headquarters HR is either nonexistent or kept to a bare minimum. The overwhelming preponderance of HR occurs in the business.
- *Unrelated diversification.* In unrelated diversification, HR's focus is to support the cash-generating activities within the differentiated businesses. Thus, HR is generally located within business units; headquarters HR remains proportionately small.
- *Related diversification.* In related diversification, the influence of headquarters HR is large relative to business unit HR. The role of headquarters HR is to leverage synergy and provide a relative uniform set of HR strategies and practices.
- *Single business units.* In single business units, the corporate HR and business unit HR are the same. Note that this is not a function of size; rather, it is a function of singularity of the business model.

What to do to be *great:*

1. Identify your company's portfolio logic. Ensure that there is agreement within the corporate leadership team concerning the corporate strategy. Allocate the HR department resources and influence in accord with the decided portfolio considerations. Try to avoid being clever by utilizing the myriad of consultant-led alternatives.
2. Organize HR to be consistent with the corporate strategy, and then get on with the business of driving business results through customer-focused HR practices.

Conclusion

In many companies CHROs and their departments may place greater focus on good HR agendas and practices than on great HR agendas and practices. On the other hand, to create the greatest value, effective CHROs and their departments do the good but also focus on the great. The key message is this: Do not let your focus on the great be inadvertently displaced by your focus on the good. Through this simple but relatively scarce logic, CHROs can create competitive advantage for their companies, their departments, and themselves.

Note

1. This work has been summarized in six books:
   - » Brockbank, W., & Ulrich, D. (2003). *Competencies for the new HR.* Ann Arbor, Michigan: University of Michigan Business School and Alexandria, VA: Society for Human Resource Management & Global Consulting Alliance.
   - » Ulrich, D., Brockbank, W., Younger, J., & Ulrich, M. (2013). *Global HR competencies: Mastering competitive value from the outside in.* New York, NY: McGraw-Hill.
   - » Ulrich, D., Younger, J., Brockbank, W., & Ulrich, M. (2012). *HR from the outside in.* New York, NY: McGraw-Hill.
   - » Ulrich, D., Allen, J., Brockbank, W., Younger, J., & Nyman, M. (2009). *HR transformation: Building human resources from the outside in.* New York, NY: McGraw-Hill Professional.
   - » Ulrich, D., Brockbank, W., Johnson, D., Sandholtz, K., & Younger, J. (2008). *HR competencies: Mastery at the intersection of people and business.* Alexandria, VA: Society of Human Resource Management & Provo, UT: The RBL Group.
   - » Ulrich, D., & Brockbank, W. (2005). *The HR value proposition.* Cambridge, Mass: Harvard Press.

Endnote

[1.] Jim Collins, *Good to Great: Why Some Companies Make the Leap...And Others Don't* (New York: HarperBusiness, 2001).

PART III

NEW LEVERS FOR COMPETITIVE SUCCESS

Chapter 7.
In Search of Execution

Kenneth J. Carrig, Scott A. Snell, and Aki Onozuka-Evans

A couple of years ago, during a strategic review process at SunTrust, our analysis of the banking financial services industry revealed something interesting: Strategy alone did not differentiate high- from low-performing firms. The true differentiator between winners and losers turned out to be how well the strategy was executed. In other words, across the industry, we found that a firm's business mix could emphasize commercial real estate, or mortgage, or consumer business, or the like, and it could still achieve upper-quartile performance in terms of revenue growth and margin (two key drivers of share price).

The data on this were fairly compelling, and it turns out the trend extends beyond banking. A recent Conference Board CEO survey identified execution capability as the critical challenge facing today's business leaders. No one seems to disagree on the importance of execution, but a study by Bain & Company found that only about 15 percent of companies truly have what we might call "high-performance organizations" (62 percent are rated merely adequate, and a surprising 23 percent actually have organizations that hold them back).[1] John Kotter, an expert on organizational transformation, reinforced this concern, noting that 70 percent of all strategic initiatives fail because of poor execution.[2] Only 37 percent of companies report that they are very good when it comes to execution.[3] Add it all up, and the conclusion seems to be glaringly obvious: (a) execution is important both strategically and operationally, (b) many of us, regardless of industry sector, need to be better at it, and (c) it is a leading cause for concern among CEOs.

Three Lessons about Execution

Over the past few years, we have been on a journey to focus on execution capability. And we have learned three principal lessons along the way. First, although most everyone seems to agree that execution is critical, there is far less agreement on what is required to achieve it. Former Honeywell CEO Larry Bossidy noted in his book *Execution* that people believe they understand execution—"it's about getting things done"—but when asked *how* they get things done, "the dialogue goes rapidly downhill".[4] Researchers at McKinsey found similar divergence; they asked senior executives, academics, and colleagues in the consulting world, finding no agreement about the keys to execution.[5] There are myriad things to consider, and seemingly just as many people with a point of view on the subject. But the approach remains elusive—there is no clear consensus on which factors matter most, or how they are connected to one another. In our experience, execution goes beyond simply implementing a plan; it has as much to do with ongoing alignment and functionality within the firm that result from the interplay of human capital (talent, leadership) and organizational capital (culture, architecture). Not surprisingly, these two factors—human capital and organizational capital—are the underlying themes of this chapter. We want to focus on them specifically.

The second lesson we have learned is that moving from theory to practice can be just as challenging. One of our priorities for the project has been to identify a set of core metrics that allow us to assess a business unit's execution capability. To be candid, our goal has never been to zero in on every isolated element that affects performance. That approach has value, of course, but exhaustive measurement would likely lead to a cacophony of metrics that most CEOs would find unusable. Rather, we embrace the Pareto principle, which states that identifying a subset of key enablers with the maximum impact on business performance may be the best first step forward. We did this with an eye toward developing a *rapid* diagnostic—a predictive execution index (PEI)—that would presage breakthrough financial performance. Neither did we want to create a lengthy, labor-intensive process that would require an army of associates to gather qualitative assessments of organizational health. Our premise has always been that the primary indicators of execution capability are discernable from data currently available within the enterprise. The challenge has been assembling the data and using them productively.

Third, we have learned that most metrics are primarily descriptive, much like a racecar's dashboard—they provide useful information, but in and of themselves they may not prevent accidents, maneuver around obstacles, or propel the car forward. We have adopted the metaphor of a navigation/guidance system that helps us make the right decisions, that improves responsiveness, and that accelerates growth and profitability. Over the past few years, we have been able to frame more clearly what execution excellence entails, but more important, we are learning what it requires. Diagnosis leads to prescription, and we have focused on using our assessments to develop sequenced action plans to address execution gaps. Our goal has not been to devise a standardized list of best practices, but rather to provide guidance in prioritizing interventions to address the most critical issues facing a business.

Our purpose in writing this chapter is to lay out for others what we have been learning along the way. This includes a summary of key dimensions that matter most for execution capability, how those dimensions interact as a system, and how we have begun to build a model of predictive analytics for managing the business. To be sure, we are not presuming to have all the right answers, and we view this chapter as an opportunity to expand the conversation to others with a mutual interest.

The 4A Model

So where do we start? At the end of the day, the performance of organizations depends on building an architecture that supports the collective abilities of individuals aligned toward achieving strategic outcomes. Many elements underlie execution excellence, but we focus on four: (1) alignment, (2) ability, (3) architecture, and (4) activation.

The 4A model is not composed of four independent factors—they are integrally related, interdependent, and mutually causal. Bossidy and Charan argued that "execution is a discipline," and we would not disagree. At the same time, we find it useful to think of execution capability more fundamentally as *building the firm's resource base to energize performance.* As shown in Figure 7.1, this is a system that combines human capital and organizational capital and that generates both potential and kinetic (in motion) energy.

Ironically, we often refer to people and organizations as "resources,"

FIGURE 7.1. 4A MODEL OF EXECUTION CAPABILITY

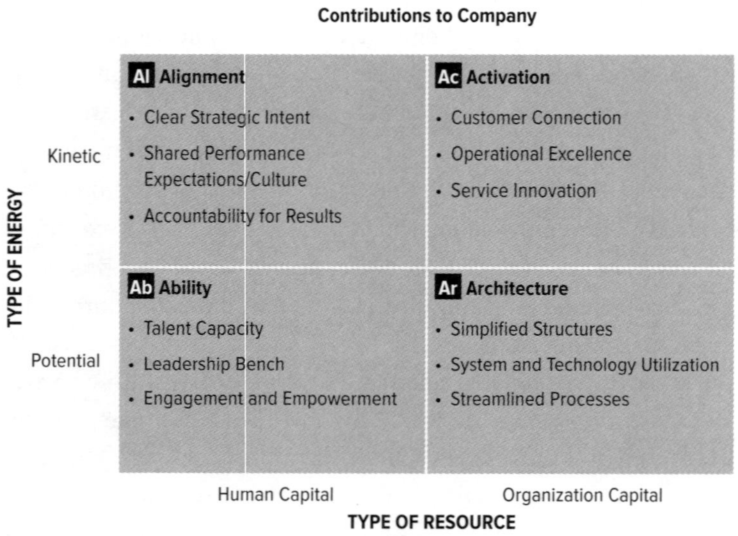

Contributions to Company

	AI Alignment	**Ac** Activation
Kinetic	• Clear Strategic Intent • Shared Performance Expectations/Culture • Accountability for Results	• Customer Connection • Operational Excellence • Service Innovation
Potential	**Ab** Ability • Talent Capacity • Leadership Bench • Engagement and Empowerment	**Ar** Architecture • Simplified Structures • System and Technology Utilization • Streamlined Processes
	Human Capital	Organization Capital

TYPE OF ENERGY (vertical axis)

TYPE OF RESOURCE

---

but less as sources of energy. In his work with senior executive teams, Jim Clawson emphasized that "leadership is about managing energy, first in yourself and then in those around you."[6] The same logic applies to strategy execution. Executives need to build the "ability" and "architecture" factors as sources of *potential* energy—the human potential and organizational potential that determine the firm's capacity to execute. At the same time, they need to foster "alignment" and "activation" as sources of *kinetic* energy—vitality that propels the firm into action. Alignment energizes performance by focusing and concentrating human resources. Activation energizes execution by channeling and accelerating it toward value-adding activities. Ask any leader with responsibility for strategy execution, and he or she will tell you, "Resources are important; managing energy is essential."

Alignment: Focusing Energy toward
Breakthrough Performance

The sine qua non of execution capability is alignment. Organizations exist only because people can achieve more together than on their own. Alignment provides coherence, focus, energy, and resilience in the face of change. And, not surprisingly, lack of alignment is a main source of divergent interests, conflict, dispersion, and decay. We like to invoke the second law of thermodynamics—entropy—that says all physical systems are predisposed toward disarray and randomness, giving off energy along the way. Organizations are no different; they tend toward disintegration, and alignment is the mechanism by which they can reverse this trend and achieve convergence toward their goals. Three underlying elements in our model focus on the cognitive, affective, and operational aspects of alignment.

Clear Strategic Intent

Although strategy per se may not distinguish top- from bottom-quarter firms, this only means that there is no silver bullet. However, the clarity with which the firms' strategy is devised, articulated, and communicated does make a difference. Two decades ago, Treacy and Wiersema described in their book, *The Discipline of Market Leaders*, that 75 percent of the executive teams they studied could not clearly articulate their value proposition.[7] The same can probably be said today, and, without a shared purpose, strategic intent, and articulated strategy, it is difficult to establish a focal point for collective action and performance. [*Metrics*: leadership unity, communication]

Shared Performance Expectations and Culture

Shared expectations, goals, norms, and values help clarify both "why" we work together and "how" we work together, that is, the rules of engagement. As the foundation of the organization's culture, shared expectations serve both as points of aspired behavior and guardrails for acceptable action. But in the context of execution, shared expectations have to be operationalized as concrete behaviors driving performance, or else they get lost in the sea of good intentions and soft ideas. Peter Drucker once said, "Culture eats strategy for lunch," and he may have been right. But a clear strategic intent that is grounded in strong performance expectations represents the vital means-ends combination for execution capability. [*Metrics*: performance management aligned to business, employee engagement, retention]

Accountability for Results

Many of those we work with assume that emphasis on accountability is a reaction to employee shirking. At some level this may true, but we think of the term more literally as "account" and "ability" combined. Without the ability to account for results toward a goal, it is difficult to create much focus for action or to energize commitment toward it. More practically, accountability requires establishing a set of performance metrics, feedback processes, and shared outcomes (rewards) for performance. The idea is not new, of course, but it is surprising how frequently the rewards of executives—not to mention others in the organization—are not clearly linked to firm-level results. [*Metrics*: performance management, pay for performance]

Ability: Building Human Potential

People are an organization's greatest asset (there, we have promulgated the cliché). But the truth is that many organizations have faltered while burgeoning with talented people. And, if we were brutally honest, we would admit that organizations traditionally have worked to take people out of the production equation to improve execution, preferring to substitute technologies for humans. But in the contemporary setting, where knowledge is a vital ingredient for both efficiency and effectiveness, that would be a mistake. We focus on three aspects of an organization's human capital.

Talent Capacity

Like any capital investment, the "make or buy" decisions for talent require tough choices about where payoffs will be greatest. Because HR budgets are often the first to be cut in difficult times, fewer dollars means more scrutinized investment. The priority with regard to execution is generating more high performers, particularly in critical roles. An internal study at IBM pinpointed "focal jobs" that make the most clear difference to success, and channeled time, energy, and resources toward these.[8] Our experience suggests that execution depends crucially on this approach to talent capacity. [*Metrics*: retention rate, vacancy rate, percent distribution of "A" performers in "A" positions]

Leadership Bench

Leadership, beyond talent alone, often comes down to mobilizing excellence through others. Cultivating leaders requires longer lead times, of course, and therefore more enduring investment. As Wayne Gretzky, the great talent guru said, "Skate to where the puck is going to be." There are many different leadership competency models, and we would emphasize four key attributes: (1) interpret/understand the business context, (2) translate that vision to energize others, (3) build collaborative networks internally and externally, and (4) empower others to excel. [*Metrics*: succession rates, "ready now" percentage]

Engagement and Empowerment

Performance is often described (by academics, at least) as a function of ability, motivation, and opportunity (hence the formula: $P = f [A*M*O]$). In this sense, an organization's ability to execute ultimately depends on engaging employees toward collective achievement. Engagement in this sense goes beyond motivation and commitment (although certainly those are critical elements) to include some degree of discretion that empowers people with the latitude to execute and improve in their roles. If execution is viewed only as a top-down initiative, the organization will miss contemporaneous opportunities that drive performance excellence from the bottom up. [*Metrics*: employee engagement, empowerment, satisfaction, retention]

Architecture: Designing Organizational Capability

The design of organizations makes a big difference in terms of reliability, scalability, and continuity of performance. So in terms of strategy execution, the organizational architecture is critical for managing resource flows, information availability, decision-making, and process. We focus on three chief aspects of the organization's architecture.

Simplified Structures

Although the adage "structure follows strategy" probably still applies, in terms of execution capability, the key is to simplify structures to eliminate needless complexity. The two fundamental purposes for structure are (a) to delineate lines of authority and decision rights and (b) to improve channels of coordination and communication. Long ago, Lawrence and Lorsch referred to these as differentiation and integration—more of one requires more of the other.[9] Elaborate structures result in conflicting priorities, duplicate communication flows, and slower decisions. The rule of thumb is to align the formal structure with how work is actually done, rather than to reflect budgetary or functional lines. [*Metrics*: organizational layers/size, spans of control, dotted-line reporting]

Information System Access/Utilization

It may come as no surprise that knowledge management is viewed by executives as the most important source of potential productivity gains over the next 15 years.[10] The role of information technology affects execution capability in three principal ways: (a) operational, (b) relational, and (c) transformational. At a base level, information systems help standardize data and automate lower-value transactional operations. Beyond that, technologies also connect people in real time, providing them with shared access to data and information and, more so, enabling synchronous collaboration and knowledge-sharing opportunities. At the extreme, technologies transform the organization by reducing or eliminating the separation of time and distance, supporting decisions that are both better and faster. Unfortunately, we often hear from colleagues that systems are more often used for reporting than for informing. The key for execution is to balance the two to make information available for decision-making. [*Metrics:* information access, connectivity]

Streamlined Processes

Technology investment without corresponding process redesign is like "paving the cow paths." A whole cottage industry has arisen around the principles of process improvement and execution. We would not duplicate that here, but only acknowledge the value of interventions such as lean six sigma and business process reengineering to eliminate variance, reduce waste (a.k.a. "muda"), and streamline the flow of work to improve efficiencies. At a minimum, execution is improved when processes and standard work are clearly defined, process owners are known and accountable, and measurement systems are used as a basis for decision-making. [*Metrics*: definition of standard work, compliance rates]

Activation: Channeling Value-Added Effort

Will Rogers, the famous humorist, used to quip, "Even if you're on the right track, you'll get run over if you just sit there." The same is true of strategy execution. In contrast to the common conception of strategy implementation, whereby someone says "go," world-class execution is nearly impossible to achieve from a standing start. It requires a base level of activation, without which nothing much really happens. Think of a sailboat analogy: Until water is moving over the rudder, it is impossible to steer or accelerate. Once moving, the design of the boat and the skill of the sailors complement each other, making all the difference in performance. We focus on three forms of activation for strategy execution, each of which provides a more proximal indicator of firm performance:

Customer Connectivity

The importance of customer engagement might be overlooked if we assume that execution is a strictly internally focused capability. In fact, the connection to customers helps clarify priorities for execution. We first need to clarify how we intend to stake a claim in the marketplace, and then design the organization's infrastructure and allocate resources to execute toward those ends. Not surprisingly, enduring customer relationships, engagement, and loyalty help ensure organizational resilience during turbulent times, increasing the degree of certainty and stability in the value stream. [*Metrics:* lifetime customer value, VOC scores, NPS]

Operational Excellence

In some ways, we might conclude that execution and operational excellence are synonymous. To some, the differences may only be semantic. In this context, we conceive of operational excellence more narrowly, as those activities driving internal efficiency (of course, strategy execution goes beyond that). Principles of continuous improvement, streamlined processes, and employee engagement all apply, and their impact on operational excellence can also be seen in their impact on costs, quality (defects/rework), and cycle time (flow rates). This applies to both manufacturing and service environments. [*Metrics*: costs, efficiency ratio, waste reduction, quality/defect, lead time]

Product/Service Innovation

Experts in the field of innovation make a distinction between two types of organizational learning: (a) exploration, which is going into new domains, and (b) exploitation, which is deeper learning within the current domain. This second type of innovation and learning is critical for execution capability. Without developing deeper expertise in current product/service domains, a firm's execution capability will stall. "New and improved" is not just an advertising slogan; it is the lifeblood of firm performance. [*Metrics*: revenue from products/service < 3 years old, IP registration/renewal]

Using the Model

Three Steps toward Improved Execution

With this in mind, we view enhancing execution capability in terms of a three-step process. Recall that our overriding priorities are to (1) profile businesses in ways that are usable by the senior team, (2) do so using operational data currently accessible in the business, (3) provide rapid diagnostics of execution capability, and (4) prioritize targeted interventions to address capability gaps.

Step One: Business Assessment. As shown in Figure 7.2, the first step is making a realistic assessment of current and desired financial performance for each business unit. Typically, we focus on two primary financial drivers (growth and margin) and a secondary driver (performance variability) of firm valuation and share price. The assessment of current and desired state has as much to do with strategic goals as it does with firm performance, and much of the decision has to do with positioning within the competitive set. Top-quartile performance may not be the goal, or it may not be feasible in the current time period. In our experience, this assessment leads to a robust discussion among the management team, which is necessary for establishing priorities for strategy execution.

FIGURE 7.2: PREDICTIVE EXECUTION

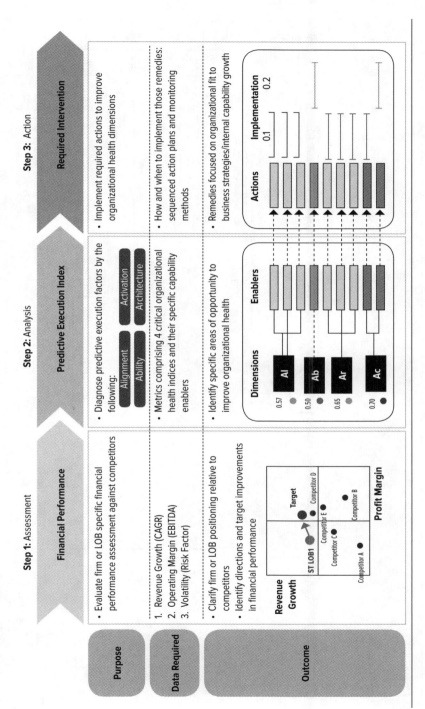

FIGURE 7.3: PREDICTIVE EXECUTION INDEX (PEI)

Assessment	Dimensions	Enablers	Metrics	Ratings (LOB)	
				CIB	BB/CML
		Clear Strategic Intent	Engagement Scores — Purpose	.92	.87
			Leadership team stability (separation)	.66	.72
			Pay-for-Performance	.88	.88
		Shared Performance Expectations/Culture	% Individual goals aligned with LOB	.76	.67
			% Team goals aligned with LOB	.84	.79
			Engagement Scores — Shared Values	.78	.83
		Accountability for Results	Pay for performance	.72	.54
			Compensation mix	x	x
			Equity (Options)	x	x
		Talent Capacity	% of 'A' players of total teammates	x	x
			% of Vacant Critical Positions	x	x
			Retention rates	x	x
		Leadership Bench	Succession pipeline	x	x
			9-box % allocation change	x	x
			'Ready Now' percentage	x	x
		Engagement and	% of Teammates with Required Courses Completed	x	x

Alignment

CIB BB/CML
.90 .81

Ability

CIB BB/CML
.90 .61

ROI

EBITDA

%

%

ENTERPRISE VALUE / BOOK VALUE

%

GROWTH IN NI/SALES

%

Architecture

CIB	BB/CML
.76	.83

Simplified Structures
- Average spans of control
- Repetitive/Dotted line reports

Information System Access
- Information access %
- System utilization rates

Streamlined Processes
- Process owners
- Standard work definitions
- Compliance rates %

Activity

CIB	BB/CML
.92	.84

Customer Connectivity
- VOC scores
- Loyalty rates
- Lifetime customer value

Operational Excellence
- Efficiency ratios
- Cost, quality, cycle time

Product/Service Innovation
- Sales from products/services < 3-5 years old
- IP registration/renewal

○ .85 – 1.0
◐ .70 – .84
● .00 – .69

Step Two: Analysis of Underlying Metrics. The second step, analysis of key metrics that operationalize the 4A model, helps us establish a PEI for each line of business (LOB). As illustrated in Figure 7.3, alignment, ability, architecture, and activation each are composed of three more specific "enablers" of execution performance. Each enabler, in turn, is operationalized by a set of common internal metrics. Aggregating across these metrics, each LOB receives a rating that is then conveyed as a PEI. Note: The figure illustrates a hypothetical comparison of two different business units. The value of this approach is that it provides a summary indicator of organizational health, but more prescriptively it also provides a set of lenses with which to probe more deeply into the root causes of any performance gaps.

As a byproduct of this analysis, we also find it useful to present the PEI data graphically to show the execution profile of a business unit. Figure 7.4, for example, illustrates (using a radar graph) a business unit with considerable strengths and some debilitating weaknesses. Specifically, the alignment and ability factors are rated within the zone of "exceptional" performance. The architecture factor is supporting at a "qualified" level, meaning that although improvements are needed, concerns are not urgent. However, this business has a rating for activation that is in the "disqualified" zone and needs immediate attention. Without targeted interventions to improve capability on this dimension, the impact of the other three will likely be compromised.

These three rating zones—exceptional, qualified, and disqualified—reinforce the evidence we have found that even superior capability in one area cannot make up for excessive problems in another. If there is a "disqualified" rating on one or more factors, nothing else much matters; execution will be deficient. On the other hand, once execution capability falls within an acceptable zone across all four factors, the model actually becomes "compensatory," in that strengths in one area can actually substitute for (some) weaknesses in another. For example, one executive told us, "Great processes make up for average talent, but great talent cannot compensate for bad processes." We would agree, within certain limits. If either of these factors falls into the "disqualified zone," excellence in another category will likely not matter.

Step Three: Action Plan for Targeted Intervention. This discussion leads to the third step in the process: establishing an action plan for

FIGURE 7.4: EXECUTION CAPABILITY PROFILE

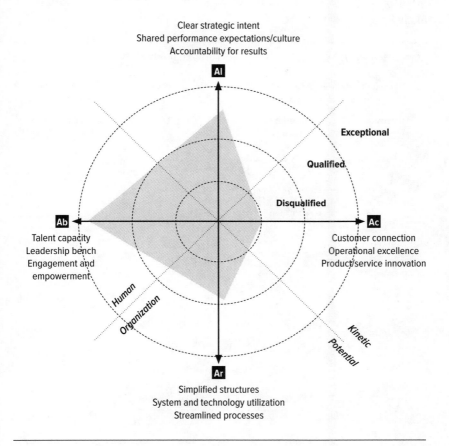

targeted remedies to execution gaps. When done right, these action plans build on information from the PEI and essentially serve as a "playbook" that allows others within the organization to act on the information. To achieve this, four conditions have to be met at this stage: (1) establish clear priorities for action, (2) identify owners of each intervention or initiative, (3) budget for all the required resources (financial, human, information), and (4) agree on timelines for action and review.

Figure 7.5, for example, shows priorities for action, targeted interventions, and timelines for implementation. Note that certain actions are both urgent and important (for example, customer relationship management, value-stream mapping) because they are remedial or corrective. Before other planned interventions will likely pay off, these have priority, and because of the larger performance gap, the timeline for intervention will likely be longer.

FIGURE 7.5: TARGETED INTERVENTIONS REQUIRED FOR EXECUTION CAPABILITY

Dimensions	Prioritized Enablers	Targeted Actions	Implementations Q4, 2014 — Q1, 2015
Alignment 0.91	Clarify strategy	Mgr focus groups	
	Perform Expect	Executive comp.	
	Accountability	Executive comp.	
Ability 0.88	Leadership	Succession mgmt	Q4, 2015
Architecture 0.78	Process	Proc. ownership	
	System	ERP review	
Activity 0.62	Cust. Connect	CRM	Q3, 2014 - Q4, 2015
	Op Excel	Value steam map	Q3, 2014 - Q4, 2015

Enablers prioritized based on their impact to business

Specific intervention selected for prioritized enablers

PEI scoring drives prioritized enablers and specific actions

Clear priorities, timelines, resources and owners established for prioritized actions

Conclusion

We have been on a journey; we have learned a good deal about the elements most critical for execution. It has enabled us to focus more precisely on those factors that matter, driving performance, and it helps create a more robust organization that leads to resilience and new strategic possibilities.

Our purpose for this chapter has been to present a model that helps business leaders frame the challenges of execution, providing them with a set of metrics and corresponding plans for action that they can use to determine the path forward toward breakthrough performance. And just as importantly, the approach we recommend emphasizes usability, simplicity, and relevance, so that business leaders might sustain momentum of the approach over time. In our experience, the upside potential for planning, communication, and performance management is significant.

Although our primary focus has been on relevance to the CEO and leadership team in general, we believe there are also clear learning points for the HR profession and chief human resource officers (CHROs) in particular. Various observers have at times argued for a more narrow definition of the HR function restricted to just talent management or just analytics, while at other times they have perhaps inadvertently separated the function from other parts of the enterprise by emphasizing "HR professionalization." We take just the opposite view; the opportunity for HR leaders is to broaden their purview and influence in a way that affects business performance in total, evolving the role of the CHRO to more like the "chief financial officer" (CFO) of human, social, and organizational capital. We would argue that when our focus is on execution capability and performance of the entire firm, narrow functional walls serve neither HR nor the organization well. Instead, our goal continues to be enabling progress toward a transformation of HR to ensure that the strategic purpose, capability, and performance expectations are understood and integrated throughout the entire organization. Doing so increases the likelihood that executional excellence will occur and be sustained over time.

Endnotes

[1.] Rogers, Paul & Blenko, Marcia, *The Decision-Driven Organization*. Bain & Company, 2005.

[2.] Kotter, J.P. Accelerate! *Harvard Business Review*, November, 2012.

[3.] How hierarchy can hurt strategy execution. *Harvard Business Review*, July-August, 2010.

[4.] Bossidy, L., Charan, R., & Burck, C. *Execution: The Discipline of Getting*

Things Done. New York, Crown Business, 2002.

5. Keller, S., & Price, C. *Beyond Performance: How Great Organizations Build Ultimate Competitive Advantage.* Hoboken, N.J., Wiley, 2011.

6. Clawson, J. G. *Level Three Leadership: Getting Below the Surface.* Upper Saddle River, N.J., Pearson/Prentice Hall, 2009.

7. Treacy, M., & Wiersema, F. D. *The Discipline of Market Leaders: Choose Your Customers, Narrow Your Focus, Dominate Your Market.* Reading, Mass, Addison-Wesley Pub. Co., 1995.

8. Lesser, Eric, Denis Brousseau, and Tim Ringo. Focal jobs: Viewing Talent through a Different Lens. *IBM Global Business Services Executive Reports.* IMG Institute for Business Value, Human Capital Management. October 2009.

9. Lawrence, Paul R., and J. W. Lorsch. *Organization and Environment.* Boston, MA: Harvard Business School, Division of Research, 1967.

10. Foresight 2020: Economic, industry and corporate trends. The Economist Intelligence Unit, *Economist,* 2006.

Chapter 8.
Creating Sustainable Culture Change

Elizabeth "Libby" Sartain

Few organizations can authentically claim they have created a sustainable winning culture. Academic studies indicate that companies with strong cultures outperform their competitors. For example, Kotter and Heskett found that organizations with cultures focused on customers, employees, and shareholders increased revenue by an average of 682 percent over 166 percent over an 11-year period versus those without this cultural focus.[1]

CEOs credit corporate culture as the foundation of organizational capability and success on investor calls or in the media. A competitor can duplicate almost any differentiator, but culture may be the only thing that cannot be copied. When an organization consistently builds and reinforces such a culture, it creates a competitive edge that is hard to replicate. So one of the top agenda items for corporate leadership teams is to drive transformation of the company culture to achieve better results or increased innovation.

On the other hand, culture is often referenced by the media as a contributing factor when an organization fails or is cited as a reason when bad behavior is allowed to go unchecked. Therefore, organizations hoping to turn around poor performance often focus on cultural changes.

Why Most Cultural Change Initiatives Fail

Even when done for all the right reasons by well-meaning teams, most culture change initiatives fail. The problem with a "culture initiative" inside an organization is that it implies intense project work for a finite period of time and with a small team of leaders working with the CEO to affect needed change.

HR is typically charged with a leading role in such initiatives. We start out with a definition of mission, vision, values, strategy, and goals. We conduct research inside and outside the organization to assess where we are and where we want to go. And, ultimately, we define a desired culture and corresponding behaviors for leaders and workers. Employing the best of change management processes, we then make changes to HR programming to reinforce the change, and we champion the culture within the organization. This work is important, and the components are essential to a strong culture. But this work alone is not sustainable.

This model does not work because it assumes that if we establish goals with corresponding rewards and consequences that we can change behaviors by changing people via the environment rather than by actually changing the culture. Most people do not change their behaviors long term, sometimes even when it is a matter of life or death—like quitting smoking or losing weight.

No workshop, team-building exercise, rewards program, nor the best of corporate communications can effect sustainable change. The change has to become a way of life, self-replicating to be sustainable. It is hard and takes dedication. It requires a functional overhaul, as well as an emotional overhaul.

A sustainable culture depends on people and practices that reinforce the culture daily. It may require an evaluation of every leader and worker to ensure their personal values align with the company's values. Values drive actions, which, in turn, reinforce culture. Every process and practice, the entire infrastructure, and all people programs must be aligned. A sustainable culture requires ongoing focus by everyone in the organization.

Elements of Sustaining Culture Change

Cultural alignment does not imply an organization of clones but one in which everyone shares a set of core values and is aligned around a common cause. In my experience there are key elements to drive this alignment:

- An employer brand that enables culture to become a way of life.
- Hiring for cultural fit, mapping individual values to corporate values.

- Cultivating leaders who promote culture.
- Adjusting HR processes, programs, systems, and infrastructure.
- Communicating, nurturing stories, developing rituals, and celebrating.
- Anointing culture keepers.
- Measuring results.

The Power of Employer Brand

Simply put, the employer brand is a way to make a culture come alive. It gives a business a consistent voice and authenticity about its relationship with workers. Done well it can be the most powerful tool a business can employ to create an emotional connection with workers that engages hearts and minds. Developing an employer brand can embed a sustainable cultural alignment.

An employer brand can be defined as how a business builds and packages its identity and what it promises to deliver to emotionally connect employees so that they, in turn, deliver what the business promises to customers.[2] Just as a corporate or consumer brand makes promises to customers, employer brand makes promises to workers. A business must create an employee experience that engages before it can expect employees to deliver a brand experience or a well-branded product to customers.

The employer brand must be applied consistently across the entire life cycle of workers from the time a prospective candidate becomes aware of your organization as a place to work to his or her departure from the organization. Over time, HR can brand the programs offered to employees from leadership development, compensation, benefits, and events. Many of these offerings are essential to the employee experience and can be branded to support cultural messaging.

Hire for Cultural Fit

The most critical cultural element is the people in the organization and their own personal values. Culture involves behaviors and years of perceptions and understandings in the hearts and minds of workers. Values are what drive how work gets done. Every interaction an employee has with another is part of the equation. Thus, everyone's values matter in a corporation. One person's behavior can affect customers or an entire team of workers. Interactions with leaders are the most important as an exemplar of what is desired.

Ultimately, culture is personal. For the culture to be authentic, the actual experience that a worker has at the business has to reflect the culture. How individuals' personal values mesh with the value sets of the others with whom they interact dictates their feelings toward the company, the team, and their managers. The experience is a collection of interactions created by all of the workers and leaders in the organization. So each worker must feel, act, and believe that he or she is part of the culture and has an opportunity to have an impact on it every day.

Hiring people whose values match company values should be one of the top competencies of an organization committed to a high-performance culture. Implementing stringent hiring practices is the most crucial step in the process. It is also the element that picks up traction the fastest. A consistent process must be used to deliver the right kind of people throughout the entire organization. By contrast, if every hiring manager is hiring a candidate using his or her values system as the lens, culture will never be aligned.

Leadership Behavior

Leaders cannot solely create the corporate culture, but they are strong influencers through their day-to-day behavior. Workers must hear from their bosses how the company will support them. Leaders must be able to clearly articulate the employee value proposition for workers answering the question, "What's in it for me to work here?" Likewise, there should be a set of expectations on how leaders act that might include a formal set of competencies to support behaviors. Face-to-face interactions with an employee's immediate leader influences what is important, valued, and rewarded, as well as, what can be ignored.

How do you cultivate the right leaders? When selecting leaders from inside or outside the company, make sure they share the desired values. A sustainable culture will both prepare leadership successors and ease the transition. The most effective way to ensure a smooth transition is to invest in leadership development programs that are aligned with values. Pick your best exemplars of the desired values, and develop them as leaders. But if you make a mistake, terminate those who are unable to work in concert with the company values. One or two visible exits will show the organization is serious about making culture a way of life.

HR Programming

Just as leadership sets the tone for cultural alignment, HR drives the day-to-day reality. HR programs and supporting technology can create the desired experience at different phases of the employment experience. Each stage of the experience will need to have a look, feel, and personality aligned with the culture's aspiration, including each learning and development offering, recognition and rewards, and finally—departure and retirement. From goal setting to performance review to compensation administration, the challenge is to view the processes and practices through the cultural lens and make the adjustment as necessary.

Communications and Celebration

Internal communications to and from the workers are part of bringing the culture and employer brand to life. Workers will look to messages coming from inside the organization to connect to the cultural elements. The unique history is powerful when crafted into a narrative to explain how the culture was created and evolved.

Today, any culture must also stand the test of social media, which gives access to limitless networks of people to share any idea or experience. Internal communication has moved beyond informing people to securing and engaging. It reaches outside to people considering the employer, as well as inside, engaging and retaining employees.

There is an inherent skepticism among workers and candidates as to whether an employer's cultural messaging is authentic. So they will check outside resources, including ratings and reviews, for validation. A multichannel approach is needed. Internal and external communities online can connect workers and prospects to ideas and causes and provide assistance for on-the-job or work/life challenges.

Celebrations of success and even light-hearted recognition of mistakes can make a culture feel real. Workers want to believe that what they do matters, that they make a difference, and that someone notices. Advancing the culture in an organization can be as simple, and as permanent, at sharing the spotlight with as many people as possible. While recognition opportunities do not have to be public, achievements can give everyone the opportunity to celebrate. And celebrations can make a culture feel alive and fun.

Providing a small budget or toolkit for managers can enable them to constantly reinforce the culture by recognizing those whose actions exemplify the organization's values, behaviors, and standards. Teams can celebrate their achievements. Formal and informal recognition reinforces desired behaviors.

Culture Committee

Southwest Airlines famously created a Culture Committee to keep the culture alive. The committee consists of approximately 120 employees who serve staggered three-year terms and meet quarterly, creating their own agenda. This committee organizes many cultural events and celebrations inside the company to keep the culture alive. Just a few examples from the author's time on the committee are below:

- Hokey Day: Committee members clean the airplanes—using handheld sweepers—to give flight attendants a break between flights.
- Maintenance barbeques: Committee members host a barbeque for maintenance workers from midnight to 3:00 a.m.
- Holiday meals: Committee members cook and serve meals to flight crews and airport employees who work on Thanksgiving and Christmas.
- New hire committee: Committee members create packets and activities to reinforce the culture for new hires.
- Adopt a break room: Committee members paint and decorate a break room for employees in a remote location.

The Culture Committee ensures that ideas from people other than top management are brought to the forefront. Sustainability relies on all workers, entry-level positions to managers, to contribute ideas and solutions. The quarterly meetings become idea sessions, and the company has the opportunity to hear fresh voices to find out what is working and what needs to be improved. It also reinforces that everyone owns the culture and is empowered to make an impact.

Assessing Cultural Effectiveness

Culture's importance is almost universally recognized, but it rarely garners daily attention because it seems subjective or anecdotal. Metrics are needed to show progress and to hold everyone accountable as keepers of the culture. To date, no universal tool has been developed to measure the value delivered and progress made on cultural effectiveness, but many organizations are working on assessments and dashboards.

To track progress, a dashboard can be developed to measure results. Metrics of success will depend on the issues the organization is working to solve, but the most common and universal metrics include the following:

1. Values assessment via brief pulse surveys to gauge the strength of the core values, the movement of the desired values, and the perception of whether the organization is "living the desired values."
2. Net promoter score (NPS) results from asking employees, "Would you recommend a friend work at this company?"
3. Engagement measures.
4. Number and quality of candidates who are a cultural fits.
5. Recruiting costs.
6. Retention rates for the right people.
7. Media coverage on the organization's culture.
8. "Best company" reports.
9. Insights gleaned from social media and listening to employees.
10. Corporate performance relative to competitors that do not focus on cultural alignment.

The Power of Purpose

Perhaps the strongest measure of an aligned, self-replicating culture is whether any employee or candidate can tell you what the company stands for. Do workers understand the business strategy and how their work and performance contribute to company performance?

Today's workers look for businesses that they can believe in and proudly tell others about. A job should be LinkedIn or Facebook worthy. People respond to values and traditions. When people know their impact on the company strategy, they are more engaged and productive. No surprise that, inside sustainable business cultures, stories about legends of the business pass from person to person to preserve the humanity of the legend and what the organization stands for.

Endnotes

[1] John P. Kotter and James L. Heskett, *Corporate Culture and Performance* (New York: Free Press, 1992).

[2] Libby Sartain and Mark Schumann, *Brand from the Inside: Eight Essentials to Emotionally Connect Your Employees to Your Business* (San Francisco: Jossey Bass, 2006).

Chapter 9.
Believe in Your People, and They May Surprise You

Michael D'Ambrose

As a proud father of two grown sons, I have thought a lot about how we raise kids. If your child is good at, say, baseball but not swimming, you do not tell him or her to work on getting better in the pool. You focus on your children's interests and talents. You build their strengths and you nurture them there.

The same dynamic happens with sport teams. We do not expect a quarterback to become a better blocker, or a lineman to work on catching the ball. When winning matters, we play to everyone's strengths. To build a great team, we give each player a specific role, and we leverage all their talents together.

We all agree about focusing on strengths with our kids and team-mates. So why would we treat our professional lives differently?

Consider this research from Gallup: Managers who received strengths feedback showed 13 percent greater productivity and 9 percent greater profitability than peers who did not receive any feedback at all.[1] Gallup also found that only 13 percent of employees—across 142 countries worldwide—were engaged in their jobs.[2] Not surprisingly, there continues to be a strong correlation between unengaged employees and business outcomes.

With statistics like these, how are HR departments—designed to support and grow people—doing? The numbers are not good. In 2014, Deloitte surveyed executives of companies with 10,000 or more employees. Nearly half, 48 percent, said their HR departments were not ready to reskill to meet the demands of the business. Even among HR executives, only 8 percent had confidence in their teams' skills and abilities to meet those demands.[3] Numbers like these call for a dramatic change in our approach to HR to achieve the performance we need.

As chief human resources officer at ADM, I encourage all of our managers and executives to believe in our people the same way they believe in people in their personal lives. This is not just a nice-to-have approach; it gets real results. It is the difference between winning and losing in our business.

We know engaged employees perform better. And the more engaged employees you have, the better your business performs. So how do you engage people? I have found some fundamental truths and effective practices that cut across industries, companies, and people. I am humbled to be part of great teams that have achieved extraordinary outcomes, and I would like to share with you some of the strategies that have worked for these teams over the course of my career.

Believing in Your People

First, I believe that everyone comes to work wanting to succeed. People want to work on things that make a difference, and they want to be trusted and respected for their work. If you approach people in this way, thinking that they want to succeed, you will give people meaningful work and a supportive environment. They will do their best work, and you will obtain the outcomes you want.

I saw this early in my career when I had my own company, which struggled in the beginning. I felt the full weight of our success or failure on my shoulders. I did not want to disappoint my people or their families who counted on them. But I did not know the industry well. It did not matter how much pressure I felt, or how much I wanted to succeed; I could not do it on my own. I had to believe in my people and trust them. And a funny thing happened. The more I trusted them, the better they performed. Together, we succeeded.

Here is another example of how trusting in people can have transformative results. After I moved back into human resources, I worked for a company that gave out a set number of sick days every year—which also became the average number of sick days that employees took every year. Managers complained, "This is so expensive; we have to reduce the number of sick days." But we did the opposite. We gave unlimited sick days. We told everyone, "We trust you. If you're sick, you're paid. But if you're healthy, please come to work." And we cut the average use in half. We continue to see this trend in the industry as more and more companies are considering policies, such as unlimited or discretionary vacation time, and its impact on company performance.[4] It is an issue to watch, and one that may continue to transform HR practices and, most importantly, company performance.

Second, I believe that everyone is great at something. With children, we recognize that each child is different. Each child has a gift, something special to offer. As parents, coaches, and educators, we help children develop their gifts with feedback along the way. We set boundaries, but boundaries that are empowering, not limiting, so they can become the great people they were intended to be.

Eventually, these children grow up. They finish school and go to work for a company. After working for a time, they receive a traditional performance review that emphasizes shortcomings rather than strengths. And they have to bend to processes and systems that assume everyone works and learns the same way. Normative rules get normal results.

If you really believed in your people and in their strengths, what would your process for setting individual priorities and goals look like? How would you go about helping them perform at their best and giving feedback that was meaningful? How would you reward them, develop them, give them new capabilities, and enhance the capabilities they have? And if you believed in people, how would you handle paid-time off and other benefits?

Bringing "Believing" to Life

Every day we have the ability to demonstrate our belief in people and to inspire discretionary performance as a result. As an HR leader, I see four broad areas: performance management, merit pay, benefits, and talent management.

Maybe the biggest area is performance management, a term I do not like. The language we use in HR sets a tone. It can encourage or discourage an organization's belief in its people. I want our supervisors to see themselves not as managers but as coaches, helping people do their best.

"Coaching" says, "How do we become great at what we already do? I'm here to help you succeed. We're all in this together." "Managing" feels more like an arms-length relationship, where I am off to the side waiting for you to perform, and I do not trust you to do well.

Performance management usually leads to ratings, which I find cause more trouble than they are worth. Usual ratings force about 70 percent of the employees to be "average." Who wants to be average? Instead of driving better performance, these labels often do the opposite by disengaging people from the organization.

Rather than set performance ratings, which focus on what people did wrong, we can train supervisors to push people to be even better at their strengths. Everyone has weaknesses, but in most cases, a strong team balances each other out, with every member complementing strengths and weaknesses. Companies have the opportunity to create lean, nimble organizational structures, whereby employees have the ability to grow and test their strengths in a multitude of efforts and settings. This creates a win-win dynamic: Employees are positioned to grow and succeed, while the company can leverage the most effective team for any given project.

Fortunately, a lot of companies are starting to rethink their policies, including performance ratings. Past practices are not achieving the level of performance required. A recent Deloitte survey found that 58 percent of surveyed executives said their current performance management approach drove neither engagement nor superior performance.[5] I believe there is an upswell coming in HR, and it is moving in the direction of believing in your people.

What does that mean? It means HR will have to do more, not less. Good feedback is tough, and it is often difficult for people to give on a frequent basis. We can help supervisors get better at it. It is easier for a manager to say, "I'm not succeeding because this person's not any good, and I have to let them go," than it is to say, "It's my job to find the goodness in that person, and I'm not succeeding at that." It takes effort and thoughtfulness to discover what people are good at. But that is part of believing in your people.

Finding the good does not mean that we accept complacency or poor performance. We must continue to acknowledge both our personal strengths and weaknesses, as well as those of our teams, to achieve personal and professional growth. What makes a chief human resource officer, or any leader, successful is the ability to understand how to leverage each employee's strengths to build high-performing teams. Through teams, we can achieve better results. And if we skillfully build teams around each person's strengths, just think about the results that we could achieve.

Merit Pay: What Really Motivates People

We have the same opportunity with merit pay. I know of organizations that used to budget for merit-based raises. Business leaders tried to control the process by dictating levels to managers based on a certain average. Then they decided to drop the budgets and just give managers a range, trusting them to give out the raises properly. They also encouraged the managers to share their thinking with others. In the end, without any kind of forcing, the raises on average were close to the previous levels. Managers got there in a way that was positive, with trust and belief, and a lot of open communication.

In any case, the main reward for performance has never really been about raises. It is about promotion. People do not work any harder to receive small boosts in salary. The people who succeed beyond expectations are the ones who attain the next job, the next opportunity. That is how hierarchies in organizations are built, and the competition to get ahead is what drives a lot of accountability.

Benefits: Aligning Benefit Platforms
with a Culture of Caring

Benefits are another way to show this kind of trust directly. Benefits are a real intersection between work and a person's personal life. Think about what a difference you can make with employees in terms of what really matters in life—a sick parent, or a child whose treatment is not covered under the health plan.

In such circumstances, we should ask whether there is another way to help that employee. Can we help cover the expense outside the plan, or perhaps even cover it out of our operating funds? We have the ability to make smart exceptions to all of our policies. We do not have to say no. We need to create situations that build trust. For example, I recall my experience with an employee whose father was dying. The employee asked if he could have an extended weekend to spend some time with his father. Rather than grant this simple request, we gave the employee the opportunity to work from home for a limited time and approved more time off to spend with his father. It was just the right thing to do.

Imagine this: What if we treated everyone as we wanted to be treated? What a wonderful world we would live in. That employee I mentioned previously? He will never forget the way that the company treated him, and he will pass on that philosophy for the remainder of his own career. Think about the impact if we treated all employees with this same level of trust and care. That is how we are going to achieve true cultural change and optimal business performance.

What we do not want is people spending time figuring out a way to beat the rule. It is better to tell people, "I trust you to do the right thing." You explain what the right thing is, and the rationale behind it, and in most cases, they will support you, without all the bureaucracy and rules around it.

In fact, people will want to reward your trust by bending over backward to perform. And if somebody does try to take advantage, before you have a chance to deal with it, in most cases other people will go talk to that person and straighten it out. They do not want to have a good environment ruined.

Talent: Rethinking the Bottom Performers

This approach of trusting and believing in people also extends to matching people to the right jobs. Some companies say that every year they are going to fire the bottom five percent and find better fits in the marketplace. But I believe in creating an environment in the HR system that allows people to work on what they do best. If people are not meeting expectations, why don't we ask if they are in the right job, at the right time in their career? Instead of saying, "This person's not any good," let's say, "What is this person really good at?"

Now, there is a thing called cultural fit, and some employees simply are not meant to be in the organization. Every company has a set of behavioral norms—not the "what" people do, but the "how." If someone cannot follow the norms, we have to ask them to leave. But that is separate from underperformance.

Part of a strengths-oriented HR environment is about bringing new people in. Your hiring process has to be rigorous. The ability to join a team that truly believes in each other has to be hard. We all know the high cost of failure when an employee does not work out. So we must be disciplined to ensure that we find the right person for the right job at the right time. And that includes a substantial onboarding process, which reinforces how the company is different from other places.

Succeed or Fail Together

When people feel believed in, when they feel supported, they take risks, and they will do the best work of their lives. As I found early in my career, teams succeed when they believe and depend on each other. Imagine if your supervisor said to you, "You're part of my team. We're going to succeed or fail together."

With shared accountability for performance, our teams can set more aggressive goals. It is not just one person or one small group's set of ideas and energy that achieve a goal; it is the *team's* ideas.

We want our teams to be bold. We want them to shoot for the moon. They may miss and land among the stars, as the saying goes, but that is a great success—we do not hold it against them. If they had not shot for the moon, they may never even have wondered about the stars. When you are trusted and people believe in you, you set greater and bolder goals. And you will be more invested in achieving those goals.

With support and trust, and making it okay to fail, it becomes safe to talk about the things that do not go well. People become open to real learning and improvement, not making themselves look good. And that is essential to improving performance, because we learn the most from disappointing outcomes.

The Best Work of Your Life

When I reflect on my career, I keep thinking about how I want to be treated. I remember when I did the best work of my life, and what kind of support I had from my organization. When people trusted and believed in me, I was able to do more than I expected, just as my children did as they grew into accomplished adults in their own chosen careers.

What usually happens to a sports team, right before it goes out onto the field? The coach brings everyone together in a circle and quietly talks about why he or she is convinced they are going to win. To the degree the coach truly believes in the players, they will perform and surprise everybody, including themselves. I have been on team after team myself, where I have listened to the coach, and I could not wait to jump out of my seat. What if we could do the same thing in HR?

A Closing Thought

These ideas apply not only to how we treat our employees, but also to how we treat ourselves. Over the course of any career, we have to make choices between our professional and our personal lives. Do I attend this critical meeting or my sons' sporting events? I often wonder what would have happened if I had said no to more of these professional obligations. Would I still have become chief human resource officer? I believe that the answer is yes. You succeed in your career based on your intelligence, creativity, and ability to create positive change. Time with our loved ones is life's biggest gift. Believe in your people, and, perhaps just as importantly, believe in yourself.

Endnotes

[1]Haralalka, A., & Leong, C. (2012, April 3). Why strengths matter in training. Retrieved from http://www.gallup.com/businessjournal/153341/why-strengths-matter-training.aspx

[2]*State of the Global Workplace: Employee Engagement Insights for Business Leaders Worldwide.* (2013). 1. Retrieved from http://www.gallup.com/services/176735/state-global-workplace.aspx

[3]*Global Human Capital Trends 2014: Engaging the 21st-century workforce.* (2014). 107. Retrieved from http://dupress.com/wp-content/uploads/2014/04/GlobalHumanCapitalTrends_2014.pdf

[4]Milligan, S. (2015, March 1). The Limits of Unlimited Vacation, *HR Magazine*, 30-36. Retrieved from http://www.shrm.org/publications/hrmagazine/editorialcontent/2015/0315/pages/0315-unlimited-vacation.aspx

[5]Buckingham, M., & Goodall, A. (2015, April 1). Reinventing performance management. *Harvard Business Review*. Retrieved from https://hbr.org/2015/04/reinventing-performance-management

Chapter 10.
Building Social Capital: An Invitation to Increased Impact and Influence

Eva Sage-Gavin

It is an understatement to say that the business world is moving at an exponential pace. There are massive and rapid changes occurring in geopolitical power, communication, international expansion, social responsibility, corporate reputation, and the fundamental ways that companies conduct business. All of us in the HR community, and in other high-impact functions, should ask if our capabilities and strategic approaches are keeping pace with change. And even more importantly, are we staying ahead of shifts with new and innovative strategies to lead?

We have a unique opportunity to build our companies' social capital, internally and externally, with customers and employees. We need to look at new ways to think about work/life integration and develop authentic relationships in our communities and with others. We need to be better storytellers and trend spotters, become more agile in our decision-making, and increase our impact and influence on others.

We are at an inflection point where we can reimagine the future and acquire the new skills we need to get there. This is our chance to build on our expertise. Similar to technology companies that design for new uber connected generations, we can build new and creative approaches to deliver services.

We must take a broader world view beyond our HR functional areas to increase value for employees, leaders, and stakeholders in the organizations we are privileged to represent and lead.

My Journey: Beyond HR

I was privileged to experience this broader scope during my tenure as CHRO at Gap Inc. The change was gradual over time but there was one day that put an exclamation point on the journey.

It was around noon in San Francisco's Moscone Center. More than 3,000 enthusiastic Gap Inc. employees from around the world had filed out of the room after gathering for the first company-wide cross-brand store manager conference in years.

It was an inspiring event for the company, one that any chief HR officer (CHRO) would be proud of, building engagement and momentum in creative and pathbreaking ways. After the room emptied, we gathered with a few key team members in the middle of the ballroom to debrief the meeting highlights. It was clearly a win for our integrated team, which included leaders from HR, communications, social and environmental responsibility, the Gap Foundation and the government, and public affairs teams. A particular high point had been the remarks of former Secretary of State Hillary Clinton, who was a surprise guest speaker.

As exciting as the event had been, we had even more pressing issues, such as how worker safety in Bangladesh was being publicly questioned. Our brand and others in the retail industry were in the middle of a complex international controversy that involved our businesses, brand reputation, and most importantly, people's lives.

The same teams who designed and delivered the store manager conference were also involved with issues in Bangladesh. They strategized and partnered with leaders attending the conference, plus our international teams, governments, nongovernmental organizations, labor, business leaders, and even industry competitors.

Of course, our "regular" work continued. That day, I had an interview with a candidate for a top HR role on our team. Separately, as a board member for another public company, I was expected on a conference call for financial strategy discussions.

I also had family obligations.

My responsibilities as the head of global HR and corporate affairs for Gap Inc. had merged into one of the most memorable and enlightening days of my career. It was a symbolic pivot point that made clear the impact our roles can have on individuals, teams, companies, industries, and even global societies. It crystallized the opportunities for new ways of leading—an inflection point for HR leaders and the HR function as a whole.

Before We Look Ahead, Let's Get Grounded in the World of Millennials and Social Media

For this kind of fundamental pivot for HR, we need to see where we are now, and look forward with an eye to future change, so we can be the cutting-edge strategic advisors our businesses need.

Demographics are changing. Baby Boomers are leaving the workforce for 2.0 pursuits, Millennials are dominating. We have an unprecedented five generations in the workplace, and diversity in all its aspects is increasing.

The business environment has grown more complex with consumers and workers connected globally. Products and services are developed and delivered all over the world. Leaders today are trying to tap into new markets and work effectively with diverse cultures in different time zones.

We also know how instantaneous communications can damage or build reputations quickly, particularly in social media. In the past, a poorly handled interaction with a customer could be managed within a store, or perhaps even overlooked. Now businesses, brands, and their supply chains are immediately visible all over the world, and we have seen how transparency can significantly damage or improve corporate reputation.

Tomorrow's consumers and employees will have different expectations of companies. Personal and professional lives are becoming intertwined, leading to a heightened sensitivity to social responsibility, and a deeper desire for an emotional relationship with companies that offer experiences rather than just a paycheck. The "social contracts" between employers and employees—salary, health care, and other benefits—are shifting. There is a new technology-enabled talent pool with freelance skills that are the business basis of companies such as Uber, Lyft, and TaskRabbit. This "e-lancer" population forms the foundation for the constantly evolving world of deconstructed work that is increasingly being performed by individuals who are not "employees" but who come together to deliver services or to complete discrete tasks in a symphony of orchestrated virtual supply chains.

There is also a growing societal demand to deliver cradle-to-grave goods and services that are renewable and sustainable. Social responsibility is growing far beyond philanthropic commitments, such as sending employees to volunteer and support local nonprofit organizations a few times per year. Today's social responsibility leaders have significant and complex roles with challenging issues to address, including international supply chains, diverse stakeholders, nongovernmental organizations, and third-party and political partners. It is a fast-changing functional area with new rules of engagement and norms formed every day.

We also must acknowledge that a baseline public assumption of trust has eroded. Some believe that companies, governments, and leaders act only in their own self-interest, and break or find loopholes. Any wrongdoing—let alone a rumor or perception of impropriety or poor judgment—can damage employee confidence, hurt sales, affect stock price, shake investors, and ruin careers.

Finally, and perhaps most importantly, we have seen that *how* companies do business has become just as important as *what* they do. While companies will always focus on expanding to new markets, staying competitive, and keeping great talent, they also need to continue to consider manufacturing conditions around the world, environmental practices, corporate governance, and community relations. This is a critical component of "social capital": The intangible assets companies possess may have a real impact on their business performance.

Social Capital and Innovation

We can find many definitions of social capital in academia, in public affairs, and among business roundtables. I operate on the core principle that by working together we can develop better outcomes, where all partners benefit.

HR can add tremendous value when we see these broader trends and fill the void by building our companies' social capital in new and innovative ways. While many large corporations have HR, public affairs, community affairs, and communications teams, these specialists often are not organized to work in integrated strategic, long-term ways to build this outcome together. Understandably, with the daily demands on each of these teams, it is easy to become mired in day-to-day crises, and as a result, miss larger opportunities for impactful leadership and long-term sustainable change.

We must develop new ways of collaborating and the discipline to maintain a broader future-oriented view. We must help our boards, CEOs, and line leaders to make the links between demographic, geographic, social, and technological innovations to all of the stakeholders whose perceptions and actions affect a business. Every day employees, customers, suppliers, investors, communities, and public officials globally are viewing our actions, and we have the opportunity to enable our companies to improve the way they show up holistically.

Building Social Capital: A Four-Part Plan

We need to be deliberate about building social capital. We must understand the gaps between our brand image and reputation. We need to learn the reputational landscape, understand the world views of our companies, and then work with business leaders to guide organizations for long-term, reputational success.

1. Understand the Authentic Reputation

A company's brand image is incredibly important and built over time, but can be damaged in an instant. HR, marketing, corporate communications, investor relations, and other teams work hard to weave an image that reflects a brand in a positive light to attract and retain customers and employees. Yet sometimes a company's reputation can be much different than the brand goals, based on what the public has "heard" or perceived through social media from events, business practices, or behavior. HR leaders must provide strategic value by understanding the authentic reputational opportunities and challenges of their organization's brand image in our transparent, "always on," digital, global world and hold up the mirror for their organizations.

2. Know the Global Footprint

The second step in building social capital is to know our organizations' global footprint in holistic ways. We should understand the nuanced complexities of operating in each country or region. We must consider economic conditions; environmental strengths, challenges, and perceptions; and work and living conditions; as well as the political environment, including influential nongovernment organizations and other stakeholders. Understanding all of these perspectives provides a snapshot of a company's social capital and reputation in different parts of the world.

3. Understand Relationships

The third step is to thoroughly understand community and political relationships locally at headquarters cities and major hubs, as well as at state, federal, and global locations. We must look objectively at relationships with vendors, labor, supply chains, nongovernment organizations, environmental groups, employees, customers, shareholders, and social media. Consider relationships with competitors, or companies in different industries, but with similarities such as supply chain operations. Assess where relationships are strong and can provide foundational partnerships during challenging times.

4. Look to the Long-Term

The fourth step to build an organization's social capital is to evaluate what you have learned and create a long-term plan. Work with the CEO, board of directors, business line leaders, and employees to determine where to focus to drive improvement, minimize risk, and help your business with growth and reputational issues. Where external relationships are strained, work to consider rebuilding these partnerships proactively. While the initial outreach could be based on short-term working agreements, it will become the foundation for something much more long-term and viable as business needs change for all stakeholders.

It is important to reiterate that while there can be short-term results, this is more fundamentally about the long term. This is about reputation, risk, and opportunities for the business, and long-term areas where the company can play a role in social, political, and environmental issues that are not always clear-cut and that constantly change. For HR and our companies, this is an opportunity to push ourselves and our colleagues to think bigger, more strategically, and to deliver broader impact.

Innovative Approaches to Reach the Goal

Just as we aspire to influence business leaders to think more broadly, we in the HR function have to think that way as well.

New Organizational Partnerships

As HR professionals, one of our strengths can be to create new organizational partnerships and bring together formerly divergent groups. At Gap Inc., I had the opportunity to oversee an organization that included HR, communications, social responsibility, foundation, and government/public affairs leaders. It was a powerful set of integrated skills and capabilities working together to understand diverse global opportunities, internally and externally. The strength of these diverse perspectives and capabilities was very impactful when working together on opportunities such as global supply chain issues, new country launches, specific Millennial and multigenerational workforce needs, and collaborative public policy opportunities.

Work/Life Integration

We also have the opportunity to refresh and update our strategies about work/life integration. In our global, virtual, "always on" lives, the concept of work/life blending is evolving. We need to support employees' and partners' wellness and engagement, and trust that the greatest creativity and highest performance comes from empowered employees with pride in their organization who feel connected to the work they do.

Authentic Relationships

Our companies need to think differently about the ways we connect with our communities. More than ever, we need authentic relationships that deliver the highest impact outcomes. The best example from the philanthropic world is the shift from task or hours-based volunteering to skills-based knowledge transfer. We have heard too often that nonprofit organizations felt they could not turn down well-meaning employees who wanted to volunteer to paint or clean. Instead, a more valuable and gratifying approach is for employees to teach their professional skills and transfer their knowledge for sustainable outcomes. The approach is more genuine and authentic, and brings greater benefits to everyone involved.

Authentic Connections

Authentic connections can have more direct business results as well. In my role as vice chairman of the national workforce development initiative called Skills for America's Future, hosted at the Aspen Institute, I saw the benefits of companies working directly with local community college leaders to build new talent pipelines for attractive jobs. When companies communicate clearly with college leaders about the skills they are looking for, schools can develop or revise curriculum to meet those needs. Everyone wins, with students getting jobs and employers building strong workforces, sustainable talent pipelines, and innovative community networks. This also builds authentic social capital that supports recruitment and employee engagement.

I have seen it work. The Skills for America's Future initiative launched in 2010 at the height of double-digit U.S. unemployment rates. In its first five years, a handful of workforce development commitments grew into a national network of hundreds of partnerships among companies, colleges, and government to fill jobs and build workforces.

At Gap, our Gap Inc. for Community College program engaged store managers to teach job skills in community colleges nationally. The participating store managers increased their public speaking and teaching skills, built community connections, identified new talent directly in schools, and generated local business in our stores. Students learned career skills, earned scholarships, and sometimes earned positions at Gap Inc. stores or elsewhere. We featured individual student success stories at headquarters, leading to joyfully tearful moments that built company pride and increased the involvement and commitment to the success of the program across the company.

Authenticity and Transparency

As we build these authentic relationships and empower employees, communities, and businesses, we also have the opportunity to improve how we share these stories. In the past we talked about goals, statistics, and revenue to explain the value and pride of a company. Today, our employees and customers want and expect more. They want an emotional connection: that lets them tell friends, family, and neighbors that they are proud of the company they are associated with.

Employees, particularly Millennials, want the freedom to tell their stories in new ways: through social media, videos, infographics, and constantly evolving technologies—when and how they want to share them. We need to build new pathways to ensure the stories transcend time zones, geographies, and generations, while keeping everyone engaged and respectful of diverse cultural expectations. We have seen repeatedly that when people have an emotional attachment to a vision, and see meaningful accomplishments along the way, they will help others get there.

Working with our communities in more genuine, authentic ways should not be thought of as a nice thing to do, but rather as a fundamental and necessary way of operating. It is the right thing to do. The concept is identified in a number of ways, including the idea of "conscious capitalism." It is a necessary step for the future, beyond the traditional corporate philanthropy of writing checks or painting a community center. As HR leaders, we have a responsibility to help companies fulfill this new norm and to anticipate and develop leading strategies in advance of changing expectations.

A Key Ingredient: Building Agility

For years, HR and business leaders have talked about becoming more agile. What exactly does it mean for HR to envision the capabilities needed to respond to a broader view of the world and the future of work?

We need to expand the traditional concept of internal organizational agility. First, it is the ability to build scenario plans, while being flexible enough to respond immediately to unanticipated crises. It is also the ability to intertwine plans with collaborative relationships externally and to create new forms and channels for innovation and growth.

Historically, as thoughtful HR strategists, we have taken pride in developing operating plans to address scenarios within the workplace. Today, we should prepare for opportunity and risk by looking externally. We need to anticipate and stay on top of global and fast-moving events and trends, then assess their potential impact on the organization—even before they happen.

Potential scenarios must include social media and consider instant global connections. Events now play out in real time, and we do not have the luxury to take linear step-by-step actions that have been laid out in advance. We need teams, leaders, and individuals who are agile enough to make key decisions and execute them efficiently, instantaneously, and authentically—in any social media channel, geography, and culture—while staying true to company values, stakeholder commitments, and brand identity. We must also leverage new technologies to help stay abreast and ahead of social media chatter. Are we ready to respond to customers, media, investors, board members, and CEOs in immediate, genuine ways that will resonate?

When Gap brand ads featuring diverse models were defaced, the company stood behind the ads and transparently shared the situation. The response was overwhelmingly positive, leading to a social media groundswell of support from individual consumers—a reach and authenticity well beyond what any planned marketing campaign would have generated. While historically we were prepared for negative feedback about ads, we were flexible enough to respond in the fast-moving social media world.

Agility also includes the ability to bring creative, innovative ideas into the discussion and to think more broadly than our functional skills, past training, or even company affiliation. Are we reflecting on our industry as a whole—or even importing relevant lessons from other industries? Are there nontraditional partnerships to build internally or externally to find new, bigger, more sustainable long-term solutions?

When safety practices in garment factories in Bangladesh were questioned in 2013 as a result of tragic fires and building collapses, the retail apparel industry built a broad coalition to address fundamental issues involving government, vendors, labor, and other international stakeholders to deliver short- and long-term solutions. Developing these coalitions was difficult, complex work that forced us to break down traditional barriers and embrace cooperation. Ultimately we built innovative, more impactful solutions to tackle an extremely multifaceted situation with numerous stakeholders.

Are we, as HR professionals, prepared to think in such comprehensive ways? How do we build and refine these new ways of thinking, build agility, and facilitate new skills and approaches? We must understand and be able to react quickly, with big ideas. We must accept that we cannot control messages as we have in the past and that authenticity and transparency have to be a given.

Why Is this HR's New Responsibility?

As I discuss these ideas with colleagues, I am often faced with one of two reactions. First, people do not always see the connections between HR, social responsibility, public affairs, and communications. Secondly, some also question why it is HR's responsibility to take on this intersection of opportunity. Most see the business value, but may be daunted by the responsibility and new skills required and do not connect it to traditional HR.

They are right. These areas have not been seen as within the scope of traditional HR. Yet they draw on the higher-order skills we have developed: leading transformational change in business and culture, strategically supporting business goals, building relationships, and engaging stakeholders in new and innovative ways. I am suggesting we use these skills and capabilities as futurists, strategists, and catalysts to influence broader audiences, beyond our workforces. While every C-suite executive brings distinct skills and capabilities, CHROs by role and training are uniquely suited to bring a holistic approach to this new future of work. We can be in a key position to leverage the diverse skills of our C-suite colleagues to deliver integrated and sustainable solutions for long-term impact.

In more than 30 years of experience in five industries and five functional areas, I have seen the power of collaborative partnerships and working globally, bridging internal and external boundaries. I have watched innovation and collaboration improve lives, create new talent pipelines, build public reputations, and become a source of pride for employees and stakeholders—positive results for all involved. Tackling this challenge tests all the skills that the HR profession demands, from strong interpersonal skills in collaboration and creative problem-solving to deep technical expertise in skill and capability building.

The opportunity for greatest impact is now. While understandably challenging to adjust to today's constantly evolving world, we need to look ahead to what is coming next. In the next iteration of the new economy, higher-order skills involving sense making, judgment, and problem-solving will be in demand. At the same time, the past traditional social contracts between employers and task-based freelancers will be changing forever. How will HR lead organizations through those changes and prepare for the next change curve ahead?

As I reflect on this unprecedented societal inflection point of change and the invitation for new forms of impact and influence, it leads me to ask—who better to lead the emerging and forever changing world of work?

Why shouldn't it be us? If not us, who? If not now, when?

PART IV

CASES IN BUILDING ORGANIZATION CAPABILITY

Chapter 11.
The Heart of Hilton

Matthew W. Schuyler

At Hilton, our people and our business are guided by our vision—"to fill the earth with the light and warmth of hospitality." To this end, our team provides exceptional experiences to the millions of guests we serve each week. We rely on the collaboration of our Team Members to deliver lasting memories for our guests, and to serve as good corporate citizens in the communities where we live and work. Our Team Members are truly the Heart of Hilton.[1]

In this chapter, I will share the story of Hilton Worldwide's transformation from a loosely controlled collection of underperforming brands with no unified vision, to one of the world's largest and best-performing hospitality companies. Along our journey, the employees of Hilton, known as Team Members, have been at the heart of our success. By providing our Team Members with a great work environment, great careers, and great rewards, we enable them to deliver excellent guest experiences, which in turn drive financial success for Hilton.

Our recent history provides an interesting case study, starting with a time where we struggled to align our many people programs with a consistent vision. We knew that a cultural transformation would require a solid foundation, built on sound values. In addition to the vision above, early in our transformation efforts we established one set of values that every Team Member lives by, from the front lines to the corporate offices:

- HOSPITALITY: We're passionate about delivering exceptional guest experiences.

- INTEGRITY: We do the right thing, all the time.
- LEADERSHIP: We're leaders in our industry and in our communities.
- TEAMWORK: We're team players in everything we do.
- OWNERSHIP: We're the owners of our actions and decisions.
- NOW: We operate with a sense of urgency and discipline.

Our ultimate success, within HR and across the company, didn't take a revolutionary idea, but rather a simple approach rooted in listening to our Team Members. First, we had to understand what Team Members wanted and needed, and where our policies and activities prevented them from doing their best work for our guests. Second, it was crucial to engage Team Members and empower them with great work environments, great careers, and great rewards. I'll share more about each of these pillars of our HR approach, but first it is important to understand where we found ourselves just a few years ago:

FIGURE 11.1: IMPACT OF PEOPLE PROGRAMS ON THE BOTTOM LINE

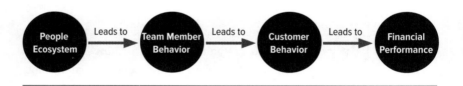

Where Hilton (Re)Started

Hilton was acquired by Blackstone in late 2007. At the time, Hilton was an 88-year-old company. Since the Blackstone acquisition, we became the largest hospitality company in the world. This milestone was achieved by increasing our overall room count by 53 percent to more than 4,750 hotels in more than 100 countries and territories. We also increased the number of rooms in our pipeline by 116 percent and nearly doubled our number of Hilton HHonors loyalty members to approximately 60 million. In 2013, Hilton became the largest-ever hospitality initial public offering.

While we are very proud of these numbers, we recognize that this success was possible only through the united efforts of our more than 350,000 Team Members around the world. Hilton had an iconic history, well-known brands, and talented Team Members, but prior to 2007, our employee programs were not aligned with our vision. Simply put, we were an underperforming company. We lacked integration, we saw average top- and bottom-line performance, and we had stagnant organic room growth. More than 80 different mission statements existed across our company. This created a lack of focus, and limited understanding of what Hilton stood for and how we wanted to be perceived.

I remember visiting several of our corporate offices and hotel properties and seeing different approaches to describing values at our company. None of them were the same. We also had more than 320 HR policies that were causing confusion. Many of these policies were out-of-date and, in some cases, made little sense for our business. This included a policy that prevented employees from being enrolled in our frequent traveler program. As a result, our Team Members were not engaged with our business. There was a general feeling of complacency holding us back from realizing our full potential.

In part, our solution was to listen more closely to our Team Members. We focused our efforts on continuously soliciting their feedback to improve the programs that they cared about the most. These efforts, and the establishment of the shared vision, have been energizing to our culture. Our CEO aptly describes our recent performance as rowers in a regatta—everyone needs to be rowing in unison for the boat to move fast and steady. This unification is clear now, because we have a clear vision and values and because we are providing all of our Team Members with a great environment, great rewards, and great careers.

Great Environment

The notion of a career is evolving. Historically, an individual aspired to stay with a company for his or her working lifetime and was incentivized with longevity rewards—pensions, retirement plans, and so on. Today's employees see a competitive and globally mobile environment that allows for more options, frequent movement, and various bespoke career paths. To retain top talent, companies need to provide something more compelling than just a great job. It starts with creating the right work environment. We found that creating a welcoming and inclusive work environment is the differentiator that separates us from our competitors.

Here at Hilton, environment includes not only the physical workplace, but also the workplace culture and authenticity of the leaders who surround you. When Team Members ask themselves "Is Hilton a great place for me to work, at this time in my career?", we want them to answer, emphatically, that it is each time they ask.

Our work at Hilton is centered on enriching the lives of guests. We need to ensure that our Team Members are not burdened by unnecessary activities that prevent them from doing their jobs effectively. Staying focused on our vision, mission, and values helps us adapt as our organization changes over time, and creates touchstones that every Team Member can rally around. This team atmosphere starts with our leaders and cascades throughout the organization.

We feel strongly that our most seasoned leaders should be challenged to inspire team performance and continuously improve the environment for the Team Members. One way we challenge our leaders is by giving them the opportunity to see the company through the eyes of our front-line Team Members as part of our Executive Business Immersion Program. This program invites senior leaders to spend three days interacting with a hotel's Team Members, and to carry out some of the key tasks that make the "machinery" of the hotel run smoothly. I have participated in the program, working side by side with our Team Members in locations such as San Diego, California, and Vienna, Austria. I have come away from each of these experiences in awe of what our Team Members do for our company every day, and inspired by the opportunity to provide what really matters to them.

As a central part of our commitment to providing a great work environment, we want to make sure that every Team Member has a great manager. To that end, we recently rolled out a new program to hold our leaders accountable and reward them for their leadership. While there is no exact formula for leadership, we have designed a Leadership Index, based on Team Member survey results (more about our annual survey below), to measure how our leaders are performing. To make sure the Index has meaning, we put an emphasis on alignment around a defined set of leadership principles that directly tie survey results to our leaders' bonus incentives.

We also recognized that physical workspaces can have an impact on how well we are engaging our Team Members. If you have ever been be-hind the scenes at a restaurant, store, or hotel, you know that the "back of the house" is rarely as inviting as the customer-facing front of these locations. While making such improvements comes at an expense, we are creating an environment for our Team Members that mirrors what we of-fer our guests. As a result, Hilton is driving efforts to make our back of house—or as we call it our "Heart of House"—more inviting and friendly. We want to be sure that regardless of the hotel or office our Team Mem-bers work in around the world, there should be great energy that drives our Team Members' engagement with their work and, in turn, great guest experiences.

Great Careers

We receive over a million resumes a year for our job openings around the world. We pride ourselves on hiring the best talent from these applicants. Once Team Members join Hilton, we must offer them meaningful learn-ing and career growth, to keep them with us, and keep them engaged to provide the best guest experiences. This requires HR to innovate beyond the traditional processes of hiring, performing evaluations, and handling departures. Instead, HR must act as an advisor in managing employee ca-reer development. By providing the tools needed for employees to pursue their passions and reach their full potential, HR can help create great ca-reers and drive Team Member loyalty.

Providing a great, long-term career means enabling employees to control their own destinies. We have implemented a diverse range of new offerings—from enhanced performance management tools to learn-ing and development opportunities—with the aim of helping Team Mem-bers take ownership of their career growth. Despite these efforts, our attrition rate increased slightly following our initial public offering, and we realized we needed to make some bold moves and re-evaluate our approach. While having the right career programs in place was impor-tant, communicating to our Team Members about them was even more critical.

Our approach to communicating about careers needed a new angle. We started by uniting our regionally-specific learning initiatives under consistent, global branding to emphasize development, recognition, and leadership. We expanded our leadership development series called "Excellence," which selects top-performing leaders from our corporate offices and properties to participate in intensive development programs. We partnered with leading educational institutions, such as the University of Virginia's Darden School of Business and Cornell University to provide world-class courses and programs on hospitality and management. We now offer training through a variety of channels (instructor-led, online, via mobile app, etc.), and we are now offering leadership development opportunities to all Team Members, through a framework known as Engage (for emerging leaders), Elevate (for established leaders), and Excel (for senior leaders). We formalized corporate responsibility and diversity functions and created global Team Member Resource Groups. At corporate offices, we established wellness teams to connect our people and offer networking events. And at our hotels, we are asking our General Managers to internally call themselves "Chief Engagement Officers," and HR Directors "Chief Engagement Champions."

We have also identified targeted Team Member inclusion programs, including recently-launched programs in military recruiting and women in leadership. Today, we are well equipped and eager to leverage these programs to tap into the energy and innovation of our Millennial generation to help build our leadership and talent pipeline. While we have seen results, including receiving Great Place to Work recognition in multiple countries around the world, as well as being named a Top 50 Company for Diversity (by *DiversityInc*) and a top employer for Veterans (by *Military Times*), our HR Team is continually challenged to evolve our approach and to focus on:

- Digital programs that implement real-time feedback to inspire performance, rather than communicating only through a traditional annual review cycle.
- Planning for the future with two generations (or more) of succession planning—creating a deep pipeline of talent and a competitive advantage.
- Using technology to transform our operations—taking HR from the back office to the front lines through mobility.

Great Rewards

In the hospitality industry, employees need to feel individually valued and recognized. While competitiveness of pay, long-term incentives, and various other compensation basics are important, a great rewards strategy must also explore ways to delight and surprise employees.

We are constantly reviewing our compensation and benefits offerings to ensure that our packages are aligned with the market. Our benefits currently provide the expected (health care and a 401(k) plan) to the unexpected (industry-leading parental leave, generous paid time off and discounts with our partners). We continue to ask: Is this enough? Are we investing in the right benefits that our Team Members care about?

Many of our offerings are a direct result of Team Member feedback from around the world. We listen to what Team Members tell us, and we act on it. Recent enhancements to important programs include our:

- Best-in-class Team Member Travel Program, which allows Team Members to stay at our properties at a greatly reduced rate, and enjoy the same experiences they provide to our guests every day.
- Global mobility program that allows for tremendous opportunities worldwide.
- Parental leave policies in the U.S., which provide industry-leading paid time off for all new parents.
- GED assistance program, to help U.S. Team Members achieve their high school equivalency diploma.
- Advance scheduling, through which Team Members know their work schedules ten days in advance, allowing them to better plan their lives.

We are continually innovating—brainstorming experiences within our Hilton locales, implementing wellness programs and onsite perks, developing healthy workplace food options, and even offering a "recognition calendar," which prompts leaders to recognize and reward a Team Member every day of the year.

Embracing the Journey

Great companies successfully engage the hearts *and* minds of their em-

FIGURE 11.2: HILTON'S TEAM MEMBER VALUE PROPOSITION

ployees. And truly great people companies know that the journey is never complete. At Hilton, we are very proud of our success over the last decade, and we continue to implement new and innovative people programs and benefits that matter most to today's workforce. Our approach continues to be holistic—addressing environment, careers, and rewards—to inspire Team Members to stay loyal to Hilton as they move through their personal and career journeys. We believe our efforts inspire engagement and trust, which in turn positively impact our guests, the communities where we live and work, and our financial performance.

We measure our progress through our Global Team Member Survey, which is completed by roughly 90 percent of our Team Members around the world each year. Our recent results tell a compelling story:

- A globally engaged workforce with 91 percent of employees reporting they are proud to work for Hilton.

- 86 percent motivated to do more than just their job.
- High trust scores—83 percent in 2015, up 3 percent from the prior year.
- 91 percent of our Team Members believe Hilton is a great place to work.

Our Team Members are the heart of Hilton. It is their efforts all around the world, every day of the year, which allow us to achieve our vision "to fill the earth with the light and warmth of hospitality."

Note

All statistics in this chapter are as of June 2016.

Endnote

[1] To read stories that celebrate the outstanding hospitality experiences Hilton teams around the world are delivering every day, see Heart of Hilton Spotlights at http://news.hiltonworldwide.com/index. cfm/misc/heart-of-hilton-spotlight.

Chapter 12.
Building Organization Capability at BASF

Judy Zagorski

As chief human resource officers (CHROs), we all know that one of the hardest things to do is help a successful company recognize the need to change, and then gather the will to actually do it. That is what was required in helping BASF Corporation reset our compass to place our customers as "true north," and embark on a journey of profound and compelling change.

We have grown from an internally focused, product- and process-oriented collection of businesses to become one company united by a forward-looking, market- and customer-driven collaborative culture. This change journey, which continues to this day, requires a company to change from the inside, encouraging successful leaders to redefine success and to adapt how they interact with each other, their teams, and our markets and customers.

With a strategic goal to deliver substantial additional sales by 2020, we have been working to provide our customers with the full power of how we create chemistry with an integrated portfolio of solutions. We began by defining an aspirational goal, broadened our horizons with an intensified outside-in thinking focused on customer success, and met these challenges with internal actions to drive change from within. As CHRO, I was at the center of a dynamic team of leaders driving strategic redirection—alternating roles as facilitator, mediator, instigator, challenger, and participant. Throughout our journey, the culture change has been rooted in helping our people see the value in taking ownership, initiative, and responsible risks.

Lessons learned have fundamentally changed the way my team and I operate, touched the core of new leadership approaches, and delivered a profoundly exhilarating, if at times maddening, experience that has value for all CHROs to consider.

One of our greatest challenges at BASF Corporation was how to more deeply ingrain a one-company mindset and "to compete at our weight class." What do I mean by that? We had to learn how to show the full value of our business portfolio to our customers. A company known for synthesizing broad aspects of our manufacturing operations (having developed what is known as the "Verbund" approach to integrated manufacturing), now had to bring that same connected, one-company mindset to the commercial side of our business.

At stake was the great potential for BASF Corporation and its affiliates to deliver unprecedented growth in North America, one of the world's leading chemical markets. The lessons we learned are not specific to the chemical industry; in fact they touch all sectors and businesses looking to reposition themselves for success, which is why I share this story.

Making It Personal

From the start, the biggest challenge did not come from being unsure where or what to change. It was in how to make the right change happen, how to sell it, translate strategic intent into actions, and build those good intentions into results. This meant touching how employees think, feel, and act on the job: What do they prioritize? How do they think strategically and act locally? One of the most difficult things to understand for employees is how they can cut through the rhetoric and make a difference.

Thus, the most important job was how to make change relatable. How did we do this? By sharing in meaningful, clear terms what we needed to accomplish together. As leaders, we had to convince people of the need to change, talk with them in ways they could understand, make it safe for them to practice and learn new behaviors, reward and recognize the right behaviors when we saw them, and do this consistently until skeptics became believers, novices became veterans, and true culture change began to take root.

There are many elements to this change effort. Rather than provide a cursory review of them all, I would like to go deeper on the critical few that I think have made the greatest difference in changing minds and behaviors. These elements were a combination of both grassroots and top-down efforts, with the intent to meet at the center and unleash the power of the "mighty middle."

- *Making TIME for Change.* The chartering of this change effort was fundamentally different from anything we had done before. At the time, the regional leadership team was essentially a group of individual business leaders who came together periodically for information sharing rather than for planning for a shared future. Changing our culture required developing a true regional growth strategy focused on entrepreneurship, collaboration, and innovation beyond just individual business unit profit and loss (P&L). Out of these discussions came Strategy 2020, a go-to-market growth strategy based in fundamental change—"It's TIME to change BASF," through an intensified focus on **T**alent, **I**nnovation, **M**arket and Customer Focus, and Operational **E**xcellence (TIME). Fundamental to this new approach was the collective realization that Talent was the most critical thread, and without the "T" there would be no TIME for change.

This realization was at the heart of resultant efforts to change. A few critical examples of these efforts are profiled here:

- *Deepening Market Focus.* A crucible for learning how to do business differently lay in the fundamental shift from a product to a market focus. With the leadership team continuing to refine the overall direction, we created the strategic framework needed to make the necessary changes happen. A deliberate outside-in perspective provided us with a more refined lens through which to see and demonstrate how our customers gain more when we unleash the full power of BASF to meet their challenges. We commissioned what at the time were novel cross-business unit teams to sell to key strategic customers; their modus operandi involved collaborating to identify and meet market needs in new ways. The cross-business teams made BASF easier to work with and explored and accelerated sales growth opportunities in attractive industries with high-growth potential. Examples included areas such as aerospace, automotive, construction, and packaging segments. These initial efforts spawned more cross-unit teams, and today the number—and effectiveness—of these teams has grown significantly.

- *Spotlight on the Future.* As in many organizations, at the start the silos were in full force at BASF. Our people identified much more with their local teams. We were coatings people, petrochemicals people, supply chain people, and yes, HR people. We knew we needed to introduce new signature behaviors that spelled out and modeled what it means to be a part of the BASF team (versus individual teams): One company, one BASF, one set of desired behaviors. We established *Spotlight Behaviors* to highlight the entrepreneurial, collaborative, customer- and market-focused, smart risk-taking behaviors that we wanted to become the "new normal" at BASF. These behaviors were embedded in our performance goal setting and were recognized through the See Things 2020 Spotlight Recognition program. Things were starting to get interesting— and different. People were seeing new behaviors, they were beginning to experience elements of culture change, they were starting to see what we meant when we talked about the unique role of the "T" in TIME. They were starting to shift their focus even more intently to our customers, with a deepening sense of what it means to be truly customer centric.

- *Daring to be Different.* To build on this momentum, we started a program called Simply Dare!—as in simply dare to make a difference. At its core were Daredevil teams, through which people were empowered to find and eliminate nonproductive work so that they could have more time to focus on efforts that really mattered for our customers and our business. This involved clearing the field before replanting it—pulling out the weeds of nonproductive and bureaucratic work to make way for real growth.

- *Pioneers for Progress.* We unleashed the power of the people to recognize the best Simply Dare! efforts through the power of the ballot box. We introduced the Pioneer Awards, which were given on the strength of region-wide voting. This sparked healthy and vocal competition among the Daredevil teams and brought further recognition to the behavior and culture change that they were meant to deliver. Pioneer Award-winning teams basked in great recognition and the satisfaction of a significant cash award shared with their chosen charity, showing the power of One BASF moving out into the community.

- *Kill 100.* Matching the grassroots involvement to cut through ineffective processes and bureaucracy, the leadership team set out to personally eliminate 100 initiatives that had outlasted their usefulness. The stated goal was to "kill" 100 unnecessary, outdated, or just plain ineffective policies and programs. This sent a powerful signal of what we meant about redirecting the power of operational Excellence (the "E" in TIME) to focus on making sure that our energy was directed at adding value to our Market and Customer Focus ("M" in TIME), not at protecting the status quo or clinging to outdated practices because "that's the way we have always done it." All eyes began to shift to the prize: uniting in our efforts to change *what* work gets done, and *how* it gets done. This took us into a different and more specific realm from simply daring to be different and contributed to an intense focus on being effective and value-adding rather than simply being busy. The goal remained to free time and energy to work on what mattered most: our customers.

- *you@BASF.* HR focused on the "I" (for Innovation) in TIME as well. We developed an innovative Compelling Total Offer that changed how we communicate the true value our people derive from working at BASF. This takes the individual components of compensation, benefits, work/life, and recognition and brings them together to present a unified value that goes beyond the sum of its parts. Not by accident, people are at the center of all these efforts; it is all about "you at BASF." Linking with our strategic goal of how we create chemistry, one of the tools in our you@BASF toolkit is a great app for engagement—a visually powerful periodic table of elements that shows our people the scope and value of programs designed to help them. It lays out for our people how we are working to improve the quality of their lives as individuals and families at the same time they are part of a company working to improve the quality of life for our customers and for the world at large.

- *Talent Management.* We upped the ante in building understanding of the importance of having the right talent needed to drive growth. This involved an integrated talent management approach across the BASF North America talent pipeline, intensifying the focus on leadership, learning, and organizational development. Much of our efforts were directed at defining our workforce capabilities for today and tomorrow, and integrating these insights into a targeted HR plan to deliver growth. The excitement of these efforts grew as we came up with new ways to enable leaders, managers, and employees to deeply engage, own and drive change by shifting their behaviors and building new capabilities.

Simply put, we worked the change equation from all sides. Operating "grassroots up" and "top down," we sent a clear message that we all have control over what we spend our time on, and it has to add value and serve a higher purpose than meeting an internal need or because "we've always done it that way." The customer is clearly at the center of our efforts. If a program or project does not help us go to market, it does not help us—period.

Art and Science

As with so many aspects of the CHRO role, there is both art and science to this kind of change. In cases like this, I think of the CHRO role as requiring the skills of a chef—and by that I mean a chef rather than a short-order cook filling one-off requests. As organizational architecture chefs, what vital ingredients do we add, and in what combinations and sequence?

One of the most important things I have learned on this journey is that the CHRO needs to acquire a certain wisdom when it comes to finding the "right recipe" for change. It is vital to find your own answers to these questions: When do I have to be the impatient voice for change now? When is it wise to sit back and have the wisdom to let change settle? How can you know the difference?

My experience is that you can never want change more than the organization is capable of wanting it. So you have to learn when to push hard, when to add ingredients, and when to take them away. When is it right to pull back a bit and let change happen, and let other leaders discover how much they want it and are capable of owning it? Finding this recipe and rhythm is one of the most challenging and rewarding aspects of a major human capital and organizational change effort.

Joining with the right partners to help you make change happen allows you to sustain momentum even in the face of significant leadership changes. Since these changes take years to make happen, they must not only survive but thrive under different leaders and market conditions. The role of the CHRO can be pivotal in pushing for this to happen at certain times, and in turning down the heat on the stove at other times to let change simmer and "set."

We started these efforts in earnest in 2008. They further evolved as part of our global "We create chemistry" strategy and its related regional priority to build the best team to drive profitable growth in each market where we do business. The second half of what we knew would be a decade-long journey is often the hardest, after the excitement of creating, launching, and building is done. We continue to work to create sustainable mindset and behavior change and embed customer centricity into our DNA—into how we develop talent, expand leadership, and create the signature behaviors guiding BASF to higher levels of performance.

We continue to learn the most from the areas where we struggle. One such area is how to build a healthy tolerance for risk within an organization that is hard-wired to engineer risk out of the system. It is about the "and" required to balance unequivocal risk management in our chemical (environmental, health, and safety) operations with smart risk-taking in business and talent development. As innovators, we need people who can experiment and take risks on new ideas. Making sure prudent risk management in chemical manufacturing does not bleed over into unhealthy risk aversion in how we select, develop, and retain talent continues to draw my attention and the efforts of my team.

Milestones in our progress have included:

- Record sales gains, with BASF North America sales of $20.6 billion in 2014, up from $17.5 billion when the journey started in 2008.
- A deepening leadership pipeline bench of market-focused regional leaders.
- Rankings in such key external benchmarks as the *Forbes* list of America's Best Employers; inclusion in the Top 50 Companies for

Diversity, ranked by *DiversityInc*; and the Most Attractive Employers list as measured by Universum.

- Significant expansion of cross-business team market activity.
- Establishment of a Welcome to BASF program to help new employees understand and become part of the change process right from the start.

So When All Is Said and Done, What Is the Role of the CHRO in Driving Change?

The answer is both simple and complex. It involves having the:

- Ability to look beyond current high levels of success to anticipate, diagnose, and provide solutions to problems that others may not—or may not yet be willing to—see.
- Wisdom to know when to push, when to prod, and when to raise and lower your voice to make change happen where it counts: from within.
- Calm demeanor of a pilot when the inevitable turbulence comes and the ability to calm the anxiety of people who think we may be losing our equilibrium and capacity for change.
- Unflinching commitment to doing what is best for the organization, its customers, its shareholders, and its people.

While this story is in many ways uniquely that of BASF Corporation, the reasons for change and the lessons learned have applicability across leading companies that are redefining themselves for a different future. It is hoped that the implications of what we have learned and shared have resonance for CHROs facing similar challenges.

Understanding and leveraging both the art and the science of managing human and organizational capital, and helping people understand how they can make change happen in their roles, are at the heart of the cultural transformation that continues to engage BASF. Doing so in a way that speaks to the heart and the mind of our organization and our people is clearly a special and rewarding journey.

Chapter 13.
Strategic Human Resources to Help Build a Global Tech Leader: A Narrative at Lenovo

Gina Qiao

As senior vice president of human resources at Lenovo, I am often asked by HR professionals about the "secret recipe" of HR's role in Lenovo's successful transformation to a global company. I do not have a magic answer to this question. In fact, HR had to explore, experiment, learn, and adapt along the way with the rest of Lenovo over the last 10 years.

Founded in 1984 by Mr. Liu Chuanzhi, Lenovo's humble start can be traced back to the equivalent of $30,000 in seed money and a guard shack in Beijing that doubled as an office. Over the next 30 years Lenovo grew into a $39 billion global company and the world's number one PC company. Today Lenovo conducts business in 160 countries, and its diversified businesses range from PCs to tablets, smartphones, servers, ecosystems, and cloud services. Ten years ago, Lenovo acquired the IBM PC business, a bold move that surprised the world and marked the beginning of our globalization journey. In 2014, we closed our acquisitions of Motorola Mobility and the IBM x86 server business to become the world's number three smartphone company and number three x86 server company.

I joined Lenovo fresh out of college and held many roles before I landed in HR. As a result, I witnessed, participated in, and learned from Lenovo's globalization process. What I learned most is that HR practices must evolve along with the rest of the company and prepare the company to tackle its most important strategic challenges at any given time. If my experience can be of value to HR professionals facing similar business transformations, I am glad to share my insights, specifically:

- How HR can help integrate cultures and build a diverse, global leadership team at a critical time after international acquisitions.
- How HR can define company culture, develop talent, optimize the organizational structure, and build trust with business leadership.

HR Plays a Critical Role in Lenovo's "Going Global"

When Lenovo announced the acquisition of the IBM PC business in late 2004, the world was shocked. Reporters and investors scrambled to learn more about this unknown company from China named Lenovo. Understandably, the IBM PC employees were nervous. It was a time of high sensitivity, and HR had a critical role to play in the acquisition.

HR worked with the leadership team to map out a two-phase journey. The first phase focused on stability and continuity. HR recognized the importance of retaining key talent and worked hard to do so, especially employees who frequently interacted with customers to ensure that our customers experienced "business as usual" throughout the acquisition. To be successful, many details, including compensation, benefits, titles, and reporting structures, had to be developed, reviewed, and implemented in a short of period of time.

In the second phase, integration, the biggest challenge was cross-cultural communication. Lenovo made the bold decision to use English as the working language for the company. This was a huge challenge for many of our managers and even senior leaders in China, but we decided that it was the best and perhaps the only feasible way of collaborating with what was now a global team. In addition, there were many cultural differences and assumptions made by each side that were not expected or easily understood. Initially, this led to frequent clashes. Yang Yuanqing, Lenovo's CEO and chairman, who was chairman at that time, was clear in his direction, "Clash is good. It's the starting point of understanding. Without it, we won't truly integrate."

Yang proposed three principles: "Be frank. Respect each other. Compromise." These became the guiding principles that enabled Lenovo to navigate a challenging and confusing period of time as the Chinese and the Westerners learned to effectively work together. It is still our guiding principle today as we work on the integration of the newly acquired Motorola Mobility and System x businesses.

The experience of combining different cultures led HR to create Lenovo's Diversity Office within the HR organization. We hired Yolanda Conyers to lead the Diversity Office and drive diversity efforts. Yolanda and I recently published a book, *The Lenovo Way*, in which we explained how Lenovo turned diversity into a competitive advantage that helps Lenovo win in the global markets. The newly created Diversity Office drove many initiatives such as East Meeting West and informal "cultural cocktails" to help build and strengthen cross-cultural teamwork at Lenovo. At the same time, HR ensured candidates of different cultural backgrounds, genders, and experiences were included in the pool when senior positions were vacant. In our people-planning process, if there is a gap in diversity, the managers are reminded of the role diversity plays in Lenovo's success.

As a result of all these efforts, and through a lot experimentation by HR, Lenovo built a new core competency—having a diverse, global team able to work together effectively at every level, from the executive committee to entry-level employees. This core competency will serve as a great foundation for Lenovo's global expansion in years ahead.

HR's Strategic Role in Defining Lenovo's Culture and Building a Global PC Leader

When a company grows larger and more global, HR must play a more strategic role. This means when the competitive environment changes, HR must be able to quickly understand the market dynamics, adjust the organizational structure, and create the right talent pipeline. It also means that for a company quickly globalizing like Lenovo, the HR team must be strong at cross-cultural management. By observing how open and visionary an HR team is and how well the members can glue the cultures together, you can tell how far a company can go.

Transforming the Culture

You can always find out why a company has a certain core competency by looking at its culture—not the culture defined on a poster on the wall but the culture in action. The culture in action tells you the employees' collective understanding of the culture as well as the shared expectations of how things should be done. After Lenovo navigated a period of confusing identities, HR helped crystallize the Lenovo Way culture based on the concepts of innovation, commitment, ownership, and a "doers" brand.

Lenovo excels at execution. Lenovo dares to dream big, but it is also fast, disciplined, efficient, and determined when executing plans. This is a unique personality of Lenovo as a company, and it is so readily apparent that everyone who joins Lenovo quickly senses it. From their first day at Lenovo, employees are immersed in a culture that emphasizes commitment and ownership, described as, "We do what we say, and we own what we do."

Initially, HR collaborated with the strategy team to summarize Lenovo's culture as four Ps:

- We PLAN before pledge. Full commitment requires we understand what is expected and be honest about what we are willing to sign up for.
- We PERFORM as we promise. If you sign up for something, then you must do everything you can to deliver.
- We PRIORITIZE the company first. Entrepreneurship is in our blood, and it takes total dedication.
- We PRACTICE improving every day. We began as a humble startup in China, and it is in our DNA to keep learning from others, and we take pride in making progress every day.

These four Ps gave us a clear identity as a company. As the market dynamics changed, Lenovo began to talk about a PC+ strategy, meaning we proactively sought growth beyond PCs, aggressively expanding into tablets and other devices. So in 2012, HR created and defined a fifth P, "Pioneering," to emphasize and encourage innovation at Lenovo.

In Chinese, we translated the word "pioneering" into "daring to be the first to try something that no one has done before." We realized this was a critical behavioral element that we must encourage in a fast-changing industry that requires risk-taking to be successful. You have to allow people to take risks and even fail once in a while.

At this time, market demographics were changing, and Lenovo recognized it must target a younger generation of consumers to acquire their brand loyalty early and turn them into long-term customers. HR again played a strategic role here. We reviewed and adapted our talent acquisition, performance measurement, and compensation strategies to recruit, retain, and unleash a different type of talent. Our CEO even set the example by posing for fashion magazines, something he probably never would have done if it were not for our drive to promote Lenovo as young and stylish to the Net Generation of customers.

Internally, we use our recent product successes, such as the Yoga Tablet and the SHAREit app to tell the stories behind the innovation and encourage the pioneering spirit. The pioneering spirit has to be something real and visible from everywhere in the company. Our culture is an asset that is reflected in Lenovo's brand image as an employer: entrepreneurial, global, diverse, and filled with opportunities to grow.

Transforming the Organization

HR drives organizational design efforts to ensure Lenovo is ahead of the curve and is well prepared to meet the needs of a rapidly and continuously changing industry. In fact, because the industry we operate in changes so fast, Lenovo completes a major reorganization nearly every year in January. For example, on the front end where we serve customers, we reorganized the company into geographic regions so they can make market-specific and customer-driven decisions to meet their commitments. At the same time, on the back end, we formed business groups to deliver the greatest efficiency when it comes to the design, manufacturing, and delivery of the products. Today Lenovo is organized into four business groups that focus on PCs, mobile devices, servers, and ecosystem and cloud services. This structure helps protect Lenovo's leadership in the core PC business and provides the necessary focus and resources in each of the new growth areas that we "attack."

Driving organizational transformation is a key role of HR. It is HR's responsibility to design the current organizational structure, anticipate new challenges, and provide direction for the future. To do so, HR must always observe the changing market and competitive landscape and create the best and most efficient organizational structure to ensure cross-regional and cross-functional collaboration.

HR also needs to help communicate the organizational changes to ensure they are understood and effectively implemented. This capability is another competitive advantage of Lenovo—we can complete a major reorganization every year and quickly start to function in the new structure. Our employees learn to adapt in this environment as well.

As we grew to be more global, our talent development strategy had to adapt. A special focus was put on developing the "global talent." Lenovo calls itself a "global local company." We hire local leaders in our key markets to run the business of that country. We have Americans run America, Indians run India, Russians run Russia, and Europeans run Europe. With this approach, leaders feel trusted and empowered, and they know their customers and their markets, enabling them to deliver the results. At the same time, they also embrace the values of Lenovo and are unified by our shared cultural identity, which we call "the Lenovo Way."

To shape the organization, HR collaborated with the senior leadership team, built trust, and ensured the best decisions were made for the businesses. In my career at Lenovo I have worked in a variety of critical business roles enabling me to develop the knowledge and credibility needed to advise leaders on organizational structure design.

I encourage the HR team to learn and understand the company's business model, the latest product portfolio, and Lenovo's customer needs. With this knowledge, the HR team is positioned to talk with the business leaders and have credibility when they propose the next strategic organizational moves for the business.

Recommendations

- Combining cultures will result in clashes and spirited, passionate discussions. Embrace them and ensure they remain respectful. Success cannot be achieved without an honest exchange of ideas and compromise.
- Diversity is a competitive advantage that must be built and fostered through initiatives and education to ensure its value to the organization is realized.
- A company's culture is an asset that can be an important part of your brand image as an employer. To attract entrepreneurs, an entrepreneurial and innovative spirit must be visible in action every day.

- HR must deeply understand the business and prepare the organization to adapt both in structure and in how it attracts and retains talent.

Conclusion

HR has an important and essential role in helping a company become global. Growth requires building trust across a diverse organization and establishing a culture that helps strengthen a company's core competencies.

HR's focus has to evolve along with the rest of the company as corporate strategies adjust to a rapidly changing marketplace. In a fast-paced industry like Lenovo's, HR must always stay ahead of the curve. Most importantly, HR leaders must stay close to the most pressing strategic challenges that the company faces and proactively prepare the company from a human capital and an organizational behavior standpoint.

PART V

MANAGING TALENT FOR SUCCESS

Chapter 14.
Talent Trumps Strategy

Rich Floersch

After over 30 years in the HR profession, and the last 10 plus as a chief human resource officer (CHRO), I have come to realize that "talent indeed trumps strategy." This is based on my experiences in consulting and at companies such as Kraft Foods, Altria, and McDonald's. Specifically, I would rather have an "A-level" talented team working on "B-level strategy" than the other way around. Obviously, having both "A-level" talent *and* strategy is ideal, but not always possible.

So, as the CHRO, there is a great responsibility to the company, its employees and shareholders as to who is placed in key jobs. Each company will have different approaches to achieving that goal, but I would like to share five critical lessons that I believe will determine whether we are successfully filling core jobs with individuals who will drive strong results for the company.

Successors Must Be Equal To or Better Than Incumbents

Let's start with a fairly simple yet powerful concept—for a successor to be considered a "ready-now" candidate, he or she must be viewed as someone who can perform at a level equal to or better than the incumbent. Sounds incredibly straightforward, but not always easy to attain.

Why? Any number of reasons. First, incumbents may have a difficult time accepting that someone could perform their job better than they can, or the decision is made out of loyalty or expedience. It is always easier to fill a job with someone who has "earned the right" to have the job, but he or she may not be the best person for the job.

In fact, if there is not a strong consensus that an internal candidate can uplift the performance of the group he or she will be leading, then it is wise to look outside the company. I have been incredibly energized by the caliber of talent that exists outside the companies I have worked with. It is somewhat more risky to go outside to fill a key job, but an external candidate is likely to generate greater upside for the organization than the "safe internal bet." You will also mitigate the risks associated with an external hire if you do a good job of assessing culture fit, properly onboarding the candidate, and ensuring that champions and advocates exist for the new hire.

The more challenging situation is convincing an incumbent that it is his or her job to develop candidates who could perform the incumbent's job better. It is so critical to reward those who do this well. Role modeling these behaviors at the most senior levels in the company ensures that the messaging surrounding succession is not hollow. Setting the right tone at the board and CEO levels goes a long way in creating the right environment for this to happen. When this does not happen and job placements are made with "safe bets," it will only be a matter of time before the overall capabilities of the organization decline and business results suffer along with it. And the decline will not happen quickly—it will be gradual, but over time the cumulative effect of suboptimal talent decisions will be significant. It is senior management and the CHRO's role to make certain that this does not happen—keeping a high bar for placement decisions starts at the top.

One final consideration: A candidate who is currently deficient should be provided with direct feedback on what would make him or her "ready now." After receiving the feedback, it is up to the individual to work on his or her areas of improvement and, hopefully, demonstrate greater capability for the job in the future. There is nothing more satisfying than seeing an individual take the feedback to heart and become a stronger candidate for the job to which he or she aspires.

Healthy Balance of "Build and Buy" Talent

I work for a company that prides itself on promoting from within. As the CHRO, I can speak with conviction and passion about our company's ability to deliver on that philosophy. It is motivating for our employees to hear that we have a bias to internal development and a development culture that supports this. I also believe this philosophy drives higher levels of engagement, as employees believe there is a commitment to developing the next generation of leaders from within.

Despite this, "buying" talent is sometimes the right decision when you are looking to turn around the trajectory of the business, fill leadership gaps, or stay abreast of changes in the marketplace.

Clearly, as a company falls short of its growth goals, it is smart to assess whether an infusion of new ideas into the organization is required. Companies go through cycles, and when the performance is strong, there is a natural tendency to believe the strategies in place remain the right ones for the future. Once the company's performance begins to show signs of weakness, it is smart to look at opportunities to inject new ideas into the system, and external hires can help make that happen. Undoubtedly, it is smarter to anticipate the downturn and start the recovery process sooner. There are a number of us who wish we had a keener sense of the future, but it is a major miss not to act when the signs are becoming clearer.

When there are gaps in bench strength, it is wise to replenish the depth of talent through accelerated development plans for internal candidates. If so, external hiring can be stepped up at key entry points within the company, that is, midmanagement levels that serve as the feeder pools to the executive and officer group.

There are also certain functions that require having a different balance of "build versus buy." Functions that are moving at faster paces of change than others, like marketing, digital, and information technology, should consider "buying" more talent. It would be wise to strategically consider where each function falls on this scale. A one-size-fits-all approach for all functions heightens your organization's potential to fall behind the curve and not recognize important market-based shifts—until it is too late.

Calibrate on Critical Success Factors

Throughout my career, I have seen a number of employees start a new job, and six to nine months into their role, I hear that they did not make the impact that the manager and organization were expecting.

Why? Often times it is the result of unclear alignment between the manager and employee on what the critical success factors are for the job, or, better said, failing to agree on the four to five imperatives that will determine whether the individual is successful and contributing to the organization in a positive way. Too often it is left up to the employee to figure out what those critical success factors are—some do it well, while many struggle.

The time to get it right is well before the employee starts the new job. The best time to determine the critical success factors is when the candidate pool is being developed and the candidates will be judged by the agreed-on success factors. Some examples of these factors include culture fit, leadership capabilities, and critical thinking skills. It is wise to identify the critical success factors with the candidate's future manager, the manager's manager, the peers and, if applicable, other stakeholder groups. Once the input has been collected, you will be in the best position to choose the right candidate. This process also helps the manager and employee construct an onboarding plan that is focused and relevant. Finally, the critical success factors also help communicate to those who did not get the position the reasons why their candidacies fell short.

Having these critical success factors clearly articulated will heighten your organization's ability to achieve a higher "hit rate" for successful placements. Taking the time to do this will pay significant dividends to everyone involved, most importantly to the person selected for the job.

Clarity of Critical Thinking and Communication Skills

Based on my experience, I have developed a perspective on the importance of two leadership attributes that are inextricably linked together—specifically, the ability to have clarity of critical thinking and then the skills to clearly communicate ideas that impart understanding. When this happens successfully, the individual and the team move in the direction intended without confusion, and when this does not happen, the opposite occurs—confusion, misdirection, and hesitation.

I spend a lot of time evaluating talent on the person's ability to demonstrate his or her capabilities on these two attributes. Some of this I glean from observing the individual with his or her peers or team, through information from employee commitment surveys, and through a structured interview process.

- Strong leaders both assess situations accurately and generate ideas that are fact-based mixed with the right amount of intuition. They then can communicate the ideas in a manner that builds alignment and action. As a leader moves up the organization and assumes more responsibility, these attributes take on greater levels of importance because the decisions become more impactful and the audiences become larger.

I would encourage those in the HR profession to build strong assessment skills on these leadership attributes, either personally or through an outside resource, and provide targeted development programs that support the importance of developing these capabilities in their leaders.

The return on investment (ROI) will be substantial, and your leadership team will lead stronger organizations. And your employees will have a clearer sense of where the organization is going and what they need to do to support the strategic direction. This breeds confidence in the future of the company and builds an energized workforce that feels empowered and not confused or disengaged.

Broader and Not Deeper Experiences

My final critical lesson learned on the topic of talent is the importance of leaders who have broad experiences. This includes cross-functional, cross-geographic, and cross-industry experiences versus someone who has deep expertise in a single function, geography, or industry. You will find that leaders with broader experiences will outperform those with deeper and narrower backgrounds more times than not.

Why? It is simply based on the premise that exposure to a number of different experiences expands the ways to approach a business challenge. Leaders are constantly making decisions that involve trade-offs—do the positive implications of a decision outweigh the negative consequences? I believe that having a wider set of experiences helps make better trade-off decisions because there is never only one way to approach a business challenge. Those who have the benefit of making decisions based on a variety of functional knowledge, cultural sensitivities, and industry dynamics will make better leaders in your company.

Therefore, a talent strategy that rewards individuals for taking lateral assignments, appreciates differences in individuals who come from outside the company or industry, and encourages and supports those who are willing to take the risk of working overseas will win in the marketplace with a diverse team open to new ideas and approaches. And, as the head of HR, your personal career history, which includes broad experiences, will make you a better leader of the function and talent strategist.

So these are the five most critical areas I suggest for building talent, and I hope you gained one or two insights from my experiences. Talent management is never going to be easy or perfect, but working hard to have "A" talent is well worth the time and effort.

Chapter 15.
Managing Your Talent Supply Chain

Jill B. Smart and Debra Exstrom

This chapter explores how the field of supply chain management can influence the work of the HR function. Supply chain principles such as resource planning, supply/demand management, and scheduling or delivery can help chief human resource officers (CHROs) understand how talent can flow optimally in their organizations. The authors share their experience at Accenture and offer insights and practical advice on how to plan and manage your own talent supply chain.

Chief human resources officers wear at least two hats, regardless of industry, type of business, or size of company. On the one hand, we are talent officers or "chief people officers": we attract, develop, and nurture our organization's people with an eye toward increasing the overall quality of talent and its positive impact on the business. On the other hand, we are operations officers: we manage talent planning, acquisition, supply, demand, and delivery such that the right people in the right numbers and price points are in place at the right time to effectively serve customers, innovate, and grow.

Accenture calls the union of these two perspectives "managing the talent supply chain."

Let's be clear at the outset: We know that people are not products or spare parts. In a business like Accenture's, much of our knowledge capital—the primary "product," or what clients buy—resides in the brains of our people. The company's leaders see and treat each person as a unique individual making a special contribution to overall success.

At the same time, if HR is to be truly relevant to the business, we need to get deeply into the heads of our executives, customers, and sales people about talent supply and demand—about forecasting talent needs, acquiring, and developing talent and delivering that talent where it is needed in a timely way. By analogy, if a products company makes a commitment to a customer to have X number of products to it by a certain date, the entire manufacturing and delivery supply chain had better be ready to deliver high-quality products on that schedule. If demand for the product suddenly increases, the system should be able to increase production rapidly to meet that demand.

Whether you are a manufacturing company or one like Accenture—specializing in strategy, consulting, digital, technology, and operations—if you swing too far toward over-supply, you find yourself with excessively high operations costs. Overbalance the other direction, though, and you find yourself leaving money on the table by failing to seize client and revenue opportunities.

This is the science—and the art—of managing the talent supply chain. It combines the hard sciences and professions, including finance, technology, and analytics, with the particular insights that only HR professionals can bring to the table regarding talent sourcing, development, and management.

Optimizing your own talent supply chain may be a significant journey for you and your organization. But the rewards are considerable: giving employees the opportunities to develop and grow, improving management rigor, providing better quality and depth of skills, and increasing HR's alignment with the business—the ability to match workforce supply with demand faster and more accurately. Ultimately it is about serving customers better, contributing greater business value, and creating a better work environment for your people.

The Talent Supply Chain at Accenture: An Overview

A talent supply chain aims to forecast, acquire, optimize, retain, and deploy the right talent at the right time in the right place, enabling customers to be served effectively while also focusing on business efficiency and employees' career development needs (see Figure 16.1). With a talent supply chain management perspective, traditional supply chain terms, principles, and approaches can be reinterpreted and applied, including:

- Resource forecasting and planning: Longer-term workforce planning based on client demand and financial forecasts.
- Supply/demand management: Shorter-term planning, balancing resource requests and availability, and determining how talent will be acquired or developed in response to business needs.
- Scheduling: Talent delivery, deployment, and redeployment.

FIGURE 15.1. THE TALENT SUPPLY CHAIN AT ACCENTURE

Resource Forecasting and Planning

Forecasting and planning for resource needs, driven by the business—at an appropriate level of detail to make good sourcing decisions
- Longer term: Capacity plans
- Shorter term: Skills/specific fulfillment actions

Supply/Demand Management

Meeting resource needs in agreed time frames and at appropriate productivity levels
- Resource pool management: Sourcing decisions (hiring, contracting, training, attrition)
- Talent acquisition and contract planning: Seamless integration across the entire talent planning and acquisition lifecycle

Scheduling

Getting talent to the right places ("delivery") and managing the deployment and redeployment process ("inventory control")
- Project resource planning
- Managing project resources

From an HR perspective, the terms used will look and sound different from those used in manufacturing supply chain management: terms such as recruiting, hiring, development, training, deployment, and so forth. Yet the rigor and predictability of supply chain management can help CHROs and their teams become more relevant and effective partners to the business.

Supporting a Changing Business

Applying a supply chain perspective to talent management provides rigor that can be especially helpful to a company undergoing extensive change and growth. In Accenture's case, the past decade has seen the company grow from 100,000 employees to more than 350,000. From a company offering technology and consulting services, it extended its offerings into areas such as operations, digital, and industry-based business services. Being competitive in those domains meant expanding the workforce presence into additional geographic regions, especially emerging countries. It also meant developing the capability and capacity to serve more clients in those developing regions. Because of the global nature of the business, the company needed a globally managed HR capability as well—coordinated efforts, with lines of sight anywhere and everywhere in the world.

The company also began drawing from different kinds of talent pools, given the more varied kinds of client services it was providing and the different demands of that work. In addition to hiring people directly from college campuses based on their aptitude and potential—for many years, its traditional approach—the need for varied skills meant that Accenture started tapping more experienced hires and more senior people, as well as contract workers.

Add this all up, and it meant a need for deeper and more specialized skills and for managing a workforce more diverse and differentiated than ever before. For all these reasons, the company adopted a supply chain approach to talent management—not just as a metaphor but in a way that influenced how it organized its HR function and how it conceived of sourcing, developing, and delivering talent.

Resource Forecasting and Planning

From a resource forecasting and planning perspective, one important question at the beginning of Accenture's own talent supply chain journey was whether it had the data to effectively guide the business with precision and confidence about what talent it had, and what talent it needed, to serve its clients and grow the business most effectively.

Initial work with measurement tools included a forecasting and planning tool integrated with finance information. The tool took the financial plans and translated those into the head count the company would likely need to drive desired results. Looking several quarters into the future, the company was able to see what parts of the business and which geographies were growing and what kind of talent it needed to support that growth. Initial work with this tool suggested that, although quite strong in general, there was room for improvement in predicting what talent the company needed, and where it was needed, to support its work.

An early insight was that the company had to predict and forecast without having "perfect" information about demand. No longer could it wait until it actually *saw* the demand; it had to forecast what the demand for talent *was likely to be* several quarters in the future so that the talent would be in place by the time the business materialized.

How precise did these estimates need to be? Today the company's rigor and precision are quite high thanks to effective processes and tools and, most recently, to analytics-based programs. But an important insight from that initial point in the journey was that Accenture could go a long way toward improving its balance of effectiveness and efficiency just with more regular, general information from its sales and delivery teams. HR needed to be included in the sales process so it could understand the sales pipeline, especially the probability of a sale.

The chief operating officer at the time, Steve Rohleder, made a big difference by making it clear to the business that getting supply forecasting right was the sales and delivery teams' responsibility as much as it was HR's. "An important step for us," as he put it, "was to change the culture of the organization, and of project management more specifically, to be more disciplined about telling HR in a timely fashion what talent was needed for the future. We also needed more timely information about when people were rolling off one project and were available for another."

One key was not to ask for this information in a way that sounded as though the request was for perfectly accurate deliverables in spreadsheets that would take weeks to create. Certainly it can be difficult to predict resource needs due to the potential volatility in the business and economic environment, as well as continuously changing client needs. However, it was possible to think about the general pipeline of demand and what skills were "hot," and then provide a rough-cut sense of the people who would be needed and where. As an example, a group might anticipate 10 percent growth in demand over a six-month period for professionals skilled in technology architectures. This projection would then be important guidance from the business, delivered in a timely fashion.

The business needed to sell work with the confidence that the right people would be available at the right time to serve on delivery teams. At the same time, those charged with hiring and development needed the confidence that there would be work for these people to do. The effort and ongoing work of resource forecasting had to be deeply collaborative.

Supply/Demand Management

In the overall information flow of talent supply chain management, re-source forecasting and planning feeds directly into supply/demand management. Resource forecasting takes a slightly longer-term and more macro perspective, looking several quarters into the future. Supply/demand management then looks at specific requests for people at clients, both immediately and in the next several months. Based on those requests and on the availability of people—those available now and those becoming available in that time frame—HR makes decisions about how to fill those needs. Traditionally the options are referred to as "buy, build, or borrow"— that is, acquire talent from the outside through recruiting, develop it internally through additional training and experience, or make use of external contractors for particular roles.

The following sections look briefly at the buy (talent acquisition) and build (talent development) perspectives.

Talent Acquisition

One of the biggest challenges in talent acquisition is having enough notice from the business that people with certain skills and in certain numbers will be needed by a certain date. So for recruiters, the benefit of being part of the information flow of the talent supply chain is the heads-up. With the knowledge coming from supply/demand management, recruiting teams around the world, in partnership with the business, can understand when they need to take action in terms of recruiting to avoid a talent gap down the road. Recruiters know they need to hire certain profiles in particular places at specified levels and costs. And they receive that request with enough time to get it done.

Without a supply chain perspective, HR has a harder time staying in lockstep with the business from a talent acquisition point of view. Every HR professional knows about the ad hoc requests that often come in: "Go hire this kind of profile." "Go hire that kind of profile." Instead, Accenture now says, "No, we have placed some very strong bets about the talent we need. Here's the recruiting plan; now it's important to deliver on that effectively."

That approach frees up capacity for recruiting teams to work on much more innovative activities—referral programs, for example, or social media relationships, or new technology applications that make interviewing faster and more effective. That is really a bonus of the talent supply chain perspective. Accenture is able to let its recruiters specialize in the candidate experience so they can help deliver the best talent possible rather than focus on "who should I go hire?"

Nurturing prehiring relationships is a critical way that the acquisition part of the supply chain can be more nimble in responding to business needs. This is an area that Ellyn Shook, now CHRO at Accenture, refers to as "talent relationship management." She envisions this set of relationships as a robust network, one much more specific to Accenture's needs than a more generalized social platform.

For example, the company's recruiters continuously network with high-potential candidates they have identified. The company may hold a virtual forum on a particular business or technology area and invite potential candidates to participate. Or a recruiter may send a candidate a relevant article or a link to some other content of interest. In many cases our experienced business professionals and leaders will be in direct contact with candidates, making them feel part of an ongoing dialogue with the company.

Having recruiters simultaneously tapped into the business and into the unique profiles of candidates also means the company can approach people in a way that is meaningful to them. That is, the manner in which the company communicates with a candidate for our Strategy business unit will often differ from how it engages with a candidate for Digital, Consulting, Technology, or Operations because each unit attracts people with different backgrounds, experiences, and interpersonal styles. And how recruiters interact with the current generation of university graduates is likely to differ from the manner in which they reach out to more experienced hires. This is in part about communicating a unique value proposition, but it is also about knowing the distinct attributes, styles, and backgrounds of people interested in different parts of the business.

Looking ahead, it is likely that the acquisition part of the talent supply chain is where the greatest changes will occur, due in part to advances in analytics. Although more effective forecasting and planning continually shrinks the time gap between the demand for talent and fulfilling that demand, two developments are dramatically changing this area and will continue to do so. The first is the use of predictive analytics to understand what skills and capabilities the company is going to need. The second is more extensive use of data mining so that HR can proactively find people—from the current employee base, the alumni network, or high-potential candidates—rather than wait for demand forecasts.

Talent Development

Talent development strengthens the overall talent supply chain in several ways. It helps ensure that our people have the right experience and skills needed to deliver excellent service to clients. Leading-edge learning principles and technologies also make the supply chain more nimble by increasing speed to competency for critical skills and for the always-evolving capabilities needed to work in a rapidly changing world. Finally, talent development provides opportunities for personal and career growth, increasing the engagement of people in their work and in the company, which in turn helps reduce attrition—something that can negatively affect overall supply/demand management.

The internal learning delivery approach, which Ellyn Shook recently launched as Accenture Connected Learning, blends a range of learning environments, including innovative learning boards, new connected classrooms, and a network of learning centers, to build the specialized professional skills and capabilities of Accenture people. Connected classrooms, for example, provide telepresence-like communication and online tools that enable people from multiple locations to participate in interactive, collaborative sessions. Learning boards are curated knowledge bases that help people find the best information and ideas from world-class subject matter experts. Accenture curators create and share expert online content in formats that include videos, blogs, digital books, and self-study training courses. Together, these technologies and approaches combine foundational learning, collaborative experiences, and ways to build awareness and understanding of new concepts at scale and at speed, so the company can continuously meet new and changing business requirements and keep the talent supply chain operating effectively.

As noted at the beginning of this chapter, the "product" of a talent supply chain is fundamentally unlike that of a manufacturing company because it is a living, thinking, growing one. People can leave the supply chain anytime they want—to competitors, clients, schools, and so forth. So it is important to make sure that people are engaged with their work and with the company and that they feel they are being given opportunities to grow in their profession. Opportunities for learning and development are a critical component, according to Accenture research and surveys, of how engaged employees are in the company.

The loss of high-performing employees can reverberate across the talent supply chain. It costs hundreds of millions of dollars for a large, global organization to recruit, source, onboard, and develop people. By improving the engagement of people in their work, companies can help optimize the supply chain, save money, and improve the service delivered to clients.

Factors such as these are now figuring into more sophisticated analytics and big data tools Accenture is putting in place that enable us to predict some of the potential disruptions in the talent supply chain before they happen. For example, the company now engages in attrition modeling to help identify employees at risk of leaving; this enables us to be proactive with those people to help them find work experiences that deepen their engagement with the company.

Scheduling

Placing talent into the right assignments at the right time is the primary outcome of the scheduling ("delivery") process; it is also one of the most challenging aspects of talent supply chain management. In part this challenge is rooted in the fact that people are deployed to a particular project but do not stay there forever. Their responsibilities on one project eventually come to an end, which means redeploying them to another. So "inventory control"—in the sense of closely monitoring when people might be available for another assignment and quickly finding them a new, meaningful role—is inherent in the scheduling process.

Scheduling is one of the most important elements of the talent supply chain because it most directly affects the business; people are put into roles that are going to serve clients today and innovate for tomorrow. Scheduling links closely to the talent development area just discussed because working directly with our clients is the most critical way by which people deepen their skills and become more specialized.

Scheduling is also where the effectiveness of the other areas of the talent supply chain becomes most evident. Ultimately, effectiveness in the forecasting area, or in supply/demand management, shows up in how the company delivers the right talent to clients in a way that also gives our people meaningful opportunities to build their careers.

Some view scheduling as transactional, but that is true only to a certain extent. When client teams identify a need for certain types of people, Accenture can use technology to do the transactional component of matching qualified people with good roles. But the human element—the expertise of HR professionals—is also critical. For example, in some cases, given the requirements identified by a project team, there may be several candidates from which to choose. In other cases, the technology may identify a number of candidates who have, let us say, two out of the three requested areas of experience. In all these instances, human decision-making—based on knowledge of the individuals themselves—will always be important.

Knowing the desired career path of candidates is part of the mix. That is, one of the stated requirements for a role may be a stretch goal for a particular employee. In some cases, matching that employee to that particular role may be exactly what the project team needs—someone especially ready for a new experience and motivated to go all out in performing to the necessary level.

Thus, making good transactions is vital to effective scheduling. But it is also important to remember that scheduling involves some of the most pressing decisions HR professionals make for the business and for people. Getting those decisions right is perhaps the most obvious part of HR that the business will note. Ultimately scheduling is about serving clients—but behind that is having highly qualified people in place on the front lines to make superior service possible.

Building Your Talent Supply Chain Management Skills

Organizing and managing Accenture's HR organization according to a talent supply chain focus has sharpened our understanding of the essential skills needed by HR people to meet the ultimate goal of effectively serving clients, employees, and shareholders alike. HR positions are now demanding knowledge-worker roles requiring specialized expertise along a number of dimensions—from finance, to relationship skills, to knowledge of particular technology platforms and solutions including analytics, to cutting-edge HR and training tools, and much more.

One way to understand the demands of these positions from a skills perspective is to look at the actual job descriptions posted by Accenture. Talent fulfillment specialists, for example, are, as a job posting has it, responsible for managing the scheduling of talent, for helping to identify and propose right talent from a resource pool to ensure fulfillment of all open roles, and for managing/monitoring people productivity targets.

Embedded in that description is the fact that these specialists have key responsibilities as (a) business operators—creating short- and long-term supply plans, exploring all sourcing channels, considering and balancing scheduling principles in making decisions, and so forth; and as (b) value creators. That is, specialists are measured not just on how well they are performing their transactional duties but also on how they are delivering positive business outcomes.

One of the biggest changes we have seen in required HR capabilities is a close knowledge of the business itself. We tell HR people: You are much more than a person filling an order; you are helping the business leader or manager understand, from a talent perspective, what that order needs to be to balance client needs, employee needs, and the efficiency of operations.

Conclusion

In large measure, HR professionals will be the drivers in establishing and managing an effective and efficient talent supply chain. At the same time, it is more accurate to think of HR professionals both as managers of, and as participants in, a larger talent management ecosystem that includes business line managers, training professionals, finance and operations, business strategists, and the executive suite itself.

With a supply chain perspective, HR professionals have the opportunity to step up to the challenge of managing talent in a way that drives better business results. A supply chain approach enables HR to define business indicators and measure them—metrics such as productivity, role fulfillment efficiency, cost of talent, and so forth. Defining and hitting those metrics are specialized skills that put HR at the epicenter of the business. People are among a company's biggest investments, so knowing what the return is on that investment is vital.

Chapter 16.

Driving Organizational Success: Addressing the Leaky Talent Pipeline for Women

Mara Swan

I have been in my fair share of talent development discussions to determine promotions into key roles within the organization. I have found over the years that something interesting happens when these decisions are being made. Often, the CEO and management team will say that James seems better for the job than Anne. For many years, I felt in my gut that this might not be right, but I took them at their word and agreed: If James has it, he has it. Later, though, I started to analyze the data, and I noticed that my original instinct was correct. Anne had equal or better skills and results than James, but they were not described in the same way. I knew then that something had to change about the way that organizations assess, develop, and leverage the talent of women.

Anne's story is illustrative of many similar decisions that I have seen throughout my tenure as a chief human resource officer (CHRO). At an individual decision-making level, I have learned over the years to elevate the conversation so that we do not miss the opportunity to leverage the talent of the Annes in our companies. At an organizational level, I have learned that as CHROs, we have a responsibility to make our corporate cultures work for women versus allowing unconscious bias to prevail and explaining away why we have no female leaders or not enough women in the pipeline ready for leadership positions.

As CHROs, we have been caught in a circular conversation over the years about why we do not have enough women in leadership positions. Are they pushed out by our cultures and the competitive squeeze to the top? Are they pulled out by better offers by our competitors? Do they leave for personal reasons? These questions have gotten us nowhere. We need to pause for a moment and admit to ourselves that for all of the effort we have put into achieving parity for women in leadership, we have not delivered the outcomes we expected. The talent pipeline remains leaky for women in leadership roles. Now, more than ever before, we need women in leadership positions.

Changing demographics and shifts in working conditions are causing a looming crisis for organizations. In Organization for Economic Cooperation and Development (OECD) nations,[1] working populations are aging, while at the same time birthrates in these nations are declining. After 2020, the working age population is expected to decline yearly from 196 million to 187 million in 2060.[2] For the first time in decades, employers will have to choose from a shrinking rather than growing workforce. Without a growing workforce, there are two primary ways to increase the talent pool: immigration or leveraging underutilized sources within the country. Immigration is something that we as employers cannot control, since it depends heavily on the legislative environment. However, tapping into underutilized sources within the country is something we can control.

Women are the most underutilized source of human capital within a country's borders. Increasingly, women in OECD countries attain higher levels of education than their male peers. In the U.S.,[3] women are achieving higher levels of education and are entering the workforce at levels equal to or exceeding those of their male counterparts.[4] They earn 57 percent of all bachelor's degrees, 60 percent of all master's degrees, and 52 percent of all doctoral degrees.[5] In a knowledge-based economy, talent is a key determining factor of the competitive success of organizations. Many companies report that the most significant barrier to growth is their ability to attract and retain a skilled workforce for the 21st century.[6] As women continue to attain higher and higher levels of education, their talent becomes more essential to the success of organizations, and companies can no longer afford to have a laissez faire approach to attracting, engaging, and developing female talent if they want to remain competitive. At the same time, it is getting more difficult to attract and retain female workers since they have more alternatives now. Today, due to technological, policy, and cultural changes, it is easier than ever for women to take entrepreneurial opportunities. When women leave organizations, they start their own businesses at twice the rate of men, and their businesses exceed average profits in eight of 13 industries and match them in two others.[7] In other words, when women leaders leave your organization, they leave to become your competition.

Women represent 47 percent of the total labor force, and over 50 percent of all management and professional occupations in business.[8] Despite this, only 16.9 percent of executives sitting on boards and barely 15 percent of executive officers are female.[9, 10] Fewer than 9 percent of top earners and only 4.6 percent of CEOs are women.[11] Though we have increased the number of women in the workplace, we have not succeeded in moving them into the key profit and loss (P&L), executive, and board positions imperative for developing core strategy and business results.

Unconscious bias, organizational structure, and outmoded views of work, especially surrounding workplace flexibility, are keeping us from retaining top talent and keeping female leaders. As women enter the workforce in greater numbers due to their educational attainment, they also come with different demands and needs. The issue now is not whether women are able to adapt to fit your organization's culture, but whether your organization can adapt to women's needs. Women with higher educational levels are prepared to compete in a knowledge economy, and although we have successfully enabled women to enter the labor force, it is time for us to take responsibility for ensuring those women make it to the top.

For the past 30 years, we have focused on programs to attract, develop, and retain women. We have changed recruiting tactics, created development and mentoring programs, conducted gender sensitivity training, and created affinity programs. Let's face it, we spent a lot of time and money, and these efforts just have not produced stellar results. Program success has been lackluster because the programs are a generic solution for a complicated issue. While recruiting tactics have brought women into the workforce, development and mentoring programs are not keeping them in. When women do stay, they largely stay in staff roles (see Figure 17.1), minimizing their chances of making it to the top.

Staying in staff roles is fine, as long as we can ensure that it is an individual choice. In my experience, however, this is not the case.[12] We need to make sure women are not making this choice because they do not feel en-

FIGURE 16.1. WOMEN OPT INTO SUPPORT ROLES EARLY IN THEIR CAREERS

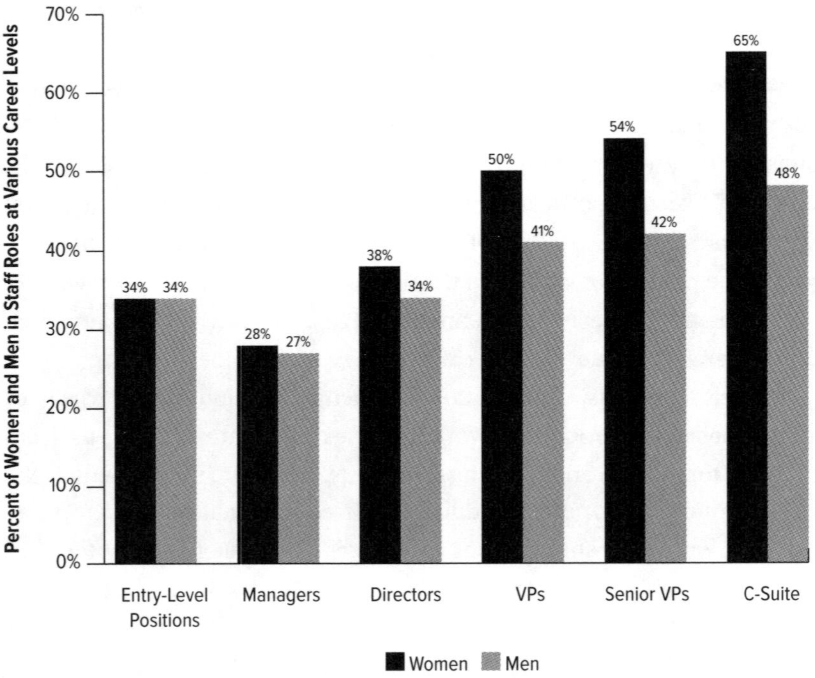

Percent of Women and Men in Staff Roles at Various Career Levels

	Entry-Level Positions	Managers	Directors	VPs	Senior VPs	C-Suite
Women	34%	28%	38%	50%	54%	65%
Men	34%	27%	34%	41%	42%	48%

■ Women ■ Men

Source: McKinsey, 2012

couraged to consider line roles, have not thought of line roles as options, or the cultural or job role conditions are not amicable to their needs. For example, 65 percent of women say flexible work options are important to them, yet only 28 percent of employers offer them.[13] Often needs like this can be met with a little creativity and flexibility.

Instead of focusing on programs, CHROs need to examine how decisions are made about Anne in their organizations and how the potential of women like Anne can be cultivated. We need to change our cultures to be more welcoming to women. Our top leadership has to walk the talk from representation of women in executive management up through the board of directors. Often we forget the ways in which we can be implicitly biased about women's behaviors. Unconscious bias, though not intentional, can have disastrous results. Recent research suggests that people think they are not biased when in fact their brains are wired that way.[14] I created a chart (see Table 17.1) based on my many interactions with hiring and promotional decisions over the years. In it are words used to explain the behavior of male as opposed to female colleagues in the workplace. Frequently, the identical personality trait or behavior held up as a strength in a man is criticized as a flaw in a woman. So the "assertive" man is contrasted to the "aggressive" woman. A man may be praised as a good "networker" while a woman is dismissed as "gossipy."

Whether you agree with it or not, Sheryl Sandberg's 2013 bestseller, *Lean In*,[15] was a success because it raised a key business issue: The business world has a culture-clash with women. If we are realistic and honest with ourselves, we have to admit that as CHROs, we need to take a stronger role in ensuring we are having the right conversations during hiring, promotional, and developmental discussions to ensure that unconscious bias is not creeping in. We need to be creative in the way we think about work in order to make certain that we attract women and keep women in key roles that lead to top leadership positions. It is hard work—but we have to do it.

TABLE 16.1. DIFFERENT DESCRIPTIONS ARE USED TO DESCRIBE THE SAME QUALITIES OF MEN AND WOMEN IN THE WORKPLACE

Men	Women
Assertive	Aggressive
Leader	Manager
Networker	Gossipy
Fair	Pushover
Innovative	Idealistic
Boss	Bossy
Tough	Pushy
Conceptual	Dreamer
Strategic	Unrealistic
Ducks in a Row	Micro-Manager
Thoughtful	Indecisive
Empathetic	Emotional
Authoritative	Overbearing
Persuasive	Argumentative

As CHROs, we need to make sure that we focus on having the right discussion every time we make an individual human capital decision, particularly for executive management, P&L jobs, and board seats. This means we must systematically look at the results our individual human capital decisions render. For example, if we have made 30 individual decisions and justified all of them, but these decisions still result in an underrepresentation of women, then we have a responsibility to look at the outcomes of these decisions and determine whether they are in the long-term best interest of our organizations. As CHROs, we are often too focused on ensuring that each individual decision is correctly made and legally defensible, rather than putting our energy into ensuring that our long-term organizational objectives and interests are achieved through each individual decision.

The bottom line is that as CHROs, we need to help leaders do a better job creating a culture in each of our particular businesses that allows for gender parity. We can do this through focusing our diversity efforts on better analytics and providing these data to the CEO and his or her leadership team. This macro analysis then allows us to gain a wider view into the micro causes of our talent problems. We can then use the analysis to target specific tactics to address parity issues particular to each of our cultures.

The solution to better gender parity in the workforce is to start with the macro-level data. If you implement a program without data analysis, it does not solve the problem and might only make it worse. By looking at the macro data, we take emotion out of gender in the workplace.

> ### How to change your culture to leverage the human capital of women:
> 1. Run analytics.
> 2. Determine outcomes.
> 3. Plan tactics.
> 4. Share progress.

While this solution sounds simple, it is much harder to actualize. There is no one-size-fits-all solution for something as complex as fixing the leaky talent pipeline, but below are some tools and guidelines to help you work through leveraging the human capital of women to the best of your organization's ability.

Step 1: Analytics

At a macro level, CHROs need to conduct a flow analysis that captures data on women's movement within the organization:

- Where do women come into the organization?
- From what positions/level/business unit do they leave the organization?
- Where do they go when they leave the organization?
- What positions/locations produce the highest/lowest turnover of female employees?

- Which managers produce the highest/lowest turnover of female employees?
- Which positions produce the highest/lowest rate of promotions for women?
- Which managers produce the highest/lowest rate of promotions for women?

This overarching analysis needs to be accompanied by a recruitment analysis, a promotion analysis, a development analysis, a distribution and pipeline analysis, and a turnover analysis. Gather the data for each category. I have provided an overview of questions each company should ask itself about its data to get an idea of each of these components. While all of these should apply, CHROs should think about their company's unique situation to see what other questions they might need to ask. It is best to think of this as an ongoing process that a CHRO conducts annually or semiannually, not a one and done solution.

Recruitment Analysis

- Which schools are producing the most/least number of female candidates/hires for our company?
- Which companies are producing the highest/lowest number of female candidates/hires for our company?
- At what point in the recruitment process do female candidates drop out and why?
- Which kinds of jobs produce the most/least successful female candidates?
- Which questions in the interview process trip up women more often than men?
- Are women and men entering the same jobs being paid at the same level?

Promotion Analysis

Look at your pool of women who have been promoted:

- Where do women come from within your company? Which jobs or regions are most likely to produce women who are promoted?
- Which educational institutions, educational attainment level, and

educational degrees, specialization, and training do they have?

- Which managers promote the most women, and how successful are the women once promoted?
- What is the promotion decision-making process?
  - » What data points are considered during the promotions process?
  - » How robust is the dialog used for promotion evaluations and conversations?
  - » Who is checking for unconscious bias during these promotion evaluations and conversations?
- What other systematic issues might be at play in the promotions process?
- Are women promoted into P&L jobs at the same rate as men? If not, why not? What changes can be made to alter the situation?
- Are women paid the same as their male counterparts when promoted?

Development Analysis

- What development opportunities do the most successful people receive in the company?
- How do these development opportunities compare to the opportunities women receive?
- What trends can you identify in the developmental feedback women receive versus the feedback men receive in your company?
- Have you used third-party developmental feedback? Has the third party assessed differences between the way men and women receive development opportunities and feedback?

Distribution and Pipeline Analysis

- Where are women working in the company (for example, position, function, country)?
- How does this compare to where the company sources top leaders?
- How many women are in P&L jobs?
- How many women are in the most competitive/highest potential business units?

- What are the key jobs that lead to P&L jobs?

Turnover Analysis

- Why do women leave your organization?
- Where do women go when they leave your organization?
- At what point in their career, at what age, or from which locations do women leave the organization?
- Do women leave from specific jobs more than other jobs? Why? What ways could your organization change the job to help keep women in it?
- Is there anything you could change about your organizational processes, culture, or policies to address turnover?

This level of analysis will allow the CHRO to engage with the CEO on the next step, which is to develop outcomes that will help the business achieve its goals. It will also allow the leadership team to work together to determine how and where to fix the parity problems in your organization, rather than invest the bulk of your time on programs that have been shown not to drive long-term sustainable success.

Step 2: Outcomes

The CHRO should be a strategic partner with the CEO to review the macro analysis and create outcomes based on that analysis. Here are the steps you should take.

Understand the Issue(s)

- Do not just run your data; take some time to analyze them. Do this from multiple perspectives and within multiple scenarios. For example, do not just check who is and is not giving promotions to women, but *why* that might be the case. What patterns emerge from your data? How do other data points like engagement surveys support or disprove the patterns you see in current data?
- Think creatively. How could we achieve better representation/ participation of women? What could we do differently to encourage women? How could we design jobs differently?

Choose Methods

- Do not go with the flow. You are there to make sure the strategies and goals your CEO puts in place get accomplished. That means you are responsible not only for *what* gets accomplished, but for *how* it gets accomplished. The means to the end are as important as the results when it comes to moving women into leadership roles.

Engage Leadership

- Nothing happens if it is not tied to business outcomes. It is the CHRO's responsibility to guide the CEO into setting shared outcomes and engaging the leadership team in developing a shared plan to achieve the outcomes.

Step 3: Tactics

Tactics are the ways you implement goals and objectives after they have been communicated to the leadership team. Some tactics might need to be implemented on a global level with the CEO. Other tactics might need to be addressed within a particular business line, with particular managers, or in specific countries. Tactics can include traditional methods, including systemic changes, leader training, programs, and cultural changes. But this time they are super-charged, primed for success with analytics, clear objectives, and leadership support.

Step 4: Progress

Accomplishing organizational objectives requires not only setting up the objectives with the business line leaders, but tracking progress against the objectives. The CEO and CHRO then need to hold the senior leadership and line leaders accountable for the results.

I believe that once you run these stats, you will find that women are not leaving your organization because of individual choice. They are leaving because we have let them leave.

Addressing the leaky talent pipeline is not going to be easy, but the facts are clear. Demographics are changing. Workforce participation and education rates are shifting. Bottom line, our economies are driven by labor force participation, and it is imperative that we tap into the underutilized source of human capital that we already have—women.

Endnotes

[1.] This article refers primarily to information from OECD countries, and specifically the United States. For information on successful implementation of top female leaders in other economies, please read my paper: ManpowerGroup "Cracking the Case: Why You Need Women Leaders." 2014. http://www.manpowergroup.fi/Global/Cracking%20the%20Case%20-%20Why%20You%20Need%20Women%20Leaders.pdf.

[2.] Armstrong, David M., and Jennifer M. Ortman. "The Difference International Migration Makes in Projections of the U.S. Population." Random Samplings: The Official Blog of the U.S. Census Bureau "2014 National Population Projections." US Census Bureau. July 1, 2013. Based on data from 2010. http://www.census.gov/population/projections/data/national/2014.html.

[3.] U.S. Bureau of Labor Statistics

[4.] National Center for Educational Statistics. Based on 2010 data.

[5.] Ibid.

[6.] ManpowerGroup 2014 Talent Shortage Survey.

[7.] Becker-Blease, J. R., Elkinawy, S., & Stater, M. (2010). The impact of gender on voluntary and involuntary executive departure. *Economic Inquiry, 48*, 4, 1102-1118; American Express OPEN. *The 2013 State of Women-Owned Businesses Report.* Retrieved from http://a10clinical.com/images/uploads/a10-news/StateOfWomenReport.pdf; The Guardian Life Small Business Research Institute. (2009). *Special Report: Women Small Business Owners Will Create 5+ Million New Jobs by 2018.*

[8.] "The Supply Problem Myth" *Catalyst.* 2012. <http://www.catalyst.org/system/files/The_Supply_Problem_Myth_Financial_Post_500_Boards.pdf>; Also cited in: "The Double-Bind Dilemma for Women in Leadership" *Catalyst.* 2007. <http://www.catalyst.org/system/files/The_Double_Bind_Dilemma_for_Women_in_Leadership_Damned_if_You_Do_Doomed_if_You_Dont.pdf>

[9.] Ibid.

[10.]Ibid.

[11.]Ibid.

[12.]LinkedIn. What Women Want @ Work: A Global LinkedIn Study; and ManpowerGroup. (2013). 2013 Women in Work Survey.

[13.]Ibid.

[14.]Yurkiewicz, I. (2012, September 23). Study shows gender bias in science is real. Here's why it matters (Web log post). Retrieved from http://blogs.scientificamerican.com/unofficial-prognosis/2012/09/23/study-shows-gender-bias-in-science-is-real-heres-why-it-matters/

[15.]Sandberg, S. (2013). *Lean In: Women, Work, and the Will to Lead.* New York: Knopf.

Chapter 17.
Great Leaders Deliver Great Business Results

Joe Ruocco

Aon Hewitt's 2014 Top Companies for Leaders study claimed that over the years, "organizations have truly raised the bar on their commitment to leadership and the benefits are evident through higher financial returns."[1] In other words, companies with strong leaders and a deep bench of talent are more likely to perform better than lesser-talented competitors. A well-designed global leadership development process and system will help produce these great leaders and produce ample talent throughout an organization. But what does a world-class global leadership development and talent management process look like? This chapter will identify the seven key attributes of one world-class process by following the journey of the Goodyear Tire and Rubber Company. Over the past decade, Goodyear developed an award-winning process and system that yielded great leaders and top talent who delivered stellar results, including four consecutive years (2011-2014) of record-setting operating earnings.

The Story

Nearly a decade ago, the Goodyear Tire and Rubber Company's leadership pipeline was weak. Only 19 percent of the top 30 or so most senior positions in the company had ready-now successors, and 75 percent of top positions were filled from the outside. Under CEO Rich Kramer, leadership development became a priority of the company. "Building talent and teams" became a leadership trait that the company measured and tied to the pay of senior leaders. Kramer made it clear that building "top talent and top teams" was a priority for the company and part of its mission and strategy, in line with Goodyear's goal of creating sustainable value.

As Goodyear's chief human resources officer (CHRO), I had the privilege to work with Kramer to implement a world-class global talent management and leadership development process at Goodyear with the goal of being able to attract, assess, develop, motivate, and retain the best talent and build a bench of ready-now successors at all levels of the organization. Importantly, all elements of this systematic and process-oriented approach were completely aligned with and designed to drive the business strategy.

The results were outstanding. In 2014, nearly two-thirds of executive jobs had ready-now successors, and 75 percent of top positions were filled from within, showing the depth of the leadership bench. Also, attrition at the senior level plummeted to less than 1 percent.

This focus on leadership development was pivotal to delivering unprecedented results for the company. From 2011-2014, Goodyear reported record operating earnings for four consecutive years. It generated free cash flow from operations of approximately $1 billion in both 2013 and 2014. Also in 2013, Goodyear reinstated its common stock dividend and implemented a stock buy-back program as part of a shareholder return program. Over the three-year period ending in 2014, total shareholder return was more than 100 percent. "The best leaders develop top talent and build top teams," said Kramer. "They create a culture of collaboration to drive business success and build the skills needed to identify and take advantage of new opportunities to grow our business."

The Seven Key Attributes for an Effective Process and System

The obvious question is how did Goodyear design and implement this effective global talent management and leadership development process. Listed below are seven key attributes found in the Goodyear system that were critical to Goodyear's success in establishing an outstanding process. The Goodyear system included:

1. Top leadership support and ownership.
2. Alignment between business strategy and talent strategy.
3. A talented HR team in place.

4. An integrated and aligned process-oriented approach.
5. A balanced "build-buy" talent game plan.
6. Metrics to hold leaders accountable.
7. An innovative best-practices mindset.

This section will cover each of the seven attributes as they relate to Goodyear's journey.

Top Leadership Support and Ownership

Goodyear's senior leadership team and members of the board of directors are actively involved in global talent management and leadership development initiatives. This involves a formal succession and talent review process, mentoring programs, informal exposure to high-potential talent, interviewing candidates for key leadership positions, and acting as faculty for executive leadership programs.

It all starts at the top of the house. Kramer spends 30 percent to 40 percent of his time developing leaders. It is important that the CEO and the board invest in identifying and developing the best leaders and talent.

Alignment between Business Strategy and Talent Strategy

At Goodyear, there is complete alignment between the talent strategy and the business strategy.

Early in his tenure, Kramer and his team developed a mission for Goodyear that included five principles as part of the company's strategy roadmap. One of the critical points was to build talent and teams. "We needed to have the best leaders and talent throughout the organization," said Kramer. "That would be key to executing our strategy."

Goodyear developed a set of leadership traits to apply globally and serve as the cornerstone for all HR systems and processes. Leaders are measured and paid not only on how they perform to objectives, but also on how they demonstrate the leadership traits. At the core of these traits and behaviors is a leaders' ability to develop teams and talent. These leadership traits serve as the nucleus of the talent and leadership process at Goodyear.

Having excellent talent and teams as a strategic priority and having the leadership traits as part of the evaluation and compensation process have created an alignment between the business strategy and talent strategy that continues to grow stronger over time.

Talented HR Team

Building a talented HR team is vital to having an effective talent and leadership development process. While business leaders are the owners of the process, the HR team members are the advocates, the facilitators, and the implementers. There are three main traits exhibited by a strong HR team. First, the HR team must know what good looks like, which in Goodyear's case required us to revamp the team and hire talent from such top HR academy companies as GE, Pepsi, Honeywell, Home Depot, and Whirlpool. Second, the HR team must be strong business partners with outstanding customer-centric skills and have credibility with its clients and the organization while constantly delivering results. Finally, the HR team must be a magnet for talent because not only do you need a strong HR leadership team, but you also need the entire function strong, top to bottom, with no weak links in talent or process. By hiring top talent from top companies and developing from within, Goodyear is now considered by leading HR search firms as an HR "talent-rich" company from which other top companies desire to recruit talent.

Integrated and Aligned Process-Oriented Approach

In 2008, Goodyear's talent management process was haphazard, with more than 100 different subprocesses that were inconsistent globally. Every division was doing its own thing, which led to a chaotic approach to talent management. This was reversed when the leadership of the company agreed to adopt nine global subprocesses around the talent management and leadership development system across all divisions and functions and around the world. Figure 18.1 illustrates this model, which became known as the "global talent management wheel." The wheel was implemented in 2008 and it includes definitions of the nine global subprocesses. Having a model that defines talent management and its key levers is the essence of a systematic global talent management and leadership development process. This process has a goal of being able to attract, assess, develop, motivate, and retain the best talent and to build a bench of ready-now successors at all levels of the organization. Having all elements of this approach completely aligned with and designed to drive the business strategy ensures that the process lives beyond the leaders who implemented it.

Need for a Balanced "Build-Buy" Talent Game Plan

As mentioned earlier, previously Goodyear hired 75 percent of top positions externally. In 2014, only 25 percent were filled from the outside. Regardless of what this percentage is in your company, having a balanced approach to hiring externally and developing from within is paramount. Goodyear calls it the "build-buy" approach. While Goodyear's goal is to fill the majority of executive positions from within, it is clear that hiring the right people externally is also needed, especially for senior-level positions. So there is a need to "build" talent from within, while supplementing this pool with what Goodyear "buys" externally.

Building

Consistent with the philosophy of promoting the majority of leaders from within the company, Goodyear transformed two core processes: the annual organization and talent review and leadership training and development. The organization and talent review involves a bottom-up assessment of key talent and high potentials in each region and function. This assessment culminates in a review with the board of directors.

As part of this review process, Goodyear implemented an automated Objective and Performance Management System to assess talent and more readily identify leaders as openings occur around the world. This system included an internal resume, career aspirations, and latest performance and potential assessments.

The leadership development philosophy involves a 70-20-10 approach—70 percent learning on the job (experiential), 20 percent learning from others (mentoring, coaching, and behavioral feedback), and 10 percent formal learning.

A new Senior Executive Development Program was established for the most senior global executives in the company. The curriculum was based on the results of a needs analysis of the top 300 global leaders. Strategic thinking, innovation, and global collaboration were high on the list. This class was designed in conjunction with Harvard University

FIGURE 17.1. SUMMARY OF THE NINE SUBPROCESSES OF THE TALENT MANAGEMENT WHEEL (2014)

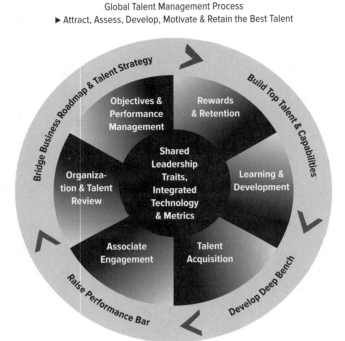

Global Talent Management Process
▶ Attract, Assess, Develop, Motivate & Retain the Best Talent

A Fully Integrated Global Talent Management Process...
Glued Together by Shared Leadership Traits, Integrated Technology and Metrics

OBJECTIVES & PERFORMANCE MANAGEMENT

A fully automated objective setting and performance management process. Associates and their managers set objectives at the beginning of the year, have a documented midyear evaluation, and finally a year-end documented review. Performance assessments against objectives and leadership traits take place. Development plans and career potential are also discussed. This process includes an internal resume and an ability to more readily identify high-potential talent.

REWARDS & RETENTION

The executive compensation process motivates and retains talent. This process is the same globally for all top leaders. This process allows for differentiation in the merit pay and variable pay for all leaders. It is a fully automated and global process. The retention process is a systematic review of all employees, highlighting retention risks, reasons for this risk, and plans to address and retain talent.

LEARNING & DEVELOPMENT

This formal learning and development process involves a 70-20-10 approach—70 percent of learning is on the job (experiential), 20 percent of learning comes from others (mentoring, coaching, behavioral feedback), and 10 percent comes from formal learning. Goodyear teamed with Harvard to design and execute three levels of executive training to develop leaders' strategic thinking, innovation, and global collaboration, and to drive Goodyear's business agenda.

TALENT ACQUISITION

All executive talent acquisition activities are coordinated globally and are locally executed. Goodyear employed a number of innovative sourcing techniques, including extensive use of social media by its in-house recruiting team. Comprehensive training in interviewing and assessment and a comprehensive onboarding process allowed Goodyear to successfully recruit external leadership talent from top companies to supplement our promotion-from-within philosophy.

ASSOCIATE ENGAGEMENT

Leaders are measured on associate engagement. An associate satisfaction index score was a key metric on the leadership balanced scorecard. Additionally, a global associate engagement survey was run every two years. Leaders were held accountable for their associate engagement metrics and required to review game plans with their managers on how to address improvement to ensure an engaged workface.

ORGANIZATION & TALENT REVIEW

This process involves a bottom-up assessment and review of key talent, high potentials, and organizational design in each region and function. The process culminates with a full review with the board of directors. The objective is to improve the talent pool and achieve a deep bench of ready-now successors at all levels of the organization. Topics covered include succession planning, organizational design, high-potential identification, diversity, associate engagement, and globalization.

SHARED LEADERSHIP TRAITS

Goodyear established a set of global leadership traits that were developed based on profiles of successful and unsuccessful Goodyear leaders. These traits have become the nucleus of the leadership development and talent management process. Leaders are evaluated and rewarded for demonstrating these traits. Internal and external candidates for jobs are assessed on these traits. Formal development and training are based on these traits.

INTEGRATED TECHNOLOGY

Goodyear's globally integrated HR technology platform became the glue holding together the global talent management and leadership development process. A number of technology tools were implemented including our enterprisewide human resource information technology (HRIT) system, HRConnect, which helps drive the HR strategy.

METRICS

Goodyear established a series of metrics to hold leaders accountable for leadership development and talent management. Goodyear leaders have targets and metrics each year on how they are building talent and teams, and one of the key metrics is the percentage of ready-now successors they have for top jobs in their organizations. The dashboard is reviewed several times a year and is integrated into the global talent management process.

and involved the senior leadership team and board members as faculty, along with prominent faculty from Harvard and other top universities. The Senior Executive Development Program and the other three levels of leadership development were completely aligned with the leadership traits.

Buying

It is estimated that at least half of senior external hires fail within their new company largely because of a cultural fit issue, not because of lack of experience or competence. To mitigate this problem, Goodyear took a three-pronged approach to the acquisition of senior leaders.

The first is innovative sourcing. Goodyear uses only top-notch search firms that are brought into the inner circle of recruiting efforts so they can be advocates of the company. The biggest challenge with recruiting senior leaders into the company is getting candidates to agree to come in for an interview. A search firm that can move someone from a "No, not interested" to a "Yes, I'll go for the interview" is worth its weight in gold. To support this innovative sourcing strategy, Goodyear established an internal recruiting organization. This group cut the recruiting expenditures in half while improving the speed of the process and the quality of hires largely through the use of social media in the recruiting process.

The second approach is the interviewing and assessment process. All interviewers clearly understand and deliver the same message to the candidates regarding the business strategy, the importance of the position, and the future of the business. Delivering consistent messages and using consistent assessment criteria are keys to successful recruitment. Candidates are assessed based on Goodyear's leadership traits through behavioral assessment interviews, competency testing, and reference checks. Once Goodyear locks in on a candidate for a senior-level position, it rarely has a problem convincing the candidate to join the company.

Finally, Goodyear takes onboarding seriously. The program involves a three-part process: a new-manager assimilation to his or her new team and peers; a written 100-day plan, including a written development plan on day one; and a 360-degree evaluation after six months on the job.

Innovative sourcing, a strong assessment process, and a comprehensive onboarding program have led to successful recruiting and retention of top leaders at Goodyear.

Metrics to Hold Leaders Accountable

You get what you measure. To move the needle on talent management and leadership development, you need to measure your leaders just like you do earnings and cash flow. To hold leaders accountable, Goodyear established a series of metrics for leadership development and talent management. "Goodyear leaders have targets and metrics each year on how they are building talent and teams," said Kramer, "and one of the key metrics is the percentage of ready-now successors they have for top jobs in their organization." The dashboard is reviewed several times a year and is ingrained in the global talent management process.

Innovative Practices

It would be safe to say that Goodyear actually invented very little of what has been implemented. You must be a magnet for internal and external best practices. Internally, during organization and talent reviews, top leadership made sure to identify best practices from the different divisions and functions and then spread them across the company. Externally, leaders have stolen shamelessly from other top companies. Goodyear leaders spend a great deal of time looking at state-of-the-art thinking on top leadership and talent development programs and implementing the best ideas.

Conclusion

These seven key attributes were critical in the development and implementation of Goodyear's leadership development and talent management process and together formed a systematic and integrated approach. While these key attributes were specific to Goodyear's success, they should also be relevant to other organizations seeking to build a strong talent and leadership development process.

On November 12, 2014, Goodyear was recognized as one of the 2014 Aon Hewitt Top Companies for Leaders. Winners were selected and ranked by an expert panel of independent judges based on criteria, including strength of leadership practices and culture, examples of leader development on a global scale, alignment of business and leadership strategy, company reputation, and business and financial performance.

"In today's complex and unpredictable business landscape, Top Companies for Leaders are passionate about cultivating resilient and engaging leaders who take the time to know and develop their talent and understand what experiences they need to rise above the rest," said Pete Sanborn, Aon Hewitt global talent practice leader. "We congratulate Goodyear on being among a select group of organizations that excel at building and growing a strong leadership environment."

Goodyear's achievement did not happen by accident. It was the culmination of years of work and commitment. But the rewards were significant. By designing and implementing a world-class global talent management and leadership development process, Goodyear developed a deep bench of great leaders and top talent at all levels of the organization. These great leaders have guided the company to the best business results in the history of the company and will continue to help drive growth in the future.

Endnote

[1.] Aon Hewitt Top Companies for Leaders Highlights Report November 12, 2014. http://www.aon.com/human-capital-consulting/thought-leadership/leadership/aon-hewitt-top-companies-for-leaders-high-lights.jsp

Chapter 18.
The Strategic Value of Talent: From Anecdote to Evidence

Robert E. Ployhart and Anthony J. Nyberg

One of the most significant and frustrating challenges facing HR professionals is demonstrating the strategic value of talent. Even though many organizational leaders recognize talent as a strategically valuable asset, generally accepted accounting principles (GAAP) recognize talent only as a cost because it is an intangible resource (Fulmer & Ployhart, 2014). Further, talent considered this way is usually an organization's single greatest cost. This unfortunate situation places the HR function at a tremendous disadvantage. First, positive returns generated by investments in talent are recorded as cost savings rather than as revenue-generating assets. Second, framing HR investments as costs creates pressure to favor metrics that emphasize cost savings (for example, cheaper, faster). For example, cost per hire is a frequent recruiting metric. The problem with this metric is that it gives the impression that an ideal situation is to minimize these costs, but such short-sighted perspectives fail to appreciate that quality hires create firm value and that good hires often require greater initial investment.

Imagine how professional sports would operate if their perspective was to view talent as a cost to be minimized. The cost-per-hire metrics would look dismal (imagine what such numbers must look like for the New York Yankees!). Yet, professional sports is an area where quite the opposite has occurred; the market has created an environment in which firms spend what may appear to be excessive amounts for talent. Why? It is not because team owners or coaches have greater insight into the nature of talent. Rather, it is because it is easier to make the connection between a top player's talent and wins, and wins are associated with financial success. It is easier to justify large salaries in professional sports because it is easier to draw the line to profitability.

Hence, HR leaders need a new way to think about the valuation of talent. Statements about "talent being the most important resource" have become cliché. They may be heartfelt, but such pronouncements undersell the value of talent and keep HR in a disadvantaged position relative to other functions. Evidence, not anecdotes, is needed to demonstrate the strategic value of talent to organizational leaders. Fortunately, new quantitative approaches can establish empirical linkages between talent and business outcomes. These approaches make it possible to demonstrate tangible financial benefits that are generated by intangible talent resources. Such approaches are similar to those described in "big data" or "talent analytics," except in contrast to those data-driven methods, the approaches followed here combine analytics with HR insight.

For years, we in the Darla Moore School of Business at the University of South Carolina have been pursuing research aimed at empirically demonstrating the strategic dollar value of talent. The vision we forward is based on nearly 20 years of scientific research and consulting experience intended to understand how to measure talent and link it to strategically valuable business outcomes in an ethical and legal manner. This approach is unique because it blends strategy and HR, with the psychology of talent and the rigor of analytics. Big data may be a current fad, but big data is not (by itself) a solution for many problems because HR expertise is necessary to make sense of the patterns detected in the data. Indeed, one should remember that any data connected to people or used to make employment-related decisions fall under the umbrella of Title VII of the Civil Rights Act and equal employment opportunity (EEO) legislation. The need for HR guidance on big data issues is an opportunity for HR professionals to create value (Ployhart, in press).

Making Intangibles Tangible

Figure 19.1a contrasts the usual way firms think of talent, while Figure 19.1b shows the vision we advocate in our research and consulting. There are two critical differences. First, the usual approach to talent (Figure 19.1a) starts with HR practices, links those practices to talent, and ultimately to firm performance. The nature of talent in this framework is vague and unspecified. In our approach (Figure 19.1b), we make a distinction between collective and individual talent resources (Ployhart, Nyberg, Reilly, & Maltarich, 2014). Individual talent refers to a person's specific knowledge, skill, or ability. Collective talent is the aggregate combination of individual talent into groups and teams, strategic business units (for example, departments, plants), and the overall firm. This distinction is important because it recognizes a tension between focusing on individuals versus focusing on the collective. HR leaders should manage the collective resource differently than they manage individual employees, in part because the collective talent resource—and not individuals—generates competitive advantage.[1] Thus, a key HR task is to manage the aggregation of talent from individuals into collective resources. Figure 19.b shows the arrows starting with competitive advantage and concluding with HR practices.

FIGURE 18.1. A COMPARISON OF TWO APPROACHES TO TALENT

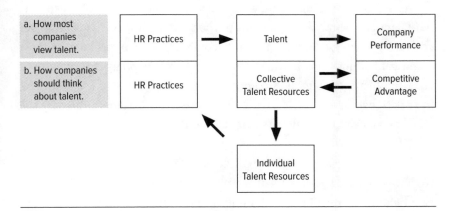

Second, the arrows lead in different directions between Figures 19.1a and 19.1b. In the usual approach, the origins of talent and firm performance begin with HR practices. This HR-centric view is problematic because it is rarely representative of an organization's actual strategy. It is now well established that HR professionals must first think like business leaders and then as HR managers (Barney & Wright, 1998; Ulrich, 1997). This means that HR leaders should begin by identifying firm outcomes and metrics that differentiate the firm from its competitors. Only then should these leaders identify the types of collective talent resources that most strongly influence those outcomes. From these collective talent resources, it then becomes possible to identify the types of individuals needed to implement the firm's strategy. Only at the end of this process is it possible to understand which HR practices are relevant and appropriate.

The key to connecting these ideas (the boxes in Figure 19.1b) is to quantify talent and link it empirically to the relevant metrics of competitive advantage. Many indicators can be used as proxies of talent quality. In our research we have used a variety of approaches to quantify talent, such as scores on behavioral assessments, including selection tests and interviews; scores on training measures; selection ratios (indicators of talent quality); and the number of training courses completed. Regardless of the specific measure used, the focus on quality is quite different from many approaches to workforce planning that focus more on talent quantity—number of people in positions. Given a minimum threshold of quantity, talent quality creates competitive advantage.

Thus, GAAP standards may define talent as an intangible resource, but talent can be made tangible for purposes of linking it to business outcomes. By making talent tangible, it becomes possible to propose and test empirical relationships between talent and firm outcomes that operationalize the firm's strategy and competitive advantage. In turn, quantifying the relationships shown in Figure 19.1b enables HR leaders to show the strategic value of talent using evidence and data.

Some Examples

We have examined variations of the framework shown in Figure 19.1b. We next illustrate some of the main implications of those studies published in the academic literature.

Collective talent helps firms be more competitive and recover from the Great Recession. Kim and Ployhart (2014) examined the effects of firms being more selective in their hiring and investing more in internal training (these served as our proxies of talent). Using a sample of 359 South Korean firms, the researchers tracked their financial performance (earnings before interest and taxes, or EBIT) over a decade. This time frame encompassed the Great Recession, so it was possible to examine how greater investments in talent influenced EBIT growth before and after the recession. The results found that firms that were more selective and invested in more internal training outperformed competitors before the Great Recession, and they recovered more quickly after the recession (primarily through the effects of selective staffing). An important implication is that investing in more generic talent skills is critical for recovering quickly from economic downturns, but training is critical for enhancing performance in more stable environments. The value of different types of talent is thus partly affected by broader economic conditions.

Collective talent creates sales growth in retail. Ployhart, Weekley, and Ramsey (2009) examined the effects of front-line retail employee talent in over 1,200 retail stores within a large U.S. retail organization. Talent was measured in terms of selection scores that employees had to complete as part of their application process (the selection scores measure customer service orientation). The researchers aggregated the individual employee scores to the store level to create collective talent resources, and then linked these collective scores to multiple performance indicators (for example, controllable profit, same-store sales, sales per employee) over multiple quarters. The results found that stores with higher-quality collective talent resources outperformed those with lesser-quality talent. Increasing talent one standard deviation produced a quarterly 6 percent increase in same-store sales, $10,000 in sales per employee, and $60,000 in controllable profit. These findings change the conversation from one of "find the cheapest and fastest way to hire retail employees" to "how can we better invest in retail employee selection?"

The supply chain of collective talent resources. Ployhart, Van Iddekinge, and MacKenzie (2011) studied how different HR practices may influence different parts of the talent supply chain, and thus cumulatively influence performance and create value. Using a sample of 238 fast food restaurants, the researchers examined how restaurants that collectively hired better-quality talent (operationalized through selection test scores) contribute to greater training effectiveness, which in turn created higher customer satisfaction and thus better financial performance. The restaurants were tracked over a period of 10 quarters, so it was possible to examine changes in talent influencing changes in performance growth. Figure 19.2 summarizes these results, in which the size of the arrows represents the strength of the relationship. Importantly, a 1 percent improvement in staffing produced a 2 percent improvement in sales per employee.

FIGURE 18.2. AN EXAMPLE OF A TALENT SUPPLY CHAIN

Note: The size of the arrow indicates the strength of the relationship (larger arrows = stronger relationships).
Source: Ployhart, Van Iddekinge, & MacKenzie, 2011.

Collective turnover undermines talent's effects. Reilly, Nyberg, Maltarich, and Weller (2014) used a systems perspective to gain insights into turnover's effects. By examining turnover, transfer, and patient satisfaction data from 12 nursing units, over 72 months in a prestigious university hospital, the researchers found that turnover effects on the unit's performance were connected closely to responses via hiring and transfers. Units that garnered replacements more quickly than other units suffered smaller detrimental effects immediately, and these negative turnover effects dissipated more quickly. In another study, Call, Nyberg, Ployhart, and Weekley (in press) investigated turnover in a large retail environment by examining 988 units over five quarters. The researchers found both turnover rate and the change to that rate to be negatively related to controllable profit. Further, the quality of the levers strongly influenced turnover's effect on performance. Thus, one consistent observation in our research is that turnover can eliminate or reduce the positive effects of collective talent resources.

Recommendations for Building a Business Case for Talent

In Table 19.1 we summarize findings and implications for understanding talent resources that have been found in scientific research (see Nyberg, Moliterno, Hale, & Lepak, 2014, for more background). These recommendations provide a broad understanding of what talent *is* and what it *does*. Beyond these recommendations (which are based on dozens of studies, thousands of organizations, and hundreds of thousands of people), we offer a few additional recommendations based on our experience:

- Finding empirical relationships with talent at the level of the firm (or similar levels) requires use of longitudinal data. Only by observing long-term performance trends is it possible to find systematic relationships between talent and firm performance.
- Small relationships, or changes in talent, do not have small consequences. Talent is just one of many factors that influence firm performance, yet even modest relationships can—over time—have important cumulative financial consequences.
- Analysis of data without understanding how those data were collected, or the factors that might influence the scores, is an almost certain recipe for trouble. You cannot start with data analytics and let it tell you what to look for. You have to give data analytics some direction and focus.
- A firm's strategy provides the appropriate focus for understanding analytics and big data. Start by trying to understand what factors differentiate your firm, and then use analytics to help understand why and how you can influence those factors.
- Numbers tell stories; stories sell numbers. Facts need flavor before they are ready to be consumed.

What Your Firm Should Do

The simplest, yet most profound, suggestion for applying the insights from our research is for your firm to leverage its existing talent data and empirically link them to the strategic metrics that matter. The HR function owns responsibility of data related to talent (for example, hiring data, performance management data, training and development data). First, recognize these data for what they are—strategically valuable resources. Second, find the people with data access and quantitative expertise to link these data to firm performance metrics that are strategically important (for example, contribute to growth or differentiation). These people must have an understanding of HR, data, *and* analytics. Third, engage key stakeholders (for example, marketing

---

TABLE 18.1. LESSONS LEARNED FROM SCIENTIFIC RESEARCH ON TALENT

1. Organizations should focus on identifying strategically valuable talent resources, and then on finding or developing people with the characteristics that create those resources.

2. Collective talent is distinct from individual talent and needs to be managed differently.

3. Culture shapes how individual talent combines into a collective resource.

4. Organizations must consider culture when thinking about how talent resources affect firm performance.

5. Talent has a stronger relationship with performance metrics internal to the firm (for example, productivity) than performance metrics external to the firm (for example, market share).

6. Organizations can use pay to shape individual and collective talent.

7. Selection and recruitment are strong influences shaping the nature of collective talent resources.

8. In addition to turnover rates, the quality and timing of turnover, and the availability and quality of replacements, all affect firm performance.

9. Organizations need to balance the portfolio of HR practices to create a holistic system that maximizes collective talent resources.

10. Relative to individuals, collective talent is more difficult for competitors to imitate and thus more likely to create competitive advantage.

---

leaders, chief financial officer) to build the story that explains the linkage between talent to competitive advantage. Thus, realize your firm already has most (if not all) of the ingredients needed to give evidence to anecdote—they just need to be combined in the appropriate manner.

Conclusion

As HR professionals, we know that talent matters, but we rarely know precisely how much talent matters, and thus we too often rely on stories and anecdotes to make the case that talent is strategically valuable and hence deserves investment. We also know that good business decisions require data and evidence, but HR, more than any other function, receives a "free pass" on providing such evidence. Yet our professional reputations and our personal effectiveness suffer every time we receive this special treatment. HR and talent are strategically valuable and increasingly so in the modern world. The studies summarized in this chapter suggest small improvements in talent can generate impressive financial returns. Let us move from platitudes to proof and place talent (and thus our profession) on the strategic platform it deserves.

Endnote

[1.]There can be exceptions, such as when key managers (for example, CEOs) or star employees are individuals who generate competitive advantage. However, for the most part, this chapter focuses on the broader organizational workforce and not the small number of employees or jobs that are strategic.

References

Barney, J. B., & Wright, P. M. (1998). On becoming a strategic partner: The role of human resources in gaining competitive advantage. *Human Resource Management, 37*, 31-46.

Call, M. L., Nyberg, A. J., Ployhart, R. E., & Weekley J. A. (in press). The dynamic nature of turnover and unit performance: The impact of time, quality, and replacements. *Academy of Management Journal.*

Fulmer, I. S., & Ployhart, R. E. (2014). "Our most important asset": A multidisciplinary/multilevel review of human capital valuation for research and practice. *Journal of Management, 40*, 161-192.

Kim, Y., & Ployhart, R. E. (2014). The effects of staffing and training on firm productivity and profit growth before, during, and after the great recession. *Journal of Applied Psychology, 99*, 361-389.

Nyberg, A. J., Moliterno, T. P., Hale, D., & Lepak, D. P. (2014). Resource-based perspectives on unit-level human capital: A review and integration. *Journal of Management, 40*, 316-346.

Ployhart, R. E. (in press). The reluctant HR champion.

Ployhart, R. E., Nyberg, A. J., Reilly, G., & Maltarich, M. A. (2014). Human capital is dead: Long live human capital resources! *Journal of Management, 40*, 371-398.

Ployhart, R. E., Van Iddekinge, C. H., & MacKenzie, W. I. (2011). Acquiring and developing human capital in service contexts: The interconnectedness of human capital resources. *Academy of Management Journal, 54*, 353-368.

Ployhart, R. E., Weekley, J. A., & Ramsey, J. (2009). The consequences of human resource stocks and flows: A longitudinal examination of unit service orientation and unit effectiveness. *Academy of Management Journal, 52*, 996-1015.

Reilly, G., Nyberg, A. J., Maltarich, M., & Weller I. (2014). Human capital flows: Using context-emergent turnover (CET) theory to explore the process by which turnover, hiring, and job demands affect patient satisfaction. *Academy of Management Journal, 57,* 766-790.

Ulrich, D. (1997). *Human Resource Champions.* Boston: Harvard Business School Press.

PART VI

CHALLENGES IN MANAGING C-SUITE TALENT

Chapter 19.
Mitigating Critical Risks in CEO Succession

Susan M. "Sue" Suver

The topic of CEO succession has long been researched, analyzed, evaluated, and refined. Best practices in the CEO succession planning *process* are well understood, yet the failure rate of new CEOs—40 percent within the first 18 months'—continues to be a concerning outcome, and , the average tenure of *Fortune* 500 CEOs is now less than five years.[2]

In public companies, the board of directors has the primary legal responsibility for appointing the CEO, but in all organizations, whether public, private, or nonprofit, the role of selecting a new CEO is one of the most significant ways the board directly influences the performance of the organization. For many boards, succession *planning* is not new, but implementing an actual CEO transition is an infrequent activity, and may be a completely new arena for many of your directors. Given the criticality of the decision, company boards should have a well-considered strategy and a rigorous execution plan for CEO selection, and this extends well beyond understanding best-practice processes.

Often, the chief human resource officer (CHRO) serves as a steward of the CEO succession planning process, invited by either the board or the incumbent CEO, or both, to assist in identifying and assessing internal candidates, coordinating with a retained search firm when external candidates are a consideration or a necessity, and serving as a coordinator of the process until the CEO successor is named and the transition executed. While it is important to be fluent in succession best practices related to candidate identification, assessment, and development processes, a greater role exists for the CHRO. When serving as a collaborative advisor to the board in mitigating significant CEO succession risks, the CHRO has a true value creation opportunity that will influence the future performance and success of the organization. Many factors contribute to the appropriate selection of a CEO and to his or her success in the role, but two of the most common impediments for new CEOs are a lack of alignment with the board of directors on strategy and the inability of the new CEO to successfully integrate into the company on a time frame that enables early acceptance, credibility, and delivery of results.

Aligning Business Strategy and the CEO Success Profile

In many organizations, planning for CEO succession begins in the *middle* of the process with the identification of a slate of possible internal candidates, and sometimes external candidates. When the succession process begins in the middle, it is often under the assumption that what is needed tomorrow is the same as today. This often occurs when the incumbent CEO is highly regarded, when he or she has led the organization for a lengthy period of time, or when the board and management team assume that the business strategy will remain largely unchanged in the future.

The velocity of externally driven changes—macroeconomic, geopolitical, innovation, and technology-based—introduces additional complexity in defining the profile of success for the future CEO. The degree to which the CEO has the predictive capability to identify and interpret on-the-horizon data and trends and to lead a strategic shift in direction is key

One of the most commonly held misconceptions is that succession planning is synonymous with replacement planning. Internal succession slates are often based on well-intended assertions that the skills and attributes of the incumbent CEO and other executives will remain largely the same in the future as they are today. As business strategy shifts, the capabilities of truly qualified CEO candidates may be materially different than those possessed by the current CEO. This misalignment of leadership capability and business strategy occurs more frequently and is not limited to just the role of the CEO. From 2003 to 2013, the percent of organizations reporting they would replace their senior leadership team if given the opportunity increased from 12 percent in 2003 to 32 percent in 2013.[3]

Boards should begin with a thorough analysis of the company's strategy and of the business and leadership attributes and skills that will be required to successfully execute at the CEO level. Often, boards begin the CEO succession planning process based on assertions that the CEO they need tomorrow will share the same profile of the CEO today. Candidate identification and evaluation should take into account whether CEO candidates possess the conceptual, strategic, and organizational skills required to operate at the level of complexity the strategy is likely to demand. No internal or external candidate identification should be undertaken until the board has clarity on a profile of success for the future CEO that has been diligently considered in light of the implications of the business strategy.

Opportunity for the CHRO #1

As the CHRO, how well versed are you in the competitive threats and opportunities facing your business? If substantive changes in the business environment or business model were required, how adept would the leadership team in your organization be in seeing the change coming and in deploying a competitive plan to seize the change opportunity? How does this inform you about the relevance of your succession plan? Have you held a strategy and talent alignment discussion with your CEO, board of directors, and senior executive team to explore impacts on talent potential, readiness, and risks as the business strategy changes? What impact does the change in your business strategy have on your definition of success for CEO succession as well as for the high-potential talent you have previously identified? Will the high potentials identified as being ready in three, five, or seven years be able to develop under the same time frames if the criteria for success are substantively different? Which individuals may be unable to develop to sufficiently meet the new capability requirements? How will you close the talent versus capability gaps?

Many unplanned CEO departures are the result of the CEO and board being misaligned on the strategic direction of the company. If a disconnect occurs between the new CEO and board before it is fully recognized, it may set in motion a cascade of decisions and actions that roll deep into the organization. The consequences may be difficult to quickly redirect, putting the near-term success of the company—and the new CEO—at risk.

Misalignment on strategy can also lead the CEO to misread the ability of the executive team to lead a change in strategy. Without experienced and capable executives who can lead consistently with strategic requirements, the strategy may fail to launch, another condition under which the new CEO may be at risk.

Opportunity for the CHRO #2

As business strategy changes, how will the current organizational capabilities of the company be challenged? Review the business strategy and evaluate which organizational capabilities need to be added, modified, or discontinued for your company to successfully deliver on the strategic outcomes. In addition to functional/technical and leadership skill changes, will your leaders and high potentials need a greater level of conceptual, strategic, and decision-making skills? As your strategy unfolds into a three- or five-year implementation plan, what impact does that have on your progression of CEO succession candidates? A similar exercise will likely apply to the success profiles for other key executive positions in the organization, and for certain high-potential roles one to two levels below.

Accelerating CEO Success through Integration and Feedback

The next major risk to new CEO failure is related to the speed and degree to which the CEO can become an accepted, credible, and contributing leader.

The integration of senior executives, including the CEO, usually takes much longer than many boards and CEOs imagine. There are many excellent books and articles written about the importance of the initial 100 days on the job. But given the complexity of the CEO's role and the degree of business transformation or strategic change he or she may be leading, full integration into the company will likely take a minimum of 12 months, long enough for the CEO to lead a full fiscal cycle and to begin execution of the business strategy. Integration plans extending to 18 months address realistic circumstances related to the phases of integration that occur when the honeymoon is over. Often, new CEOs spend a significant portion of the initial six months just accelerating their understanding of the business and competitive forces, navigating the company's culture, and building early relationships with key stakeholders. In times of strategic change, some of the most challenging work for a new CEO may not begin until after this initial familiarization and planning period. If the board were to discontinue its monitoring and support of the CEO at this early juncture, it may miss important opportunities for feedback and coaching.

When the CEO is hired or promoted, the board should outline specific performance expectations and outcomes, and in most cases should have time frames associated with the major deliverables. This becomes the basis of early performance feedback and coaching and ensures clarity between the parties at the outset. Defining outcomes and expectations is an essential discussion between the board and the CEO, and with the support of the CHRO, a tracking mechanism can be established to enable the directors to attain a real-time read on how well the CEO is integrating and performing.

In addition to addressing key expectation and deliverables, a robust integration roadmap also becomes a GPS for navigating the company culture related to being viewed as accepted and credible. In the early weeks and months, the organization will interpret the new CEO's intentions based on what is said or not said, what is delivered, where the CEO spends his or her time, and the level of engagement with internal and external stakeholders. If the CEO is viewed as significantly disconnected from the organization's culture at the outset, management and the broader employee population may be unwilling or unable to accept the CEO. Even when wrong, these early perceptions can present significant roadblocks to acceptance, and ultimately to the CEOs success.

This is a critical value-creating moment for the CHRO—an opportunity to work with the board and new CEO to outline an 18-month integration roadmap—not a hard-wired plan, but a flexible, living document that assumes that events will occur as the CEO progresses that may require the integration plan to be modified, while keeping in sight the major deliverables and expectations previously agreed to by the board and CEO.

For a CEO new to a company or industry, the integration roadmap points him or her to stakeholders, issues, and events that fall into the category of "you don't know what you don't know," and can serve as a compass in the earliest months of integration. However, an 18-month integration plan is equally important for a CEO promoted from within. In this case, the integration plan serves as a reminder of new or different areas of focus for CEOs: how they engage, with whom they engage, how and where they spend their time, and how and what they communicate. For first-time CEOs, additional emphasis should be placed on what they should stop doing or should delegate, as well as what they should begin doing differently. In the spirit of "what got you here, won't get you there," there is no other role so uniquely constructed as that of the CEO. Being successful requires CEOs to be discriminating about what they are involved in; constructing a matrix of the behaviors and actions they need to start, stop, and continue can be a useful tool in this regard. For first-time CEOs, what they do and do not do are equally important, and the integration plan serves as a helpful reminder about avoiding activities and behaviors that may have been very relevant and appropriate in their prior role(s) but are distractors or hindrances on the journey to becoming a highly effective CEO.

CHRO Opportunity #3

Does your board have a well-defined integration roadmap and plan for the successful candidate? Are early performance milestones defined and monitored, and does the new CEO receive timely feedback from the board about integration progress and potential problems? As the CHRO, how involved are you in that process, and how can you add value for the board and your new CEO?

Work with the board to create a high-impact, simple-to-track CEO integration roadmap that is constructed around four fundamental topics:

1. What does the CEO need to learn and know? What are the logical and critical time frames?
2. Who does the CEO need to know? Which stakeholders will require the CEO to build influential relationships? What are the critical time frames for each stakeholder or stakeholder group?
3. What are the critical deliverables, outcomes, and results to be achieved by the CEO? What are the critical milestones within the stated outcomes, which if missed, potentially derail the organization?
4. What is the cadence the CEO wants to establish related to leading and running the company? How frequently does he or she meet with executive direct reports as a group? Individually?

How frequently does the CEO convene the officers of the organization (if this is a larger group than the CEO's direct reports)?
How frequently does the CEO engage with the top leadership
levels of the organization (annually, semiannually, quarterly)?
How does the CEO use these opportunities to set expectations,
engage in dialogue and decision-making, establish strategy, ensure execution and outcomes are on track, report on progress,
celebrate success, and coach for performance improvements?
What is the agenda and purpose of each of these leadership engagements? How do they establish the CEO's vision and strategy, build and develop other leaders in the organization, and
create line of sight to company objectives for all employees in
the company?

For first-time CEOs, and CEOs promoted from within, a fifth topic is
often helpful:

1. What are the critical behaviors or actions that new CEOs need to
    start, stop, or continue to differentiate themselves from their pri-
    or roles (or to reset how they are perceived by the organization?)

Just as leadership is situational, so is CEO selection. A sound CEO
succession process rooted in the business strategy and based on prospective business and leadership capabilities will increase the chances
of identifying and developing successful CEO candidates and of selecting an executive with the ability to quickly integrate and deliver on
expectations. Clearly articulated CEO selection criteria and a three- to
five-year succession planning time horizon are basic elements for success. Additionally, when guided by a flexible integration roadmap that
extends to 12 to 18 months, the new CEO's chances of success are likely
to be accelerated.

The CEO selection and integration process can serve as an opportunity for the board to take stock of the company, its leadership team, and
talent pipeline, and creates a window for organizational renewal. No member of executive management is better suited to serve as a steward of this
important work than the CHRO.

Endnotes

[1] Dan Ciampa, "Almost Ready," *Harvard Business Review*, February 2005.

[2] Michael Jarrett, "CEOs Should Get Out of the Saddle Before They Are Pushed," *Harvard Business Review*, November 2013.

[3] "Three Critical Talent Conversations for Every Board of Directors," The Corporate Executive Board Company, 2013

Chapter 20.
Choosing the Next CEO: Assessment Practices and Challenges

Patrick M. Wright, Donald J. Schepker,
Anthony J. Nyberg, and Michael Ulrich

The challenge of CEO succession has emerged as one of the most important governance responsibilities faced by boards of directors. After HP's
series of failed CEOs without any internal successor available, boards increasingly attended to the process of developing internal successors to
the CEO. The later observations of failed CEOs at Procter & Gamble and
McDonald's illustrated that even when internal successors are chosen, the
process may have resulted in wrong decisions. The costs of a poor process
are significant for firms, with CEO succession failures costing large firms
more than $50 million in direct costs alone. Despite the importance placed
on succession, in today's environment approximately 25 percent of CEO
turnover is involuntary, suggesting the wrong leader was chosen at some
point. Clearly the choice of who should serve as the leader of any corporation may determine its future success or failure, yet little is known about
this process.

Elevation to the CEO role results in a tremendous change in the level of complexity with which the individual is required to operate. Within
the organization, CEOs might have to understand an array of businesses
located in diverse industries or dispersed across a large number of geographic regions. Externally they must deal with a larger and more varied
set of stakeholders, including shareholders, analysts, and the press. Being
able to gather information to best predict who will be most able to make
this transition presents an immense challenge to organizations.

The 2014 HR@Moore Survey of Chief HR Officers sought to examine how firms assess the skills, competencies, and potential of possible

successors to the CEO. Assessments are a means by which firms can evaluate candidates to determine their ability to perform effectively, particularly in challenging or unexplored roles. A history of research across a variety of jobs suggests that assessments are valuable tools in selecting appropriate candidates with significant profit implications for firms that use them successfully. To understand assessment techniques used in the CEO succession process, we first presented chief human resource officers (CHROs) with a list of potential assessment tools and asked them which tools they have used or are using to assess their internal and external CEO successor candidates, respectively.

As can be seen in Figure 21.1, for internal candidates the past performance accomplishment profile was by far the most used assessment tool. Of our respondents, 95 percent of CHROs indicated their firms used this technique for internal candidates. In addition, 88 percent reported that past development needs were used as an assessment tool. The third most used assessment technique for internal candidates was 360-degree evaluations, used by 80 percent of the CHROs. Finally, 69 percent of CHROs reported their firms conduct unstructured interviews with internal CEO candidates. All of the remaining assessment techniques were used by less than a majority of the firms for gathering information on their internal CEO candidates.

Regarding evaluating external candidates, 87 percent of CHROs indicated using reference checks, followed closely by 85 percent using past performance accomplishment profiles. Unstructured interviews were used by 72 percent of CHROs with structured behavioral interviews (71 percent) close behind. Past development needs (61 percent) and personality testing (51 percent) were the other assessment techniques used by a majority of the firms to evaluate external candidates.

Comparing the differences between assessment techniques used for internal versus external candidates reveals few surprises. For instance, firms use reference checks much more frequently for external candidates (87 percent) on whom they have less information than for internal candidates (38 percent). Similarly, because the data exist within the firm, internal candidates are much more likely to be assessed with 360-degree evaluations (80 percent) than external candidates (30 percent).

The most surprising result stems from the relatively low use of for-

FIGURE 20.1. WHICH OF THE FOLLOWING HAVE YOU USED OR WOULD YOU USE TO ASSESS YOUR INTERNAL OR EXTERNAL CEO SUCCESSOR CANDIDATES?

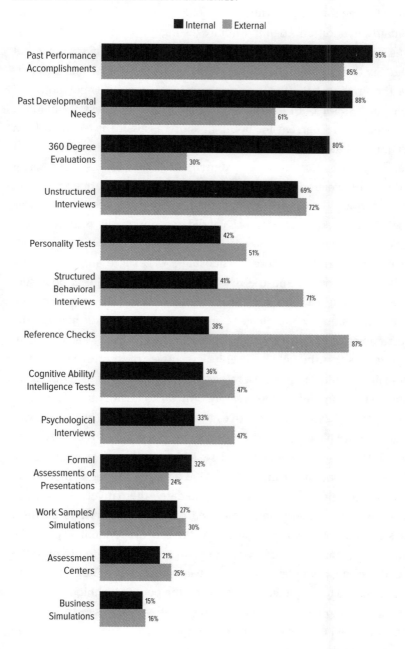

mal, professionally developed, and relatively objective tests for both internal and external candidates. While 51 percent of companies use personality testing for external candidates, only 42 percent do so for internal candidates. In addition, cognitive ability testing, psychological interviews, and assessment centers were more likely to be used to assess external candidates than internal, but these were still used by less than a majority of the firms. In addition, few firms use work sample/simulations (30 percent or less for both internal and external) and business simulations (approximately 15 percent for both). In short, assessment techniques on internal candidates rely on information gathered by the firm throughout the employee's history, whereas external candidates are assessed using additional information sources as a means to reduce information asymmetry regarding the candidate's capabilities. However, neither processes for selecting internal or external candidates optimized recommended techniques.

Given the sensitive nature of choosing a CEO successor, the various pitfalls in the process, and the risk associated with making a poor succession decision, it seems that firms that invest in gathering more objective information would have a greater foundation for making the correct choice. Preliminary research on mistakes in hiring senior executives suggests that the failure of senior executives most often stems from personality or culture problems, rather than from a lack of technical competence. These problems, however, are difficult to identify in a normal interview process, as senior executives and board members are unlikely to be trained in behavioral interview techniques designed to identify such issues. Further, board members and senior executives may unknowingly take it easy on potential candidates to find a reason to hire an individual, rather than to reject him or her as a candidate. Alternatively, some companies have found that using structured behavioral interviews by third parties adds objectivity and expertise to the process to identify potential other red flags that may exist with candidates. This is not to discount the value of the most popular assessment techniques, but to suggest the incremental value to be gained by expanding the pool of techniques.

In addition to the question about the use of various assessment techniques, we asked CHROs which techniques they had found to be the most valuable for gaining information on both internal and external CEO candidates. This changes the nature of the question from descriptive (what does your firm do?) to prescriptive (what do you think your firm should do?).

As can be seen in Figure 21.2, the vast majority of CHROs reported that they viewed using multiple assessments as the most valuable approach to assessing internal (75 percent) candidates. They either specifically said "multiple assessments" or listed multiple assessments as part of their answer.

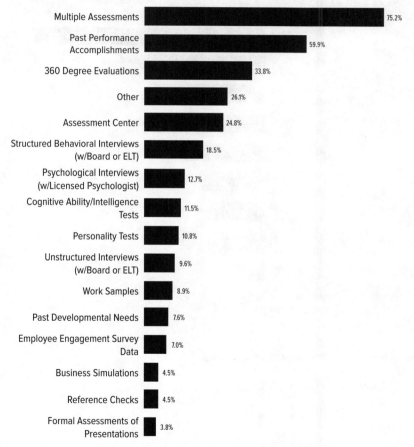

FIGURE 20.2. WHAT ASSESSMENT TECHNIQUES DO YOU BELIEVE PROVIDE THE BEST INSIGHTS REGARDING AN INTERNAL CANDIDATE'S POTENTIAL TO FILL THE CEO ROLE AND WHY?

Technique	Percentage
Multiple Assessments	75.2%
Past Performance Accomplishments	59.9%
360 Degree Evaluations	33.8%
Other	26.1%
Assessment Center	24.8%
Structured Behavioral Interviews (w/Board or ELT)	18.5%
Psychological Interviews (w/Licensed Psychologist)	12.7%
Cognitive Ability/Intelligence Tests	11.5%
Personality Tests	10.8%
Unstructured Interviews (w/Board or ELT)	9.6%
Work Samples	8.9%
Past Developmental Needs	7.6%
Employee Engagement Survey Data	7.0%
Business Simulations	4.5%
Reference Checks	4.5%
Formal Assessments of Presentations	3.8%

However, regarding specific techniques, past performance accomplishments topped the list for internal candidates (60 percent), far exceeding the next highest, 360-degree evaluations at 34 percent. Assessment centers (25 percent) and structured behavioral interviews (19 percent) also were noted as valuable. Consistent with the previous data, few pointed to formal testing (psychological profiles, personality, or cognitive ability) as valuable tools.

Regarding evaluating external candidates, as Figure 21.3 shows, again CHROs pointed to using multiple assessments as the most valuable approach (73 percent) to gaining information on potential successors. Refer-

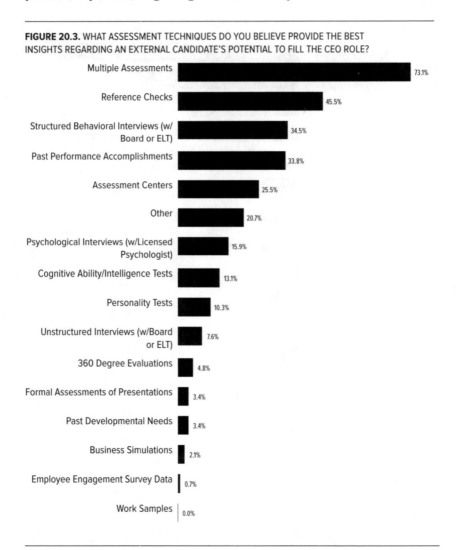

FIGURE 20.3. WHAT ASSESSMENT TECHNIQUES DO YOU BELIEVE PROVIDE THE BEST INSIGHTS REGARDING AN EXTERNAL CANDIDATE'S POTENTIAL TO FILL THE CEO ROLE?

Technique	Percent
Multiple Assessments	73.1%
Reference Checks	45.5%
Structured Behavioral Interviews (w/ Board or ELT)	34.5%
Past Performance Accomplishments	33.8%
Assessment Centers	25.5%
Other	20.7%
Psychological Interviews (w/Licensed Psychologist)	15.9%
Cognitive Ability/Intelligence Tests	13.1%
Personality Tests	10.3%
Unstructured Interviews (w/Board or ELT)	7.6%
360 Degree Evaluations	4.8%
Formal Assessments of Presentations	3.4%
Past Developmental Needs	3.4%
Business Simulations	2.1%
Employee Engagement Survey Data	0.7%
Work Samples	0.0%

ence checks (46 percent), structured behavioral interviews (35 percent), past performance accomplishments (34 percent), and assessment centers (26 percent) were also acknowledged as valuable tools.

The risk inherent in choosing a new CEO is clear. Again, CHROs have often noted that moving from a role as a direct report to the CEO to the role of CEO requires a step change in cognitive, emotional, and energy requirements. In exploring how firms seek to gain information on those who aspire to the role, it seems that three generic dimensions of the candidates require assessment, as depicted in Figure 21.4. "Performance" refers to a track record of past accomplishments that indicate a requisite level of business savvy, leadership, and accountability. This dimension is clearly captured through reliance on past performance profiles and past development needs. However, the weakness of this dimension is that because the nature of the CEO role is so unique, there is no guarantee that past performance will be indicative of future performance.

"Capability" refers to the basic competencies, leadership style, and other characteristics that one would expect in the CEO. This could be eval-

FIGURE 20.4. DIMENSIONS TO ASSESS IN CEO SUCCESSION

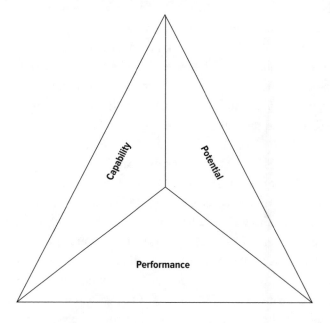

uated through assessment centers, behavioral interviews, work simulations, business simulations, and cognitive ability tests. This dimension is probably correlated with the performance dimension, but does have some aspects that could be missed by solely relying on past performance.

The "potential" dimension describes the ability of the individual to quickly and effectively adapt to the new requirements of the CEO role. This dimension seems the most important area of risk, and the least developed in terms of assessment tools to effectively evaluate individuals. Based on decades of assessment research in the personnel selection literature, it seems that firms might reduce this risk by relying more on existing (for example, personality testing or psychological assessments to evaluate adaptability) and developing (assessment centers or business simulation aimed specifically at the new requirements in the CEO role) techniques. Perhaps this is one area that CHROs can add significant value to the board of directors' CEO succession process. The ability to develop an appropriate capability profile and create assessments (either internally or in conjunction with third-party assessment services) to test candidates against that profile could create significant value for the firm. Furthermore, given that many executives fail due to personality or culture clashes, CHROs may serve as a trusted advisor to the board or use outside trusted advisors to provide information regarding candidate fit with both the position and the company. When examining potential CEO candidates, candidates must be able to adapt to both the technical and personal skills required by the position. CHROs are likely to be in a crucial position to help the board understand the multidimensional nature of the job of the CEO within the firm's context and the skills that are needed to be successful.

Conclusion

The risks inherent in making poor CEO succession decisions can have tremendous short- and long-term financial consequences. Making the right decision requires having all of the right information about the potential successors. This survey revealed that the most popular assessment methods seem to focus primarily on a candidate's past performance. While valuable, a sole focus on the past may miss meaningful information regarding the capability and potential of successor candidates. Furthermore, given the rapidly changing business and technological environment in which firms are operating today, prior performance and previously developed capabilities may not be beneficial in successors in the future. Failure to look forward as to the necessary future capabilities needed may create misalignment between company leadership and the company's competitive environment. Because boards frequently look to the CHRO as an expert in aspects of the CEO succession process, CHROs have an exceptional opportunity to structure the architecture, process, and information used. Thus, they have the potential to encourage a more comprehensive gathering of assessment data that can serve as input into the board's ultimate decision. This may be an area in which CHROs can add informational value by developing a more rigorous and comprehensive assessment process.

Chapter 21.

Best Practices vs. Best Fit: Challenging Conventional Wisdom in Incentive Design

Michele "Shelly" Carlin

In the wake of the financial crisis and a tepid economic recovery, the current state of executive compensation has come under attack from multiple stakeholders—institutional and activist investors, proxy advisory firms, the media, organized labor, and government officials—all of whom have an interest in the outcome. Rising levels of executive pay have been cited by some as a contributing factor to income inequality, and even among the defenders of the current system, many boards of directors feel constrained by the one-size-fits-all mentality of the say-on-pay era.

Driven by the leverage of the proxy advisory firms over the voting decisions of some institutional investors, boards face increasing pressure to approve incentive plans that conform to proxy firm guidance instead of tailoring their plans to meet the specialized needs of their firms. Though this trend may ensure satisfactory say-on-pay outcomes, it is unclear whether such an approach is in the best long-term interests of the company.

HR professionals play a key role in ensuring that the decisions made regarding pay design—especially the selection of the performance measures on which incentives are based—reflect the distinct needs of their businesses and are aligned with their companies' strategic plan.

The Homogenization of Executive Pay Design

A move toward "sameness" in pay design is not new—for decades, companies and their compensation consultants have crafted executive pay programs with a studied eye on the practices of their competitors. The increased transparency required by proxy disclosure rules has made it easy to discover what everyone else is doing—and that information has evolved from being a reference point to setting "best practices."

But there is something different about the recent similarity in incentive design, and it is related to the advent of mandatory say on pay and the corresponding rise in the influence of proxy advisory firms, principally Institutional Shareholder Services and Glass Lewis. Proxy advisors now play a significant role in shaping executive compensation plans, and their policies on how best to measure performance and what constitutes the appropriate form of pay have contributed to the current homogenization. While most large institutional investors conduct their own independent analysis of a company's pay practices and plans, many smaller investors lack the resources to carefully evaluate the proxies of the many companies whose shares they hold, and as a result, are inclined to follow the proxy advisor recommendation.

Companies understandably seek to avoid a low say-on-pay vote and often have focused attention on identifying those actions that will help secure a "for" recommendation from the proxy advisory firms. Many of the resulting changes have been positive—the most egregious pay practices of the past are disappearing, and the pay-performance link is growing stronger. But it is less clear that changing fundamental pay designs to conform to the preferences of proxy advisors is a positive development.

Of particular note is the increased use of total shareholder return (TSR) as a performance measure in long-term incentives. The prevalence of performance-based long-term incentives has increased dramatically since say on pay became a reality, and they now comprise, on average, over half of the total long-term compensation opportunity for executives. And TSR is by far the most commonly used measure in those performance plans.

The focus of proxy advisory firms on TSR as the definitive performance metric has played a major role in its increased prevalence. But while TSR is arguably the ultimate measure of management's performance, it is also similar to the score at the end of a baseball game. That is, TSR is the best measure of the final outcome, but it is not particularly helpful in determining what it takes to actually win.

The Case for a New Approach

Human resource professionals have the opportunity to shape this debate and lead their organizations in a process of reimagining executive pay. And the playbook for how to do so comes from an unlikely source: Major League Baseball.

In the early 1990s, the Oakland A's delivered superior results with the third-lowest payroll in baseball by ignoring conventional wisdom when it came to identifying the predictors of a player's success. Instead, the As employed the practice of sabermetrics—the empirical analysis of the vast wealth of baseball statistics—to objectively identify what differentiates high performers.

Just as sabermetrics has been described as the search for objective metrics about baseball, it is time to make the case that incentive plan designs should begin with a search for objective metrics about the true drivers of a company's performance. This search should be based on the fact that while total shareholder return is the ultimate measure of outcomes—of *how much* value was created—it fails to tell us *how* that value was created in the past or will be created in the future. Why is this important? Because in addition to providing the means to reward executives for performance, an incentive plan plays a key role in communicating how an organization seeks to achieve its goals. A better understanding of the "how" will ensure that incentive plans are based on measures that clearly communicate to executives and investors what drives sustainable value creation.

Instead of adopting the de facto standard of TSR as the optimal performance metric, HR professionals can play a leadership role by insisting that incentive plans be linked to those measures that are the true indicators of a company's ability to create sustained shareholder value—the measures that, over time, will drive superior TSR performance. The right measures may be financial (measuring capital return or cash flow, for example) or operational (reflecting a company's ability to drive innovation, customer retention, or manufacturing efficiency). The central point is that, rather than focus management only on the final score, effective incentives should also communicate and measure the actions needed to win the game.

A Data-Based Approach to Incentive Design

By adopting a data-based, quantitative approach as a key component in the selection of performance measures, HR professionals will be better prepared to improve their companies' ability to design, communicate, and defend their pay programs.

While the actual work may require the analysis of large amounts of data over varying time periods, the basic approach is simple. It starts with the idea that superior value creation is the result of sustained high performance on industry-specific financial and nonfinancial drivers over time. Because businesses and industries differ dramatically with regard to customers, markets, suppliers, talent, company culture, and numerous other factors, no single measure or a set of measures will be correlated to shareholder value for every company, in every industry, for all time periods. For some industries, value creation depends on revenue growth; for others, cash flow or capital returns are key. The question is even more complex for companies that compete across multiple industries.

So how do you discover the measures that drive value in your industry? After all, most HR organizations are still in the early stages of developing expertise in financial metrics and statistical analysis. As a result, the most practical approach involves a partnership between HR and the business strategy and financial experts in the company. They have the data, the expertise, and the tools to conduct the analysis.

Using your company's strategy as a starting point, reimagining incentive plan design is a process of discovering the financial and nonfinancial drivers that are most likely to result in sustained shareholder value over time. This process consists of four basic steps.

Step One: Identify the Measures

The first step is to identify the measures to be tested. One logical place to start is with the measures your company is currently using in your incentive plan or in other management processes (such as annual budgeting or capital investment decision-making). But it is important to recognize that the analysis need not be limited only to your current measures—or even to financial measures. Any quantitative measure for which adequate data are available can be tested. What measures do your investors care about? What about your competitors? For example, if your incentive plan uses a capital return measure, but investors continue to question your company's prospects for growth, it may be appropriate to consider a revenue measure.

Once you have selected the measures to be tested, you will need to gather historical data for these measures and for TSR. It is important to gather these data over a long enough time horizon to make sure the analysis reflects the appropriate investment and product life cycle horizon for your industry.

Testing the selected measures for more companies than just your own is also crucial. A group of companies is preferable—ideally, those in your current compensation peer group. This will provide a more robust data set, improving the validity of the analysis.

Understanding Financial Measures

There are many types of financial measures used by a wide variety of stakeholders, including investors, accountants, regulators, and executives. When it comes to incentive design, the most popular measures used in short-term plans are revenue, operating income, and earnings per share (EPS), whereas relative TSR, EPS, and capital return measures are most common in long-term performance plans.

Step Two: Test Correlations for Single Measures

Once you have gathered the data, you can use basic statistical analysis to determine the correlation between each selected measure and TSR. At this step, you should calculate the R-squared for all the selected measures independently (that is, one at a time) over multiple time periods. Then you can compare the outcomes to determine the measures most highly correlated to TSR.

Understanding R-Squared

R-squared (also r^2 or R^2) is a measure of how well data fit a statistical model. It is a statistic used when the main purpose of the analysis is either to predict future outcomes or to test a hypothesis. Also known as the coefficient of correlation, the value of r2 ranges from -1.0 to 1.0. In general, the closer r^2 is to 1, the better the model fits the data.

At this point, it is important to make sure the time frames you are using for the analysis reflect the fundamentals of your industry or industries. Investment cycles differ dramatically between industries, and some segments are more sensitive to macroeconomic forces and global business cycles than others. It is also important to test for correlations over a relatively long historical time frame, so that the impact of various economic conditions (recession and expansion) can be taken into account.

Step Three: Test Correlations for Multiple Measures

What if the single measure analysis does not result in strong correlations? It could be because multiple factors, operating in combination with each other, have a bigger impact on TSR than any single measure alone. For example, a company's ability to both grow top-line revenue and simultaneously improve operating margins could have a bigger impact on value creation than either growth or profitability alone. You can test this using multiple regression analysis—more complicated than single regression but easily completed using today's standard spreadsheet software.

Step Four: Using the Outcomes

Measuring the correlation of potential incentive plan measures to TSR is a useful input to the incentive design process—but not an absolute answer. By definition, the analysis is backward looking—it shows how various measures have been correlated to changes in TSR in the past. As a result, it might not adequately reflect changes in your company or industry that will change how value is created in the future.

Correlation is not causation. While the analysis can determine which measures in the past have had the highest statistical relationship to shareholder value, it does not guarantee that focusing solely on those measures will create value in the future.

That said, by employing a data-based, quantitative approach to discovering the facts about performance, HR professionals can give compensation committees and boards a foundation to help tailor incentive designs that resist the "best-practice" mindset and seek to achieve "best fit" instead.

PART VII

BUILDING CHRO TALENT

Chapter 22.
CHRO Succession: Are We Practicing What We Preach?

Mirian Graddick-Weir

Chief human resource officers (CHROs) typically play a key role in CEO succession. A report by Wright, Nyberg, Schepker, and Ulrich (2014) provided an excellent summary of the critical partnership between the CHRO, the CEO, and the board of directors to ensure there is a well-executed process in place to identify the next CEO. Spencer Stuart (2014) also highlighted the strategic role that CHROs play during the CEO succession process. Over the past 10 years, CHROs from *Fortune* 500 companies have consistently rated executive succession and development as one of their top five most important priorities (HR Policy Association website), and we have all seen how the quality of these efforts can significantly affect the success of the business.

But what about the CHRO succession process? Shouldn't we be equally adept at managing a robust succession planning process for this critical role? Recent data from a CHRO succession survey revealed that nearly 60 percent of CHRO positions are currently filled with an external hire (Wright et al., 2014 and Wright, Call, Nyberg, Schepker & Ulrich, 2015). Stated differently, since 2010, the number of CHROs who were promoted through an internal (within HR) succession process has trended between 31 percent and 38 percent. For these same companies, CEOs (70 percent) and CFOs (57 percent) were far more likely to be promoted internally (Wright et al., 2015).

The reality is that even with the most thoughtful and well-planned CHRO succession process, there are inherent complexities and challenges. For example, CEOs increasingly rely on the input from other key stakeholders before making their final decision, including the compensation committee of the board. Wright et al.'s (2014) survey data showed that boards are involved in the CHRO selection process by advising, approving, or interviewing candidates 68 percent of the time. Clearly their input and perspective are becoming even more critical, especially as the environmental and regulatory demands become more complex (for example, Dodd-Frank, say on pay, activists investors). And of course succession plans can change when a new CEO is recruited into the position. These new CEOs will have their own ideas about the type of person they want in the role.

The purpose of this chapter is to shed further light on the complexities of the CHRO succession process and to identify lessons learned and key strategies for the successful execution of a robust and thoughtful CHRO succession plan. Furthermore, I will highlight some useful approaches for grooming an internal candidate and identify when an external candidate may be the best alternative. The goal is to learn from one another's experiences and ensure we do not become the "shoemaker's children" in an area in which we should demonstrate world-class thought leadership. I will draw on data from a recent CHRO survey, my own experiences as someone who was both promoted into a CHRO role and hired externally into a CHRO role, and relevant experiences of several colleagues.

Recent Survey on CHRO Succession

To set a context for where we are, I will reference data from Wright et al.'s annual survey on C-suite succession conducted in 2014 and 2015. The 2014 survey was sent to 560 chief HR officers at *Fortune* 500 companies as well as CHROs that are part of a large CHRO professional society, and the authors received results from 223 individuals (40 percent response rate). The 2015 survey was sent to a slightly larger group of chief HR officers (over 600) with a 30 percent response rate. While both surveys focused on a variety of C-suite succession topics, I will highlight the data relevant to CHRO succession.

CHRO Succession Challenges

When a CHRO job becomes vacant, only 31 percent of the CHROs say that it was a normal retirement; rather many left by "mutual agreement." One hypothesis is that people who leave without it being considered a normal retirement are perhaps not in as much control of whether their succession plans are actually implemented based on their recommendations. When CHROs were asked why they were brought in from the outside, half said that there were no internal talents available. On further examination—people cited that the CEO was looking for people who could transform the HR function, bring a new or more strategic perspective to the role, and help change the culture and who had previous experience working with boards and had more international experience. This suggests that in many cases the CEO and the board have decided that they want a CHRO who has a track record of driving change and brings a level of sophistication to the role and that they believe they do not have the luxury of time to develop someone into the role. Several of my colleagues have stated that their CEOs and boards were adamant that they wanted a CHRO who already had experience working with boards even if they were coming from a much smaller company.

The survey also revealed that only 25 percent of CHROs currently have a ready-now candidate—so if they were to leave their jobs today, the company would be forced to look externally or have to take a chance with a less senior person knowing that it is a risk. While 40 percent of CHROs indicated that they have a "ready within one to two years" successor, this should still raise a concern since so much can happen in a company within two years.

Another sobering statistic comes from the HR Policy Association (HRPA) survey (HR Policy Association website), which introduces yet another element of complexity as we tackle CHRO succession. Of the 326 HRPA members, half of the CHROs have been in their roles less than three years. These individuals are less likely to be concerned about grooming their successors versus figuring out how to be effective in their relatively new roles.

Lessons Learned—Effective Ways of Developing Internal Candidates

I would like to share a few of the lessons I have learned along the way and reference data from the CHRO surveys as appropriate. As with other C-suite positions, CHROs should have the ultimate goal of developing a pool of top-quality candidates internally. Wright et al.'s survey (2014) high-lighted what respondents felt they needed as they assumed their first CHRO role. When CHROs were first appointed, they were least prepared for dealing with the board (24 percent), felt they needed additional experi-ence in the more complex elements of executive compensation and other regulatory topics (27 percent), and felt less prepared to deal with the C-suite dynamics (9 percent). The previous work assignments that best pre-pared them for the role were HR business partner (33 percent), benefits (15 percent), international assignment (12 percent), and executive com-pensation (11 percent). These results should be considered when looking for opportunities to develop potential successors.

Board Exposure

There is no doubt that having exposure to the board is an essential component of developing an internal candidate. Individuals who have executive compensation experience or who lead the global talent group will most likely have had exposure to the board. If not, typical ways CHROs have provided their internal candidates exposure is through board presentations, informal sessions such as lunches or dinners, the opportunity to attend succession planning discussions, and compensa-tion and benefits (C&B) committee meetings. I believe it can be help-ful to work with your CEO and C&B committee chair to determine the most effective way for the board to get to know the internal candidate. For example, in addition to my core responsibilities, my predecessor at AT&T gave me responsibility for compensation and benefits for an interim period of time so that I could attend the C&B committee meet-ings alongside our executive compensation leader. The board knew that this was an interim structure designed to expose me to the issues and to better understand the C&B committee dynamics. If the candidate is in a business partner role, another approach is to give him or her the opportunity to present the talent strategy for the division the candidate supports or to allow a board member to spend one-on-one time with him or her during one of the board member's site visits. The board (es-pecially the C&B committee) will no doubt influence the selection deci-sion, and you must find ways for board members to get comfortable with the succession candidate.

C-Suite Dynamics

One strategy in ensuring the success of an internal candidate is to deliberately align your potential CHRO successor with the executive who is being groomed as the next potential CEO. If they both end up in their respective top roles, their transitions will be easier because they have already had the chance to cultivate a trusted partnership. Another essential part of the development strategy is for your internal successor to have the opportunity to build strong relationships with other C-suite executives, particularly the CFO and general counsel. One of my colleagues highlighted how beneficial it is when the other key C-suite executives are personally invested in helping the new CHRO transition effectively into the role.

Relationship with the CEO

It is critical that the internal candidate builds a strong relationship with the CEO. My experience is that this involves a combination of the candidate being viewed as competent and credible, having "chemistry" with the CEO, and having the chance to build trust. If the candidate has not previously worked with the CEO, you must deliberately create opportunities to allow the two to cultivate the relationship. You can give the candidate a project and let him or her work with the CEO directly (without you being involved). Alternatively, you can arrange for the candidate to spend quality time with the CEO, sharing his or her perspectives on the business he or she supports (including leadership and cultural issues) or traveling to a region with the CEO without you accompanying them. These interactions need to be substantive, and we have to acknowledge that it is difficult for our potential successors to build a relationship with the CEO if we, as CHROs, are not comfortable creating these opportunities.

HR Team Dynamics

To adequately prepare internal candidates, you will need to provide them with unique developmental opportunities. They have to realize that there may be resentment among their peers and accept these "special" roles with humility and grace. Should they become the CHRO, they will need to retain some of these colleagues to be successful in the role. If they do not have a compensation background, they particularly need to form a good relationship with the person who has responsibility for executive compensation. Most of my colleagues would agree that having a top caliber executive compensation/benefits senior leader in the CHRO role is critical. From the perspective of the CEO and the C&B chair, this is the last person you want to lose during a CHRO transition. Managing the team dynamics within HR can be challenging, particularly if multiple individuals believe they are qualified for the CHRO role. Just as you are being thoughtful about the development of your lead candidate, you also need to be transparent with those on the HR leadership team who are not immediate successors and discuss their potential next opportunities and career paths with them.

Lessons Learned—When an External Hire Is the Prudent Path

After examining your options for an internal CHRO successor, you will need to recognize when recruiting externally is the optimal strategy to pursue. Several factors make going outside the right path forward.

Major Transformation of the Business or HR

The CHRO survey indicated that a major reason companies go outside is because they want someone who can bring an outside-in perspective and not be comfortable with the status quo. The CEO may want to pursue major changes with key C-suite members or need someone who can drive more transformational versus incremental change. Alternatively, the CEO may want more radical changes within the HR department. It is important to step back and consider the leadership dynamics and future challenges within the company and the external marketplace. A crucial question we should not be afraid to ask is whether a more transformational leader is desired rather than someone who has grown up in the existing culture.

Desire of the Board

The C&B committee members are under increasingly greater scrutiny as they manage the dynamics of key external stakeholders such as proxy advisory groups, like Institutional Shareholder Services and activists, and regulatory issues such as Dodd-Frank in the United States. They too may prefer a more seasoned CHRO who already has some board experience. As you develop your succession plan, elicit regular input from the C&B committee chair. You do not want to be blindsided by the board's opposition of promoting an internal candidate into the role. I have personally seen board members put pressure on the CEO to recruit a more experienced CHRO, especially if they believe that promoting the internal candidate is too much of a developmental stretch.

New CEO

In many ways, all bets are off when there is a new CEO (either an external hire or an internal candidate). The new CEO will undoubtedly have a different style of operating and will want to select someone who can help him or her advance his or her agenda and vision, and someone who the CEO thinks can be a close partner and trusted confidant. If the new CEO is a result of an internal promotion and he or she has worked with the candidate, then there is a higher probability of that person being a legitimate candidate for the CHRO role. Otherwise, you have to test your succession planning assumptions with the new CEO and assume that those assumptions might need to change.

Another interesting scenario is that the new CEO might prefer to keep the experienced incumbent CHRO in the role for a longer period of time than the person was planning to remain in the position (or with the company). If you believe you have someone who can be a strong candidate within a reasonable period of time, the CHRO may need to stay a bit longer to ensure the CEO is more comfortable with that person. Additionally, the new CEO also has time to gain comfort in his or her role and establish a good working relationship with the board.

Like with other C-suite positions, the key is to engage your stakeholders in the process and recognize that they may have a different perspective than you. A principal lesson is that the board and other C-suite executives will have significant influence during the selection process. Most importantly, the CEO—not the CHRO—is the ultimate decision-maker.

Through engaging the board and the CEO in candid conversations about their succession plan, several of my CHRO colleagues realized that they would need to recruit an existing CHRO to succeed them. Well ahead of retiring, one colleague started to have dinner sessions with CHROs from smaller companies to get to know them. This was a terrific way to begin to develop a short list of external candidates well ahead of actually launching the selection process.

Framing the Key Issues as You Build the Optimal CHRO Succession Plan

There are many inherent complexities in developing a CHRO succession plan. Although CHROs are specifically qualified to develop an optimal plan, we should frame the issues in the same way we would for any other C-suite position. From my perspective, I would assign the main questions or topics to four major categories, as seen in Figure 23.1.

FIGURE 22.1. FRAMING THE DYNAMIC AND CRITICAL CHRO SUCCESSION ISSUES

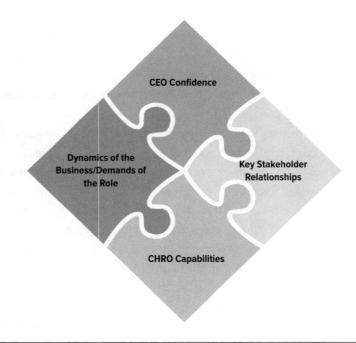

Dynamics of the Business/Demands of the Role

What are the major challenges facing the business; how well positioned is HR to drive change and address those business challenges? For example, will large acquisitions be a part of the business strategy, and does the HR team have the core capabilities to support a major transaction? Does the CEO want to drive major culture change, which may require recruiting new senior leaders and exiting others? Will there be multiple upcoming C-suite retirements, including the need to replace the CEO? How credible is the HR team, and what is the depth of the talent pipeline in HR? The bottom line is to have a solid understanding of the context within which a CHRO will need to operate effectively and be ruthlessly honest about whether the internal candidate(s) has the capabilities, experiences, and sophistication to drive significant change. If the CHRO role is complex, another pertinent question is whether the person can make the leap from his or her current position to the CHRO position or would the candidate be more successful initially moving to a smaller CHRO position in another company.

Required Capabilities of the Next CHRO

Much has been written about the CHRO role and the critical competencies required for success (Wright et al., 2015, and Ulrich, D., Younger, J., Brockbank, W., & Ulrich, M., 2012). But we need to ask which competencies are the most important for success, given the internal and external challenges and demands over the next three to five years. The common characteristics often mentioned are having credibility, trust and courage, strong business/financial acumen; translating insights on external trends into business implications; bringing innovative solutions to problems; championing change; and driving operational efficiency. However, a frequent reason my colleagues cite for new CHROs failing is the complexity of the role and the many relationships that need to be cultivated and managed. CHROs find it incredibly difficult to effectively juggle the multiple demands of the role (for example, C-suite dynamics, CEO demands, board dynamics, executive compensation challenges, and managing the HR function). The daunting reality is that you are never really fully tested as to whether you can effectively manage this level of complexity until you actually move into your first CHRO role. As part of the development process, CHROs should spend quality time with their potential successors sharing the "day and the life of a CHRO." Even my direct reports comment that parts of my job are somewhat "invisible" to them, particularly managing the politics and how to handle difficult interpersonal scenarios and conversations. Sharing those experiences and perspectives along the way can take some of the elements of surprise out of the role. Finally, while most of my colleagues would acknowledge that having high "EQ" (emotional intelligence quotient) is essential, one of my colleagues emphasized the importance of CHROs having high EQ with an "edge" to gain the appropriate respect necessary to drive large-scale change. Senior line leaders sometimes complain about necessary changes, and CHROs must have the confidence and courage to defend pivotal actions that need to be taken (for example, aligning HR policies and practices to the marketplace versus maintaining historical practices).

Key Stakeholder Relationships

There is no doubt that a successful CHRO must cultivate and manage relationships with sophisticated senior leaders. Wright et al.'s (2015) survey results had an interesting and new finding related to the importance of cultivating relationships. They asked the CHRO survey participants to describe 2-3 areas where the previous CHRO was weak. The most frequently mentioned area was in building trust with the board, CEO and the executive leadership team. The CEO will want a CHRO who can easily establish these relationships to become a better coach and confidant to him or her. Yet the real challenge comes from having the ability to navigate complex, politically charged, and nuanced situations with credibility, and courage, while continuing to engender trust. An HR business partner who has supported a president of a large division and has had to work with his or her direct report team has had some experience in this arena. But the risks and stakes are so much higher, particularly when it involves the board. Helping the internal candidate become aware of pitfalls and landmines and learn how to develop strategies for managing various scenarios can be beneficial.

CEO Confidence

Finally, at the end of the day the CEO is the ultimate decision-maker. If he or she is not totally confident about the candidate, it is a nonstarter. One must assume that a CHRO would only recommend a candidate who has the capabilities and credibility for the role. Therefore, trust and chemistry can be the enablers or the deal breakers. This is why allowing the candidate opportunities to spend quality time with the CEO at least gives the candidate a chance to determine if the relationship can work. If a CHRO has a terrific relationship with the CEO, of course the CEO's first choice will always be to have the CHRO remain in the role. However, if the CHRO has a qualified successor, the CEO must recognize when it is best for the company and the shareholders to move on and let the candidate or successor move into the role rather than risk losing a key asset.

Summary and Conclusions

C-suite succession is challenging, but doing it well can positively influence the success of the company. As CHROs, we are qualified and expected to help the CEO and board execute the process well. However, the trend of only 31 percent to 38 percent of CHRO jobs being filled through a thoughtful internal plan is not acceptable. As Kadar (2014) pointed out: "It's one thing to plan the succession of someone else. It's quite another to do it on your own behalf." If the CEO and board are happy with their CHRO, they are likely not exerting the same pressure or sense of urgency to have a realistic plan. So we have to make sure we are holding ourselves accountable for our own function. It takes a thoughtful plan and willingness on the part of the CHRO to give the internal candidate the assignments and exposure necessary to adequately prepare him or her for the role.

Ideally our goal should be to develop a qualified internal candidate. However, we need to embrace the feedback from the board and the CEO and be brutally honest with ourselves about whether an internal candidate can meet the evolving demands of the role. We should not be embarrassed if key talent within our organizations takes CHRO roles in smaller companies to sharpen their skills. Many of them ultimately become the talent pool for bigger and more complex CHRO roles over time. The ultimate contribution is the meaningful role we should all play in developing the next generation of CHROs.

Finally, an interesting, recent statistic is the number of CHROs at *Fortune* 500 companies who are in their positions less than three years (50 percent) and less than two years (40 percent) (HR Policy Association website). Another priority for current CHROs is to help ensure these individuals are successful in their roles, or we run the risk of the CHRO succession issue becoming even more challenging than it is today. There is clearly more evidence-based work that needs to be done to better understand what factors most contribute to CHROs not being successful in their roles and generally what factors contribute to CHRO turnover. But I think we would all agree that we need to challenge ourselves to "practice what we preach" and ensure that the CHRO succession process is one that people reference as world class!

References

HR Policy Association. (2015). Retrieved from http://www.hrpolicy.org

Kador, J. (2012). CHRO succession at the crossroads. Human Resource Executive Online. Retrieved from http://www.hreonline.com/HRE/view/story.jhtml?id=533350839.

Kelly, C. L., & Ogden, D. (2014). CHRO at the center: Five recommendations for managing an effective succession planning process. Spencer Stuart. Retrieved from https://www.spencerstuart.com/~/media/pdf%20files/research%20and%20insight%20pdfs/ceosuccession_chro_final-10jul2014.pdf.

Ulrich, D., Younger, J., Brockbank, W., and Ulrich, M. (2012). HR from the outside in: six competencies for the future of human resources. The McGraw-Hill Companies.

Wright, P. M., Nyberg, A. J., Schepker, D. J., & Ulrich, M. D. (2014). CHRO succession. Center for Executive Succession, University of South Carolina, Darla Moore School of Business.

Wright, P. M., Call, M. L., Nyberg, A. J., Schepker, D. J., & Ulrich, M. D. (2015). The chief HR officer role. Center for Executive Succession, University of South Carolina, Carla Moore School of Business.

Chapter 23.

Courage:
A Critical Attribute for Success Amidst the Competencies HR Executives Need

Debra J. Cohen

What does it take to prepare HR professionals to ascend to the top HR position in an organization? What competencies do they need, and how do they obtain these competencies? Do most organizations have a formal documented plan for developing HR professionals? In addition to certain competencies, what are the attributes that HR professionals need to be successful in the competitive environments in which they operate? According to a survey of HR professionals, only 17 percent of organizations have a formal documented plan for developing HR professionals, but nearly one-half (48 percent) identify high-potential HR professionals through succession planning (SHRM, Developing HR Professionals survey, 2011).

Just as organizations need to create value for their customers and shareholders, HR needs to create value for its organization through the development of its HR talent. For the chief human resource officer (CHRO)[1] to develop his or her firm's human capital as a weapon against competitors, the CHRO must create an army of HR professionals capable of selecting and deploying this capital in an effective manner. The productive capacity of a firm depends, at least in part, on the productive capacity of the HR function that serves and leads the organization. There is both an art and a science to developing HR professionals.

In preparation for this chapter, the CHROs[2] who contributed to this book were asked the following question: *In your opinion and based on your experience, what are the key behavioral attributes that are most important for HR professionals to develop during their career to ascend to the top HR job in an organization or simply to advance in the HR profes-*

sion? Their responses were insightful and quite consistent with existing validated research.

Courage and Business Acumen

One attribute stood out loud and clear and underscored all the other competencies that the CHROs noted: courage. Courage can be thought of as a person's ability *and* willingness to confront such things as fear, pain, danger, shame, uncertainty, scandal, or intimidation (Woodard, 2004). Courage is about perseverance, leadership, and ethics. And like other qualities or "muscles" that a person has, it is strengthened by use. And courage is something that the CEO wants from HR. Mark Twain once said that "it is curious that physical courage should be so common in the world and moral courage so rare." It has also been said that courage does not mean you do not get afraid; courage means you do not let fear stop you. According to the CHROs who responded about what CHROs need, the courageous CHRO is one who is consistently able to confront people and situations and who demonstrates decisiveness, innovation, and the ability to say what needs to be said at the appropriates times and places. They described the moral courage that Twain speaks about. As one CHROs put it, "purpose and being purpose-focused in HR" can be taught, and this is then displayed through courage. But to have courage and to ultimately be influential, the respondents noted that the CHRO must have business acumen and be insightful about what the organization needs by balancing strategic and operational priorities.

HR is responsible for identifying and developing talent in the organization. But how do HR professionals rate with *HR* talent development? Research by Wright and Collins (2012) indicated that HR does a good job of developing others but not its own HR professionals. CHROs say they do not have the competence that they need within their own function (Wright and Stewart, 2011). If this is the case, then perhaps the way in which many HR professionals have been developed has not been effective in the past, or the focus has not been in the right areas. Although business acumen is a key competency and courage a core attribute that facilitates the application of competencies like business acumen, there are additional competencies that a researched HR competency model embodies and which CHROs identify as the behavioral attributes that are most important for success.

HR Competencies

HR competencies provide a CHRO with a way to define in behavioral terms what it is that HR professionals need to do to produce the results that the organization desires and in a way that is in keeping with its culture. By defining competencies, you allow HR professionals to know what they need to be productive. When properly defined, competencies allow the CHRO to evaluate the extent to which behaviors HR professionals exhibit are effective or to demonstrate where they may be lacking. These insights speak to the behavioral attributes that CHROs know set them apart. And it allows a CHRO to focus on developing the next cadre of HR professionals who will be successful.

Competencies do not establish baseline performance levels; rather, they are used to raise the bar on employee performance. For example, communication at an entry level may refer to communicating policies and procedures for new employees, whereas for executives it may refer to negotiation with stakeholders to reach the best possible solution. As one CHRO noted, strong leadership communication skills are needed, and this is often an "underutilized and underemphasized" competency. It will likely take many years of professional development and experience to progress from communicating HR policies to mastering successful negotiations. Competencies provide professionals with a roadmap to increase their capabilities incrementally over time. Competencies focus development on how results can be achieved rather than on simply the end result. In this manner competencies bridge the gap between performance management and employee development and are critical components of personal and professional development plans for ascending in HR. Following a competency model and applying it in your organization can allow CHROs to identify and develop HR talent.

How do HR professionals decide if they want to ascend to the top HR position in an organization and whether they want to work in a small-, medium-, or large-size enterprise? The job can be quite different in a 500-person organization than in a 5,000-person organization or even larger. How does an HR professional develop the knowledge, skills, abilities, and other characteristics (KSAOs) that will allow him or her to do the job of a CHRO and to thrive as an executive among a team of equals who are leading other functions in the organization? Research from the Society for

Human Resource Management (SHRM) revealed that the HR competencies HR professionals most want to develop vary by career stage. Table 24.1 shows the characteristics of four HR professional career levels (SHRM, 2014). For example, and not surprisingly, entry-level or early-career professionals are most likely to want to develop their Human Resource Expertise, while HR professionals at the executive career level most want to develop their Leadership and Navigation competency (SHRM HR Jobs Pulse Survey, 2014.) As another CHRO described, CHROs think and act strategically—"they see the bigger picture and understand how to connect the dots."

TABLE 23.1. HR PROFESSIONAL CAREER LEVELS AND DESCRIPTIONS

Early
- Is a specialist in a specific support function, or is a generalist with limited experience.
- Holds a formal title such as HR assistant, junior recruiter, or benefits clerk.

Mid
- Is a generalist or a senior specialist.
- Manages projects or programs.
- Holds a formal title such as HR manager, generalist, or senior specialist.

Senior
- Is a very experienced generalist or specialist.
- Holds a formal title such as senior manager, director, or principal.

Executive
- Typically is one of the most senior leaders in HR.
- Holds the top HR job in the organization or a VP role.

Source: https://www.shrm.org/LearningAndCareer/competency-model/Documents/Full%20Competency%20Model%2011%202_10%20 1%202014.pdf.

CHROs set the tone and direction for other HR professionals in their organizations with respect to what is expected, and more to the point, how they are developed. HR expertise is a necessary ingredient, but to develop courage and insight, the less experienced HR professional must be exposed to many different situations and opportunities to flex and strengthen the muscles that give them the courage to lead and navigate in their organizations. Understanding and possessing HR expertise is a basic foundation, but at some point to be an effective CHRO, one must cross the threshold from being primarily an HR practitioner to being the strategic business practitioner and partner, supported by his or her HR expertise. In fact, one CHRO stated that CHROs "need to be a business professional 'first and foremost,' even before being an HR professional."

> *Is there a specific pathway to become a CHRO who has the necessary courage, business acumen, and other attributes needed—or to develop the attributes necessary to become a CHRO? If so, what is it?*

There are multiple pathways from beginning a career in HR to achieving the top spot in HR. A person working in HR cannot ultimately be successful without knowing or understanding the functional components of HR. Competencies, on the other hand, are attributes that are tied to successful performers. Competencies have gained popularity among organizations looking at ways to identify, hire, and retain top talent. In day-to-day activities, you display competencies, and you look for competencies in others. Even when faced with a similar situation, you often need to behave differently to be successful. Competencies, once developed, are things that you carry with you throughout your career. With respect to courage, one CHRO commented, "The complexity of the job, and the num-

FIGURE 23.1. SHRM COMPETENCY MODEL

TABLE 23.2. INSIGHTS FROM SITTING CHROS

In addition to having courage, CHROs offered the following traits for ascending to the top:

- Can analyze complex situations—breaking down into small, more manageable parts
- Can balance strategic and operational priorities
- Can build influential relationships with CEO, board members, and other executives
- Can build talent and teams
- Can read people and situations and has perspective and judgment
- Can coach, influence, and inspire
- Has curiosity and authenticity
- Has flexibility and grit
- Knows the business and has financial acumen
- Manages and drives change
- Is a problem solver and critical thinker
- Is a steward of culture
- Has strong leadership communication skills
- Is a team player—and selfless
- Is a trusted, visible and approachable leader
- Upholds highest integrity and ethics—strong internal compass

Source: Attributes presented in alphabetical order. Responses from the following individuals were received: Susan Suver, Marcia Avedon, Kevin Cox, Michael D'Ambrose, Ken Carrig, Joe Ruocco, Mara Swan, Jill Smart, James Duffy, John Murabito, James Bagley, Mark Schuyler, and Eva Sage-Gavin.

ber of situations requiring the demonstration of courage, is constantly growing. Business pressures are more pronounced than ever—and those pressures create a cauldron in which dilemmas, compromises, ethical breaches, sins of omission and sins of commission boil and bubble. I find myself looking harder at the courage dimension/attribute among my up and comers within HR."

So what does a comprehensive competency model for HR look like, and how does it jive with what CHROs describe? Using thousands of HR subject matter experts (SMEs) at all levels of the profession, SHRM researched and developed a competency model for the HR profession that can be used as a roadmap to help set the tone and direction for HR professionals as they progress through their careers (SHRM Competency Model, 2014). A graphic of the model can be seen in Figure 24.1. The input from CHROs, summarized in Table 24.2, shows an amazing overlap with the SHRM Competency Model. In addition to business acumen and courage, they highlighted integrity, influence, collaboration, accountability, communication, cultural sensitivity, and more.

SHRM Competency Model

The SHRM Competency Model is a framework of nine competencies that together define the characteristics needed for successful performance in HR. This model includes one functional competency, HR Expertise, and eight behavioral competencies:

- Business Acumen.
- Communication.
- Consultation.
- Critical Evaluation.
- Ethical Practice.
- Global and Cultural Effectiveness.
- Leadership and Navigation.
- Relationship Management.

Results of a content validation study provide strong support for the model (SHRM, *Content Validity Study of the SHRM Competency Model*, 2014). The study of 32,000 HR professionals showed that all nine competencies are important and that the mean importance for each competency increases in each of the successive four levels (shown in Table 24.1). For example, at the entry level the mean importance for consultation is 1.5 and moves to 2.1, 2.4, and 2.6 for mid-, senior-, and executive-levels, respectively. The same pattern of results is seen in each of the nine competencies (SHRM, *Content Validity Study of the SHRM Competency Model*, 2014). The model includes the ability, demonstrated through *behaviors*, of HR professionals to meet complex job demands by drawing on all of their resources, including knowledge, skills, abilities, and *behaviors* in a given context. HR professionals, as noted by the majority of CHROs, need to have a wide range of competencies, not just in HR, to face the complexity of challenges that exist today. *Behavioral competencies* are what make top HR performers stand out among those who are not able to demonstrate them, because like courage, behavioral competencies are visible and measurable and distinguish good performance from mediocre performance.

The intent of the SHRM Competency Model is to provide a basis on which HR professionals can learn, develop, and grow. Implicit in the model is the assumption that knowledge is necessary but not sufficient for success, since there is often a gap between knowing something and acting on that knowledge. This gap can be thought of as our courage attribute, developing that willingness to do, to persevere, and to lead. The model is an excellent source for understanding career growth and career potential, for bridging the gap between what you know and how you get there, and for providing guidance on how to take that next step to become an effective HR business leader.

Developing Future CHROs

Few, if any HR professionals will be expert performers in all nine competencies identified for the HR profession; thus, the model can be used to help them with their career growth within one organization or across multiple organizations. HR professionals need a wide range of competencies to face the complex challenges of today's world. Table 24.3 offers some detailed examples of proficiency standards by HR level from the SHRM Competency Model[3] to demonstrate how the proficiency of an HR professional will need to evolve over time to be successful. It will take much development over time, and focus on both learning and gaining experience through practice, to develop these behaviors. The proficiency statements for senior- and executive-level HR professionals in the SHRM Competency Model are quite consistent with the input from CHROs. One of the critical leadership traits of the CHRO as noted by one responding CHRO is that of building "talent and teams," and several CHROs noted that they are problem solvers and deliver results.

HR executives must be aligned and integrated with the overall organizational mission, vision, and strategy if they are to be effective. This is no different than any other executive in an organization. HR brings value to the organization in a variety of ways; perhaps no better way is by focusing on preparing other HR professionals to sit in the top spot and lead the organization effectively.

It is important to develop HR talent in a structured way that will lead HR professionals and guide them toward the competencies that they need, building their confidence along the way. One CHRO talked about the evolution of the behavioral skills necessary to be successful in HR: "Administrative proficiency and subject matter expertise are table stakes in today's business environment." Today's requirements, he went on, "beg for those

TABLE 23.3. SHRM COMPETENCY MODEL: A SAMPLE OF PROFICIENCY STANDARDS BY HR LEVEL

Competency	Proficiency Standards by HR Level			
	Entry	**Mid**	**Senior**	**Executive**
HR Expertise Ability to apply principles and practices of HRM to contribute to the success of the business.	• Provides service to stakeholders • Follows relevant laws and regulations	• Reports trends to senior leadership • Applies compliance knowledge to protect organization	• Determines best practices to support organizational direction • Designs strategy for organizational culture	• Educates and advises executive team on strategic HR issues as a factor in decision-making • Oversees HR issues involving legal and financial risk to organization
Relationship Management The ability to manage interactions to provide service and to support the organization.	• Provides first point of contact for employee questions • Serves as frontline liaison with vendors/suppliers	• Mediates difficult interactions, escalating problems to higher level when warranted • Oversees interactions with vendors/suppliers to maintain service quality	• Develops policies/practices for resolving conflicts • Designs programs/policies to cultivate a strong customer service culture in the HR function	• Oversees HR decision-making process to ensure consistency with HR and business strategy • Proactively develops relationships with peers, clients, suppliers, board members, and senior leaders
Consultation The ability to provide guidance to organizational stakeholders.	• Conducts initial investigation for HR-based transactional issues • Gathers, and when appropriate, analyzes facts and data for business solutions	• Coaches direct reports and others throughout organization utilizing HR expertise • Develops HR and business process improvement solutions	• Designs creative business solutions utilizing HR expertise/perspective • Designs long-term business solutions in partnership with HR customers	• Identifies opportunities to provide HR and business solutions that maximize return-on-investment for the organization • Recognizes excessive HR liabilities and provides proactive strategic guidance for remediation

continued on next page

TABLE 23.3. SHRM COMPETENCY MODEL: A SAMPLE OF PROFICIENCY STANDARDS BY HR LEVEL (continued)

Competency	Proficiency Standards by HR Level			
	Entry	Mid	Senior	Executive
Leadership and Navigation The ability to direct and contribute to initiatives and processes within the organization.	Acts consistently with and represents the culture of the organization Seeks new ways to improve and recommends improvements to HR processes, transactions, and outcomes	Manages programs, policies, and procedures to support the organizational culture Serves as the principal liaison to frontline managers for HR strategies, philosophies, and initiatives within the organization	Establishes programs, policies, and procedures to support the organizational culture Drives alignment and buy-in at all levels in business units across organization	Serves as the influential voice for HR strategies, philosophies, and initiatives within the organization Gains buy-in for organizational change across senior leadership with agility
Communication The ability to effectively exchange with stakeholders.	Promptly responds to stakeholder concerns via written, verbal, or electronic communication Communicates policies, procedures, culture, etc. to new and existing employees	Translates organizational communication strategies into practice at the operational level Crafts clear messages that inform frontline HR staff of relevant organizational information	Solicits feedback and buy-in on HR initiatives from organizational stakeholders Creates channels for open communication across and within levels of responsibility	Articulates the alignment between organizational HR initiatives and organizational strategy Negotiates with stakeholders to reach best possible outcomes
Global and Cultural Effectiveness The ability to value and consider the perspectives and backgrounds of all parties.	Respects differences and promotes inclusion on a transactional level Demonstrates awareness and appreciation for the global multi-dimensional and diverse perspectives in organization's line of business	Designs, recommends, and/or implements diversity/culture programs Employs cultural sensitivity in communicating with staff	Fosters culture of inclusiveness within organization Implements initiatives to ensure global effectiveness in strategic business units	Sets the strategy to leverage global competencies for competitive HR advantages Sets the vision that defines the strategic connection between diversity and inclusiveness practices for employees and organizational success

continued on next page

TABLE 23.3. SHRM COMPETENCY MODEL: A SAMPLE OF PROFICIENCY STANDARDS BY HR LEVEL (continued)

Competency	Proficiency Standards by HR Level			
	Entry	**Mid**	**Senior**	**Executive**
Ethical Practice The ability to support and uphold the values of the organization while mitigating risk.	• Documents and escalates reports of unethical behavior to management • Maintains employee confidentiality throughout appropriate business processes	• Reinforces difficult decisions that align with organizational strategies and values • Influences others to behave in an ethical manner	• Establishes oneself as a credible and trustworthy source for employees to voice concerns • Serves as a role model of ethical behavior by consistently conforming to the highest ethical standards and practices	• Challenges other executives and senior leaders when potential conflicts of interest arise • Develops HR policies and internal controls to minimize organizational risk from unethical practice
Critical Evaluation The ability to interpret information to make business decisions and recommendations.	• Reports on data entry and key metrics • Develops basic working knowledge of statistics, research methods, measurement concepts, and metrics	• Asks critical questions to prepare and interpret data studies/metrics • Conducts assessments to address problems and implements solutions within business units	• Leads research and evaluation and provides resources for specific issues studied • Validates processes to ensure that they meet desired and reliable outcomes	• Analyzes information needed to direct, evaluate, and use data and other information to make effective decisions • Challenges assumptions and critically examines all initiatives and programs
Business Acumen The ability to understand and apply information to contribute to the organization's strategic plan.	• Gathers, assembles, and reports HR metrics, Key Performance Indicators, and labor market trends • Develops familiarity with business terms and acronyms	• Utilizes appropriate business terms and vocabulary in interactions with employees and leaders • Defines critical activities in terms of value added, impact, utility derived from cost-benefit analysis	• Applies consistently the principles of finance, marketing, economics, sales, technology, and business systems to internal HR processes and policies • Implements solutions with analysis of impact on ROI, utility, revenue, profit and loss estimates, and other business indicators	• Maintains expert knowledge of key industry and organization metrics—"knows the business" Examines all organizational problems with a sense for integrating HR solutions designed to maximize ROI, profit, revenue, and strategic effectiveness

*Note: This is a subset of proficiency standards derived from the SHRM Competency Model. The full model with all validated proficiency standards can be found on the SHRM website at: http://www.shrm.org/HRCompetencies/Documents/Competency.pdf.

who are practical, action-oriented, anticipatory and have the capability to understand digital technology and other future business disruptors." How can HR professionals be prepared for these disruptors or go in front of the board of directors? What KSAOs must they possess? What leadership capabilities would you expect an HR professional to gain by moving out of HR for a period of time? What should be gained through international exposure?

In a study by SHRM (2011), HR professionals were surveyed regarding developing HR professionals in their organizations. Only about one fifth of the HR professionals surveyed indicated that they had formal, documented plans for developing HR professionals. About half of the respondents reported that high-potential HR professionals were identified through succession planning. How can these HR professionals be developed in a systematic way that will provide meaningful results to the organization? The CHROs' comments consistently talked about integrity, judgement, influence, accountability, and business. The "business" may be learned through study, but attributes like influence, integrity, accountability, and judgment must be gained through a heavy dose of experience.

If an individual has the ability to do a job correctly—we call him or her competent. To be competent, an HR professional needs to be able to interpret a situation in the context in which it occurs, have a range of possible actions to take, and be prepared for these possible actions. Regardless of education or training, one's competency can grow through experience and the extent to which an individual is able to learn and adapt. To become competent and then to distinguish themselves, HR professionals must, according to one CHRO, be "self-aware" of their behavior and be willing to put themselves in situations in which they will be able to grow and develop the KSAOs that will allow them to be effective. In addition to the *Content Validation Study* conducted by SHRM, a *Criterion Validation* study was also conducted with four large organizations that looked at performance data for HR professionals (by supervisors) as well as their own self-assessment using a tool designed for the study. The result of this study also suggests that the behavioral competencies in the model predict job performance over and above both HR Expertise (HR Knowledge) and demographic characteristics. This finding is especially relevant because it empirically demonstrates that the job performance of HR professionals is determined not only by technical knowledge but also by the domain-specific KSAOs that make up the behavioral competencies in the SHRM Competency Model (SHRM, 2015).

Self-assessments, contextual or department assessments, and pursuing advanced degrees and certifications will be helpful in focusing an HR professional on what is needed.[4] And while such developmental opportunities exist and are broadly available to HR professionals, keep in mind what CHROs themselves have stated as the attributes needed to ascend to the top. As one CHRO remarked, "The best HR leaders of today and tomorrow are trying to drive massive change in their organizations and find growth, drive productivity, and embrace a digital world." Using a proven competency model as a roadmap will, over time, result in changing the outcome that Wright and his colleagues have seen about the preparedness of HR professionals to ascend to the top spot in HR.

Many tools and opinions exist about what HR professionals must do to ascend to the top. Many differences exist based on the size, sector, or industry where the position resides. On the other hand, as evidenced by input from CHROs who answered the question above, there are also many commonalities. Each of the attributes/competencies today's CHROs identify allows them to be successful, and more important, allows them to know what to look for in future HR executives. CHROs set the tone for developing HR talent, and through their experience they are clearly able to articulate what is needed by the "up and comers" they cultivate. Given the notable overlap with the SHRM Competency Model, perhaps the way forward for HR professionals and the organizations in which they work is to apply the guidance such a model offers for HR professionals at all levels.

A final word about courage. It is incumbent on the CHRO to ensure that HR professionals are guided to develop the necessary competencies to ascend to the top, or to choose a better aligned HR position for their KSAOs. This may include the courage to help some HR professionals understand that a midlevel HR professional does not necessarily refer to years of experience but rather to a meaningful result of one's career attainment. Not every HR professional will or should ascend to the top. HR needs highly competent professionals at all levels to contribute to overall HR success. Business acumen at a "sophisticated level," said one CHRO, means that CHROs do more than understand the business—they understand it to "the point where they can predict and affect the human capital issues that are driven from the business problem"—solving business issues with HR solutions.

Endnotes

[1.] The term "CHRO" is used in this chapter to refer to the senior most HR professional in the organization and could hold a different title such as executive vice president (EVP) or senior vice president (SVP).

[2.] Responses from the following individuals were received: Susan Suver, Marcia Avedon, Kevin Cox, Michael D'Ambrose, Ken Carrig, Joe Ruocco, Mara Swan, Jill Smart, James Duffy, John Murabito, James Bagley, Mark Schuyler, and Eva Sage-Gavin.

[3.] To see the detailed proficiency statements for each of the nine competencies in the SHRM Competency Model, visit: http://www.shrm. org/hrcompetencies/pages/default.aspx.

[4.] SHRM has developed a host of diagnostic tools and a competency-based certification tied to the SHRM Competency Model to assist in this regard. For more information about SHRM Certification, visit: http://www.shrm.org/certification/pages/default.aspx and http:// www.shrm.org/hrcompetencies/pages/tools.aspx.

References

Society for Human Resource Management (SHRM). (2011). Developing HR Professionals: Shedding Light on the Business of HR. Alexandria, VA: SHRM.

SHRM. (2014). *Content Validation Study of the SHRM Competency Model*. Alexandria, VA: SHRM. Retrieved from http://www.shrm.org/ HRCompetencies/PublishingImages/14-0705%20Content%20Validation%20Study%203.pdf

SHRM. (2014). The SHRM Competency Model. Alexandria, VA: SHRM.

SHRM. (2014). *HR Jobs Pulse Survey Report*. Alexandria, VA: SHRM.

SHRM. (2015). *Criterion Validation Study of the SHRM Competency Model*. Retrieved from https://www.shrm.org/HRCompetencies/ PublishingImages/15-0412%20Criterion%20Validation%20Study_FINAL.pdf

Woodard, C. R. (2004). Hardiness and the concept of courage. *Consulting Psychology Journal: Practice and Research, 56*, 173-185.

Wright, P., & Collins, C. (2012). The Chief Human Resource Officer: Key Challenges and Strategies for Success. Center for Advanced Human Resource Studies (CAHRS), ILR School (Industrial and Labor Relations), Cornell University.

Wright, P., & Stewart, M. (2011). "What does today's CHRO look like? In P. M. Wright, J. W. Boudreau, D. A. Pace, E. Sartain, P. McKinnon, & R. Antoine (Eds.), *The Chief HR Officer*. San Francisco, CA: Wiley.

Chapter 24.

Are the Best CHROs Developed or Recruited?

James M. Bagley

The challenge for every organization when filling the top seat in human resources is whether to develop leadership talent internally or to recruit a candidate who brings new insights, experiences, and vision. While the CEO may want to raise leaders from within, internal candidates may not have all of the experiences or skills to implement talent solutions that match the organizational strategy. External candidates may have the background and capacities, but they do not have the connected relationships of someone who is already trusted throughout the company and by the board.

In every case, CEOs want an HR leader who:

- Possesses the core skills to implement human and organizational capital solutions that produce measurable value.
- Leads with behaviors that can handle the complexity of global organizations.
- Builds confidence in his or her abilities from the first interview.
- Matches the pace and cadence of a company's culture.

The Path to the Top Historically, chief human resource officer (CHRO) transitions have relied on specific HR experiences and the belief or feeling that the person had the right personality for the job. Today, CEOs' needs in an HR chief are not only being met with traditional candidates.

In the 2012 Russell Reynolds Associates (RRA) study of 97 CHROs at *Fortune* 100 firms, 57 percent had served as a regional or divisional head of HR, 41 percent had run learning and talent, and 36 percent had led compensation. But of the other 14 core HR and non-HR experiences surveyed, no other leadership experience tallied higher than a third of the CHROs at the world's leading companies.

Of these experiences, while 32 percent had been CHROs previously, the non-HR backgrounds varied widely. The highest percentages included 29 percent who had international experience, 27 percent who had been general managers, and 21 percent who had led a finance function. Although *Fortune* 100 companies are a unique sample, these data points reveal that candidates came to their HR officer positions from surprisingly diverse backgrounds.

Not only do candidates emerge from outside the HR world, but they do not match a neat picture of core experiences. The statistics point to the new reality: Companies look for the right skills, behaviors, and cultural fit in a candidate rather than a particular route to the top HR seat.

Do We Already Have Our Next CHRO?

A CHRO candidate may come from outside the human resource department, be part of a well-articulated and implemented succession plan, or, in some cases, come to the CHRO position after a sudden, unexpected retirement or transition. What is consistent among hiring committees is the analysis of candidates to determine if they can meet the CEO and the board's needs.

The diagnostic on whether an internal candidate can succeed as a CHRO begins with *HR proficiencies*. For instance, a CEO may want his or her director of compensation and benefits to be the next CHRO, but the candidate also needs capacity in talent management as well as the leadership readiness to interact with the board.

Every CHRO needs to be proficient in *core skills*, including:

- Broad HR disciplines such as organizational development, labor and employee relations, compensation and benefits, and executive compensation.
- Talent acquisition as well as development and retention.
- Strategy linking talent solutions to growth and profit.
- Communication both internally and externally.

- Independent thinking: The individual needs to have visionary ideas and a history of providing creative value.
- Team-building: Plain and simple, the CHRO that develops the best team wins.

Second, the person needs *broad business experience*. Although internal candidates know the organization they work for, have they worked in other companies in the same industry? Do they have international experience or experience in other verticals? Have they worked at the highest levels, including with boards? Can they handle the scale?

Third, do people *trust* the candidate? Organizations are either based on transactions or relationships. In a retail company where success is based on sales, the level of relationships the person has within the company will not be as important as in a relationship company. In insurance, for instance, in which trusting a leader's judgment can decide which risks are taken, and billions of dollars can rest on a single bet, the CEO needs to trust that the talent and organization under the CHRO's leadership will keep their promises.

Fourth is *loyalty*. Will an internal candidate keep more talent within the organization or cause other leaders to seek new roles elsewhere? Some leaders attract great leaders; others, no matter how many coaches they hire, cannot work well with a team. The ability to inspire loyalty spreads throughout a culture, and an internal candidate has to keep the best people from seeking new positions.

The fifth category internal candidates need to satisfy is their *leadership*. Do they have the ability to build a culture? Can they work with the CEO? Can they be the lightning rod for conflict, keep confidences, and ultimately develop stronger relationships at different levels and around the world? Most importantly, can they live out their role as a leader that creates a team of leaders ready to engage global challenges?

HR proficiencies are the foundation of choosing the next CHRO. And a competent internal candidate will not succeed if he or she does not have the behavioral traits essential for leading HR in this generation.

The Four Behaviors of Today's CHRO

CEOs, boards, and the HR community have always had an instinct about what makes a CHRO effective. In the spring of 2013, RRA engaged 20 top CHROs to scientifically define their behavioral traits.

Each participant was given three validated questionnaires, the Occupational Personality Questionnaire (OPQ), the Sixteen Personality Factor *Questionnaire (16pf)*, and the Hogan Development Survey (HDS), to capture their personality attributes. Participants were then interviewed, and their quantitative and qualitative results were compared to other HR professionals (for example, heads of compensation and benefits, heads of talent, and directors of HR).

Fifteen individual scales revealed statistically significant differences between the two groups. These results distinguished four distinct categories of leadership behaviors exhibited by the CHROs.

Social Dexterity

CEOs have always known that they want a CHRO who can confidently meet with the board as well as influence diverse constituencies within an organization.

The RRA study revealed that CHRO participants exhibit higher levels of social confidence than other HR professionals. Whereas their HR colleagues are less likely to attempt to change people's minds, CHROs have a willingness to sell ideas in every part of the organization.

Their confidence is most valuable because they work to understand others, and their insight is magnified by a desire to adapt. Whether speaking with different levels within the organization or with customers around the world, they comfortably adjust their social style to each new situation.

Bias Toward Action

CEOs have always known that they wanted a CHRO who could provide not only functional HR skills but also talent strategies for what are now global business challenges.

The RRA study revealed the behavioral evolution in the HR function from specifically running an efficient operation to today's CHRO who delivers competitive advantage by being decisive, vigorous, and conscientious.

Whereas their HR colleagues are comfortable providing options, CHROs seek the right solution, backed by data, that moves the organization to action. CHROs thrive on lots of activity, and they need to get things done for their own personal satisfaction. They are bellwethers who persist until tasks are complete and problems are solved.

Appetite for Change

CEOs have always known that they need a CHRO who can handle both the daily challenges of people problems and the crisis moments that threaten an organization's future.

The RRA study illustrated that successful CHROs thrive in the velocity of change promoted by 24/7 connectivity and social media attention. They cut through bureaucracy because they work comfortably without clear guidelines, and they do not let the rules stop their pursuit of results. They prefer novel approaches and new or unfamiliar situations.

The CHROs assessed were able to handle a diversity of people, environments, and crises because they are independent minded and exhibit high levels of managerial courage. They are not cautious with new ideas. They value innovative strategies and are not afraid to offer those ideas openly.

Setting a Constructive Tone

CEOs have always wanted a CHRO who can create a winning culture—an environment where the best talent is attracted, develops, and thrives.

The RRA study clarified that successful CHROs create a culture in which people want to stick around because the CHROs are trusting, modest, and positive.

Today's CHROs hear all the challenges and frustrations both within in the organization and among fellow leaders. The result of their core personality traits is the ability to build trust even among people who do not like each other and during situations that create the inevitable stress on an executive team or between competing units.

CHROs who can set a constructive tone, the study revealed, are not arrogant; they focus on their people rather than on personal reward, and they tend to see the positive opportunities in difficult situations.

How to Know the Right Candidate

HR proficiency and exemplary leadership behaviors, however, are still not enough in this century's international and interconnected climate. Historically, CEOs and boards needed HR efficiency; today, they need a confident executive who *models the character* expected from every executive and employee.

The ideal scenario is a succession plan and a pool of strong candidates ready to fill the HR officer role. Unfortunately, too few internal candidates are ready to flawlessly lead the HR function *and* create competitive advantage. That is when organizations look for an outside leader.

Outside candidates come from diverse backgrounds because organizations have clear outcomes they want from the role. They still have to be the competent, affable head of the HR department. The best HR leaders have always made it easy for other executives to close the door and process the people problems inherent in every business.

And CHROs now must also find the best people, they have to strategically develop them for today and tomorrow's unexpected scrums, and their work is now measurable. If they seem to have the right skills, experience, and behaviors, how can an organization know if it has the right leader?

Consider two external candidates. Both have a proven track record of competent HR and innovative talent solutions in diverse companies. It turns out that the confidence in a leader, which can produce what CEOs and boards need over the long term, begins at the moment of a formal offer.

Candidate one: She researches all the facts publicly available about the potential company. She is open about the situation she is leaving and specific about what she needs personally and organizationally from the new company recognizes the expectations and compensation that will make sense to the board and CEO, and her negotiation is organized, focused, and clear.

Candidate two: He enters the final meeting with a detailed compensation package matching his responsibilities. At the end of the meeting, he says to the CEO, "I definitely want this to move forward." While the CEO thought he and the candidate had reached an agreement, candidate two was not up front about everything he wanted. In asking for additional benefits, candidate two did not exhibit the ability to handle the CHRO role's nuance and complexity. If a candidate cannot handle the negotiation gracefully, how can he or she lead an international team against global competitors?

Candidate one, on the other hand, began building rapport from the first conversation with the leaders of her new company. At the final contract meeting, she crystalized her functional competence and behavioral leadership during the kind of interaction she will repeat thousands of times in negotiations and in other sensitive, high-impact conversations as HR chief. Her character inspires confidence.

A Unified Theory of the CHRO's Role

With the HR competence, leadership traits, and the right first impression, an internal or external candidate's *style still has to match an organization's environment.* Companies' cultures reflect the products, services, and life cycles that drive profit.

When finding the next CHRO, a company has to truly define its culture by answering three questions:

- What does this company do?
- What is the pace and cadence of activity?
- How are decisions made?

When a CEO of a chemical company says he or she wants to drive change, the CEO means over the next seven years. Change to a retail CEO, on the other hand, means over the next seven minutes.

The CHRO who fits an organization's culture, therefore, has to have the personality to match the pace and cadence of an organization. In retail, advertising, or fast food, CEOs make decisions quickly as trends and tastes change. In a paper company, growing trees takes a long time. In an insurance company, CEOs are huge risk takers, but deliberate.

A candidate who is smart and has the resume but likes to be deliberate with changes will not be happy in a company where the CEO adjusts strategy at every Monday meeting. On the other hand, a candidate who loves innovation and solving crises will fail a CEO in a business like big oil, where a single decision, like which land to develop, will affect the company for years at a cost of billions of dollars.

A candidate who fits will be able to show the diverse impact groups of a company that they actually need the same thing. In private equity, for instance, the candidate must satisfy the partners, CEOs of portfolio companies, and the resource groups.

Each CEO has different hopes from his or her new CHRO leader. The right candidate has the academic background to satisfy the partner's desire for complex models, the personality to help busy CEOs navigate daily people problems, and the broad HR skills so every group in the company has the talent, training, and strategy essential in affecting the business.

Within many firms, there will be huge disagreement about the role of HR. And that is just one more opportunity for effective CHROs today to build stronger relationships with other leaders and a culture that matches the company's core business and pattern of activity.

The reason CHROs have been hired from diverse places both inside and outside of organizations is that the skills, personality, immediate impact, and ability to match a company's pace and cadence are rare. We have captured, however, the clear portrait of who these leaders need to be.

The Future CHRO

In the past, CHROs could have the skills or the personality to fill the role. They did not have a seat with other executives or at the board table because the position was functional or relational. That has changed, and as a result, the choice of who can lead HR in the future is no longer straightforward, and it is dramatically more important to the longevity and profitability of a business.

The objective of the RRA *Fortune* 100 and CHRO behavioral studies was to validate what CEOs and boards have always thought about the best CHROs but also to differentiate what the future CHRO looks like. We now know that the path to CHRO is not singular and that specific behaviors signal a leader is ready for the role.

And the final word on whether to hire within or externally begins with a question: As a CEO, if you did another search, would your best internal successor be a candidate? CEOs and hiring committees have to step back to see clearly whether a person checks all the boxes. A generalist with no compensation experience or a head of compensation, benefits, and operations without talent experience may have the right behaviors, but can he or she truly represent the identity of the firm in a global market?

Whom firms hire as CHRO will be a statement about what they want to be as a company. For internal candidates, raising up a leader from finance or operations versus promoting from within the HR organization reveals the expertise a company plans to use to grow the business. When the new CHRO comes from an outside company that has world-class talent, world-class products, and is one of the world's best places to work, the person's background tells a story. If a CEO and board recruit a head of HR who has been the professional brought in to fire people at six companies, and this person has done the dirty work of reducing head count, the optics of the person declares what the company plans to be.

Since the next CHRO is a signal to the market about the organization's future direction, the hire needs to be better than the functional needs he or she fulfills. The CHRO has to be additive to the culture, bringing talent and ideas the firm does not already have. To recruit someone who fits the culture is an odd statement. Why hire a CHRO who simply fits when the new leader can transform a successful company into an even better and more profitable organization?

To fulfill the need for HR executives with broader talent, the HR field has to work harder to be as disciplined and valuable as other business specialties. If HR advises other parts of the organization to focus on succession, it has to take its own advice. HR has to contribute commercially and want to improve organizational culture, but it is hard to lead change without producing measurable results. The future CHRO has to do both.

The new dynamic of HR leadership is that CHROs can have a place at the executive table; the bad news is that finding that leader who has the competence, behaviors, character, and style is hard to raise and difficult to find. If firms can promote complete candidates from within, they should. For talented leaders, the route to the C-suite in HR can be faster than in finance or in operations because too few complete executives are ready to head the function and contribute commercially.

But HR efficiencies and competitive advantage through talent strategies cannot be mixed up. Flawless payroll, benefits, and training and development could also be led by another function. Creating competitive advantage is harder, and it is the innovative necessity of future HR leaders. HR leaders who can master the science of their field, who possess the leadership traits that CEOs need, and who create business solutions through human capital are the leaders who will be hired from both within and outside a company.

Conclusion: Creating Value through Human Capital: The Journey Ahead

Patrick M. Wright, Dave Ulrich,
Richard L. Antoine, and Elizabeth "Libby" Sartain

This book highlights some of the leading thinking on how firms seek to create value through their human capital. Through bringing together chief human resource officers (CHROs), thought leaders, and researchers to share their insights on the CHRO role and the HR function, we show how they can help firms not only compete but gain a competitive advantage through their people and organizations. Some authors answer this question through frameworks, others through case studies, and others through research. However, across all the approaches, the focus remains on creating value through a firm's human capital.

At a molecular level these diverse approaches and stories may seem somewhat confusing. However, stepping back to a broader perspective, the various chapters can be summarized by a few integrating themes. We highlight these below.

The Only Constant Is Change

This phrase, while trite, remains true. The exponential change in technologies alone requires organizational responses. Retailers have moved from selling at brick and mortar stores to selling through the Internet, to now creating omni-channel capabilities allowing customers to seamlessly navigate a retailer's offerings via computer, mobile device, telephone, or physical presence. Recruiting has moved from accepting mailed-in resumes to accepting them online, to searching out passive applicants through social media sites such as LinkedIn. The pace of change has even increased, and no one expects that to end soon.

When the business strategy or business model changes, the CHRO and CEO need to examine and decide if changes to the culture or talent are required. If faster cycle decision-making is needed in a new product or service sector, the CHRO must lead the effort to change from a slower, more bureaucratic culture. If the strategy now has a new geographic component, then the CHRO needs to significantly change the talent sourcing approach.

We titled this chapter "The Journey Ahead" with this in mind. While all the frameworks, company stories, and research provide insights into how firms create value through people and organization today, we note that they differ from how firms accomplished this 20 years ago, and will differ from how firms will do so 20 years from now. This book provides a snapshot into a much longer movie and provides foundations from which future efforts will emerge.

Culture Eats Strategy for Lunch

To understand the relative importance of culture over strategy, one must first define culture. Traditional definitions of culture focus on patterns of thought and action inside an organization. Edward Schein offered one of the original definitions of organizational culture as "a pattern of shared basic assumptions learned by a group as it solved its problems of external adaptation and internal integration, which has worked well enough to be considered valid and, therefore, to be taught to new members as the correct way to perceive, think, and feel in relation to those problems." However, sociologist Daniel Bell defined culture through a societal lens, more broadly than within any specific organization as "the effort to provide a coherent set of answers to the existential situations that confront all human beings in the passage of their lives." This latter definition suggests that people, as social beings, seek both order and meaning in all aspects of their lives, including their work lives. Just as societal culture provides that in their non-work lives, organizational culture creates the stable guiding framework for their work lives. It helps them answer the existential questions of purpose of their organization as well as their purpose within it. Consistent with this societal view, we have defined culture as the identity of the firm in the mind of the key customers, made real to employees. This means that culture is not just any random pattern of activity, but activities that translate a firm's brand, reputation, or identity outside to employees inside.

Think back over your work experience. How many times has your organization changed its strategy? While firms may make revolutionary strategic changes somewhat infrequently, evolutionary changes happen constantly. For employees seeking a "North Star" to help them navigate their decisions and actions, a constant culture provides far better guidance than a constantly changing strategy.

This does not suggest that culture cannot or should not change. With an outside-in view of culture, culture inside a firm should change when the firm's external brand or identity changes. Changing the culture may mean helping people step back and reframe the questions for why the firm exists and why and how they can contribute to it because the culture inside reflects promises outside. Louis V. Gerstner, in his book *Who Says Elephants Can't Dance?*, told of the opposition he faced when he changed the IBM dress code. He noted that the blue suit, white shirt, red tie uniform was based in the cultural value of "dress like your customer." When IBM's customers were bankers, the uniform fulfilled the value. However, when the customers changed, the value was still right, but the operationalization of it had become misaligned. Thus, when IBM's customers evolved, it led to an evolution of the IBM firm brand and identity, which in turn required a new culture inside IBM.

When firms build cultures inside aligned to external identity outside, they provide meaning and motivation for employees to act the right way. Strategy simply provides ways for firms to make choices and allocate resources to steer their way through the competitive environment, but culture provides the necessary thrust to move them forward.

Talent Eats Strategy for Breakfast

If culture eats strategy for lunch, then talent eats it for breakfast. This is not to argue for the unimportance of strategy, but to recognize both its limitations and interdependencies. Regarding its limitations, little differentiation can be seen in terms of core strategy. Many retailers are simultaneously moving to an omni-channel strategy. Consultants sell new "strategies" to multiple companies. While differentiation still exists, much of strategy today seems to be more about "keeping up with the Joneses."

However, even where differentiation in strategy exists, its effectiveness depends on both culture and talent. If the strategy does not translate to customer expectations that lead to culture shifts, its execution ends up dead on arrival. And if the firm does not possess the talent required by the strategy, implementation will suffer.

More importantly, in today's competitive environment, talent often drives the strategy. A seasoned executive once told us, "If I pick the right person for the right job at the right time, I don't need to worry about strategy. But, if I pick the wrong person, the strategy will never be right." The corporate and business strategies emerge from CEO and business leaders respectively. The strategic opportunities often stem from the ideas and outputs of innovative scientists or software engineers. Thus, one cannot conceptualize of strategy absent the talent that created it, and as competition intensifies, firms with better or unique talent will continue to dominate.

Never Forget the "Human" in Human Resources

As the spotlight has increasingly focused on talent, usually meaning the leaders and innovators who drive disproportionate value for firms, many have lost sight of the rest of the employee base who may lack fame, but not importance. Training budgets shift toward the high-potential talent and away from everyone else. Those deemed top talent reap great monetary rewards, but the remaining employees continue with incrementally small opportunities to significantly increase their financial positions. From an economic standpoint, these trends makes sense. But from an organizational effectiveness standpoint, they may miss the mark.

Charles Plumb tells the story of being approached by a man at a coffee shop. The man asked if he was Charles Plumb, if he had flown jet fighters in Vietnam, if he had been shot down, and if he had parachuted behind enemy lines and served six years as a prisoner of war. Charles said yes, and asked how he knew all that. The man answered "because I packed your parachute." Plumb then ponders how he, as an officer or the "talent" probably paid no attention to the lowly sailor, yet his success, and even his life, ultimately depended on the skill and effort of this ignored man.

Similarly, some of the company stories presented in this book have taken a much broader view of talent to encompass the entire workforce and each member's contribution to firm success. While it is easy to get caught up in the C-suite issues and the focus on the high potentials, CHROs need always to remember the importance of the unsung heroes in firm success, that is, those who pack the parachutes.

People Are the Center of Competitive Advantage

Much attention has focused on how firms gain competitive advantage or sustainable competitive advantage. Competitive advantage stems from having resources or capabilities that customers value and that are rare within the competitive landscape, whereas sustainable competitive advantage exists when competitors cannot imitate those resources and capabilities.

Certainly technology and financial capital can only temporarily provide competitive advantages as technologies can be imitated or leap-frogged and financial capital readily flows to any good idea. What firms find difficult to imitate are all the aspects of the organization that include people and culture.

First, economists refer to human capital as the characteristics of people that can provide value to a firm, such as knowledge, skills, and abilities (KSAs). Every firm seeks to have "world-class" talent, but with all firms competing for the same skills, one may find it difficult to attract and retain a workforce that is superior to its competitors in terms of raw KSAs. However, just because an individual works for a company does not mean that he or she works most effectively for that company. If two people have the exact same skill set, but one possesses a significantly higher level of engagement, he or she will certainly contribute more to the firm's success. Additionally, often an individual's contribution depends on relationships with others, so firms that create opportunities to build relationships will outperform those that do not. Thus, the workforce (people) and the workplace (culture) are both key factors in overall human capital. Finally, firms that have people with good KSAs, who relate well with one another and who share beliefs and values about the firm's purpose and their purpose within it, will run on all cylinders. Building such a firm takes time, effort, and consistency, making it extremely difficult to attain. However, if attained, that workforce and workplace of human capital create value in a special way that competitors will find difficult to imitate, and thus the firm will possess a sustainable source of competitive advantage.

Opportunity Knocks: CHROs and
HR Functions Must Answer

All of us, at some point in our lives, have faced friends or relatives who complain about their situation—a bad marriage, a dead-end job, a dysfunctional relationship, and so on. However, more troubling are those in such situations who constantly complain yet never seem to do anything about it.

No longer does strategy seem the monolithic determinant of organizational success. Today culture and talent have moved to demand equal attention and equal investment. These areas exemplify the sweet spot for those in HR, places where we bring knowledge, expertise, and experiences far greater and deeper than other functions. Thus, the new demands of competition require firms to create value through their human capital. This creates a tremendous opportunity for CHROs and HR functions to leverage their expertise to make it happen, and therefore increase their value, reputation, and impact. The question is, will we seize it?

Index

Italic *f* and *t* appended to page numbers indicates *figures* and *tables*.

About the Editors

Richard L. Antoine is president of AO Consulting, a human resource consulting firm working with CEOs and chief HR officers on leadership, talent development, and HR strategy. He is the past president of the National Academy of Human Resources, the organization that recognizes outstanding and sustained excellence in human resources. Antoine retired from Procter & Gamble in 2008 after a 39-year career in supply chain and HR—most recently after 10 years as P&G's global HR officer reporting to the CEO, A. G. Lafley. During his P&G career, Antoine lived in several U.S. locations and in Kobe, Japan.

Antoine is the chair of the board of the University of Wisconsin Foundation and serves on the boards of Northlich Advertising and IRC (Industrial Resources Counselors). He is also on the advisory boards for the University of Wisconsin College of Engineering and the Center for Brand and Product Management. He was elected a fellow in the National Academy of Human Resources and is a member of two professional HR organizations (PRT and HRPI). Antoine has a chemical engineering degree from the University of Wisconsin and an MBA from the University of Chicago.

Antoine has a wife of 44 years and a daughter in the NYU School of Medicine's Ph.D. program. He and his wife live in Longboat Key, Florida.

Elizabeth "Libby" Sartain, SHRM-SCP, SPHR, is now an active business advisor and board member after a distinguished 30-year career in human resources.

As CHRO of both Yahoo Inc. and Southwest Airlines, Sartain led significant business transformation initiatives as a member of executive leadership teams and guided global human resource efforts focusing on attracting, retaining, and developing employees. Her focus has been growth companies where she developed employment brand strategies that helped grow the workforce exponentially while establishing company reputation as a leading employer of choice. Both Yahoo and Southwest were listed on the *Fortune* 100 Best Companies To Work For in the United States and the *Fortune* 500 during her tenure.

Sartain serves on the boards of directors of ManpowerGroup and AARP. She was a director of Peet's Coffee & Tea, Inc., from 2005 to 2012. She is on the board of the SHRM Foundation and is a trustee for the National Academy of Human Resources Foundation. She advises several start-ups and *Fortune* 500 organizations on HR, employer branding, and talent management.

Sartain served as chairman of the board of the Society for Human Resource Management (SHRM) in 2001 and was named a fellow of the National Academy of Human Resources in 1998. *Human Resource Executive* magazine named her as one of the 25 most powerful women in HR in 2005.

She holds an MBA from the University of North Texas and a BBA from Southern Methodist University.

Sartain co-authored *HR from the Heart: Inspiring Stories and Strategies for Building the People Side of Great Business* (AMACOM), *Brand from the Inside: Eight Essentials to Emotionally Connect Your Employees to Your Business* (Jossey-Bass), and *Brand for Talent: Eight Essentials to Make Your Talent as Famous as Your Brand* (Jossey-Bass). She contributed to and edited *The Chief HR Officer: Defining the New Role of Human Resource Leaders.* Recent e-books include *Cracking the Culture Code* with Brent Daily and *The Rise of HR: Wisdom from 73 Thought Leaders* with Dave Ulrich and William Schiemann. She is a frequent speaker and is often quoted as a thought leader in human resources in the business media.

Ranked as the #1 management guru by *BusinessWeek*, profiled by *Fast Company* as one of the world's top 10 creative business thinkers, and recognized on Thinker's 50 as one of the world's leading business thinkers, **Dave Ulrich** has a passion for ideas with impact. In his writing, teaching, and consulting, he continually seeks new ideas that tackle some of the world's thorniest and longest-standing challenges.

His bestselling books and popular speeches set the corporate agenda. He has influenced thinking about organizations by defining organizations as bundles of capabilities (in *Organizational Capability*) and worked to delineate capabilities of learning (in *Organizational Learning Capability*), collaboration (in *Boundaryless Organization*), talent management (in *The Why of Work*), and culture change (in *GE Work-Out*). His work has articulated the basics of effective leadership (in *The Leadership Code*), connected leadership with customers (in *Leadership Brand*), and synthesized how to ensure that leadership aspirations turn into actions (in *Leadership Sustainability*). He has shaped the HR profession and been called the "father of modern HR" by focusing on HR outcomes, governance, competencies, and practices (in *HR Champions, Value Added, Transformation, Competencies*, and *HR from the Outside In*).

Ulrich's current work on *Leadership Capital Index* (Berrett Koehler, September 2015) creates a "Moody's index" for leadership. This work shows the impact of leadership on market value and helps not only internal leaders to become more competent but investors to rigorously measure leadership to realize a firm's full market value.

He is the Rensis Likert professor of business at the University of Michigan and co-founder of the RBL Group (www.rbl.net). From this body of work, he has received numerous profiles, accolades, and lifetime honors. Passionate about learning and perennially curious, Ulrich is one of the most in-demand business speakers worldwide. So far, he has worked in 87 countries.

He gives back to the profession and others, having served as editor of *Human Resource Management* for 10 years and donated time to the *Rise of HR*, an anthology focused on what is next for HR professionals. He works as a trustee and advisor to universities and other professional groups. At the peak of their careers, he and his wife took a three-year sabbatical to run a mission for their church.

The Ulrichs have three children and seven grandchildren, and derive their greatest glee when their grandkids' eyes light up at seeing them, when they want them to read a book, or when they simply go on a walk together.

Patrick M. Wright is Thomas C. Vandiver bicentennial chair in the Darla Moore School of Business at the University of South Carolina. Prior to joining USC he served on the faculties at Cornell University, Texas A&M University, and the University of Notre Dame.

Wright teaches, conducts research, and consults in the area of strategic human resource management, particularly focusing on how firms use people as a source of competitive advantage and on the changing nature of the chief HR officer role. He has published over 60 research articles in journals and over 20 chapters in books and edited volumes, and has co-authored two textbooks and two books on HR practice. He is the Editor at *Journal of Management*.

He has conducted programs and consulted for a number of large organizations. He currently serves as a member on the board of directors for the Society for Human Resource Management (SHRM) and the National Academy of Human Resources (NAHR) and is a former board member of HRPS, the SHRM Foundation, and WorldatWork (formerly the American Compensation Association). From 2011 to 2016 he was named by *HRM Magazine* as one of the 20 Most Influential Thought Leaders in HR. In 2014 he received SHRM's Michael R. Losey Human Resource Research Award.

About the Contributors

Marcia J. Avedon is senior vice president of human resources, communications, and corporate affairs at Ingersoll Rand and a member of the company's enterprise leadership team. She has global responsibility for all aspects of human resources and also oversees the company's corporate communications, branding, government affairs, and community relations practices. Under Avedon's leadership, Ingersoll Rand was recognized as the No. 1 Industrial Machinery company on *Fortune*'s Most Admired Companies list, designated one of the Best Companies for Leaders by *Chief Executive* magazine, and named to the *Workforce* 100, a listing of the world's top companies for human resources.

Prior to joining Ingersoll Rand, Avedon was chief human resources officer at Merck & Co., with global responsibility for human resource strategies, programs, and policies. Before her post at Merck, Avedon held a variety of leadership roles in human resources and communications at Honeywell, and also worked in human resources at Anheuser-Busch Companies. She began her career as a management consultant with Booz Allen Hamilton.

Avedon is a recognized expert in talent management, succession planning, executive compensation, change management, and leadership strategy. She serves on a number of professional, community, and academic organizations, where she contributes time and expertise to help shape the future of human resources, leadership effectiveness, and workforce development. Avedon is a member of the boards of directors for the Center for Creative Leadership, the HR Policy Association, and the Cornell University Center for Advanced Human Resources Studies. She is the inaugural chair of the University of South Carolina's Center for Executive Succession and serves on the board of directors for GCP Applied Technologies.

Avedon was recently named to the HR Honor Roll and recognized as one of the Most Powerful Women in Human Resources by *HR Executive* magazine, and in 2013 was elected a fellow by the National Academy of Human Resources. She holds a bachelor's degree in psychology from the University of North Carolina at Wilmington, and a master's degree and a Ph.D. in industrial and organizational psychology from George Washington University.

Based in New York, **James M. Bagley** has been with Russell Reynolds Associates for more than 25 years. He is currently the global head of the firm's HR practice, leading engagements for clients across all industries and geographies. He focuses on chief human resource officers and other senior human capital and talent management leadership roles at the world's most successful organizations in industrial, consumer, technology, financial services, health care, and the non-profit sector. Bagley previously co-managed the firm's New York office and led the global corporate officers sector.

Prior to rejoining Russell Reynolds Associates in 1998, Bagley was the senior vice president, human resources, at MasterCard International, where he had global responsibility for the firm's comprehensive human resources activities. Bagley was recruited to MasterCard from Russell Reynolds Associates, where he joined the firm in 1984 as the director of human resources. Earlier Bagley was a benefits and compensation consultant with Alexander & Alexander Services, Inc., and worked with State Mutual Life Insurance Company.

Bagley contributed to the book, *The Chief HR Officer: Defining the New Role of Human Resource Leaders*, which was spearheaded by the National Academy of Human Resources and published as part of a series focused on senior business leadership by John Wiley & Sons, Inc. In addition, Bagley has led research focusing on the experiences and behaviors that contribute to success in the CHRO role.

Bagley received his B.A. from Fordham University.

Wayne Brockbank is a clinical professor of business at the University of Michigan's Ross School of Business. At the Ross School of Business, Brockbank is a co-faculty director and core instructor of the Advanced Human Resource Executive Program. He is also the director of strategic HR executive programs in India and the United Arab Emirates. Over the past 20 years, these executive programs have been consistently rated as the best HR executive programs in the United States and Europe by the *Wall Street Journal, Business Week,* and *Leadership Excellence.* He has been on the visiting faculty at universities in Saudi Arabia, Kuwait, Australia, China, Indonesia, Hungary, United Kingdom, the Netherlands, India, Korea, and the Czech Republic. In 2013 he was acknowledged as one of the top 20 global HR thinkers by *HR Most Influential.*

His research and consulting focus on (1) linkages between business strategy and human resource practices, (2) creating high-performance corporate cultures, and (3) key levers that drive business performance. He has published seven books (with colleagues) on these topics and numerous articles in the *Annual Review of Business Strategy, Human Resource Management Journal, Harvard Business Review, Human Resource Planning,* and *Personnel Administrator* and has contributed numerous book chapters. In 1990, 1995, and 2000, he received the best paper of the year award from the Society for Human Resource Management and the Human Resource Planning Society.

Brockbank has consulted in these areas with major corporations on every continent. Among his clients have been General Electric, BAE Systems, Cathay Pacific Airways, Unilever, Harley-Davidson, Citigroup, Shell, Lafarge, Wyeth, Microsoft, IBM, Tata Group, Handelsblatt, ICICI Bank, Perez Companc, Sony-Ericsson, Cisco, Godrej Group, Rolls Royce, Walt Disney Corporation, General Motors, Boston Scientific, Saudi Aramco, Texas Instruments, Exxon-Mobil, Wal-Mart, JP Morgan, and Hewlett-Packard. He has served on the board of directors for the Society for Human Resource Management and the Human Resource Planning Society.

Michele Aguilar "Shelly" Carlin is executive vice president of the HR Policy Association and its Center on Executive Compensation. Carlin joined the association in August 2014 from Motorola Solutions, where she was senior vice president (SVP), human resources and communications.

During her tenure at Motorola, Carlin led the HR function through a period of substantial change, from the spin-off of its consumer cellphone business to a major transformation of how HR services are delivered. She also implemented the CEO Leadership Forum, a business-driven learning program for the company's top 20 high-potential executives.

Prior to serving as the head of HR, Carlin was corporate vice president (VP), global rewards. Before joining Motorola in 2008, she was VP of compensation, benefits, and HR technology for the Campbell Soup Company. Carlin's earlier positions included VP, HR rewards and operations, for TIAA-CREF; VP of compensation and benefits for Sears, Roebuck and Co.; and SVP of executive compensation and corporate unit reporting for Bcom3 Group, Inc.

Carlin currently serves as vice chair of the board of directors for Skills for Chicagoland's Future, an initiative to match local employers with qualified unemployed job seekers in the Chicago metro area. She earned a BA and MBA from the University of California, Los Angeles (UCLA), and was an Academic All-American in softball and a member of UCLA's 1982 NCAA National Championship team.

Kenneth J. Carrig is corporate executive vice president and chief human resources officer for SunTrust Banks, Inc. In this role, he oversees human resource strategy, talent management, employee benefits, compensation, staffing, human resource systems, operations and payroll, compliance, employee relations, and human resource policies, as well as training and development.

Prior to joining SunTrust in June 2011, Carrig was executive vice president of human resources for Comcast. He previously held similar roles with Sysco Corporation and Continental Airlines during his 30-year human resource career.

Carrig earned his undergraduate degree in labor economics from Cornell University and participated in leadership development education and training at Columbia University and Yale University. He is a member of the advisory board of the Cornell Center for Advanced Human Resource Studies, a fellow of the National Academy of Human Resources (2004), and was named the Academy of Management Distinguished Human Resources Executive (2010). He is also a member of the advisory board of PearlHPS, a predictive execution analytics software company. He also serves on the board of Operation HOPE and the Atlanta Botanical Garden.

In 2006, Carrig co-authored the book *Building Profit Through Building People*, the proceeds of which benefit Share Our Strength, an organization dedicated to fighting childhood hunger.

Debra J. Cohen, Ph.D., SHRM-SCP, is a speaker, author, and senior advisor to organizations, nonprofits, and academic organizations. With more than 25 years of experience, she brings her practical, results-oriented approach to projects and provides leadership and insight to her clients. Cohen is a noted speaker and has a strong track record of performance in knowledge and content development in higher education and association management. As a former senior vice president with the Society for Human Resource Management (SHRM), she was responsible for the Society's Knowledge Division, where she oversaw the HR Knowledge Center, Research Department, Academic Initiatives, and the development of SHRM's comprehensive Competency Model. Cohen spent nearly 16 years with SHRM and started as the director of research.

Prior to joining SHRM, Cohen spent 15 years as an academician teaching HRM at George Washington University (10 years) and George Mason University (5 years). She has published over 50 articles and book chapters and has been published in such journals as *Academy of Management Journal, Personnel Psychology, Human Resource Development Quarterly, Journal of Management, Human Resource Management, Journal of Small Business Strategy, Journal of Business and Psychology, Training and Development Journal, Journal of Management Education* and the *Journal of Business Ethics.* She is a co-editor for a book titled *Developing and Enhancing Teamwork in Organizations: Evidence-based Best Practices and Guidelines* (2013) and co-author of the book *Defining HR Success: 9 Critical Competencies for HR Professionals* (2015). Her latest book, *Developing Proficiency in HR: 7 Self-Directed Learning Activities for HR Professionals (2016),* is sole-authored, and Cohen is delivering talks and professional development highlighting the key points.

Cohen received her Ph.D. in management and human resources and her Master's Degree in labor and human resources from The Ohio State University. She received her Bachelor of Science (in communications) from

Ohio University. She is a frequent presenter at both national and regional conferences and has spoken to a wide variety of audiences. Prior to her academic career, she was a practicing human resources manager (in training and development).

James Duffy has been an HR practitioner for nearly 40 years. He has significant experience in multiple sectors of the economy, primarily industrial and financial services. Duffy is currently the chief human resource officer (CHRO) for Ally Financial, Inc., a leading automotive financial services company powered by a top online banking franchise. Previously Duffy was the CHRO for CIT, Inc. During his career he has worked for General Electric, Citigroup, AlliedSignal, and Ingersoll-Rand. He received a BS in industrial and labor relations from Cornell University.

Debra L. Exstrom is managing director for HR strategic transformation and global delivery at Accenture. In this role she is responsible for Accenture's talent forecasting and planning, supply-demand management, and scheduling process/technology design, as well as manages operational targets across the business and geographies to drive desired business outcomes. Prior to her work in HR, Exstrom worked with clients primarily in the utilities and financial services industries.

Rich Floersch, recently retired as McDonald's executive vice president and chief human resource officer. While in that position he oversaw McDonald's HR function for its 400,000 company employees in 118 countries. As a member of the senior management team, he was responsible for the company's talent management, leadership development, rewards, and employment branding programs.

At McDonald's, over the past 10 years, Floersch has helped execute four CEO transitions, worked on overhauling all of the company's reward programs to ensure pay for performance and sound governance practices, and provided strategic direction to new talent management and leadership development programs.

In 2003, Floersch joined McDonald's from Kraft Foods International, where he had served as senior vice president of human resources for five years.

Prior to this post, he was vice president of corporate compensation at Philip Morris.

Floersch is vice chairman for the HR Policy Association, a public policy advocacy organization representing the chief human resource officers (CHROs) from more than 350 leading employers across the U.S., where he chairs the association's Center on Executive Compensation. He is also on the executive committee of the Personnel Roundtable, a group of CHROs from over 50 leading companies.

In 2008, he became the fifth recipient of the Hunt-Scanlon Advisors' HR Leadership Award and was also named by *Human Resource Executive* to its Honor Roll.

In 2009, Floersch was inducted into the National Academy of Human Resources (NAHR).

Floersch earned his bachelor's and master's degrees in business administration from the State University of New York at Buffalo. He enjoys traveling back to Buffalo to meet with UB's business students, faculty, and the dean.

Floersch lives in the Chicago area with his four children.

Mirian Graddick-Weir is executive vice president, human resources, at Merck, with responsibility for all aspects of human resources for 68,000 colleagues located in over 90 countries. Graddick-Weir joined Merck in 2006 from AT&T, where she was executive vice president of human resources and employee communications for five years. Prior to that role, she spent 20 years at AT&T holding numerous positions in HR and several operational roles.

Among her many awards, Graddick-Weir received the Distinguished Psychologist in Management award in 2003, the HR Executive of the Year in 2001, and the AT&T Catherine B. Cleary Woman of the Year award in 1990. Graddick-Weir was also awarded the Lifetime Achievement Award by the University of Michigan in 2012, and she received the 2014 Academy of Management's Distinguished HR Executive Award. Most recently, in 2015 she was named by *Black Enterprise* as one of the 50 Most Powerful Women, and she was recognized by *Human Resource Executive* as one of the 15 most influential women leading HR.

She is a member of the board of Yum! Brands, Inc., the Human Resources Policy Association (chair), and the Cornell Center for Advanced Human Resource Studies (CAHRS). She is also a fellow of the National Academy of Human Resources (NAHR) and a senior advisor to the Jersey Battered Women's Services (JBWS).

Graddick-Weir earned a bachelor's degree in psychology from Hampton University and a master's degree and a Ph.D. in industrial/organizational psychology from Pennsylvania State University.

Edward E. Lawler III is distinguished professor of business in the management and organization department of the Marshall School of Business at the University of Southern California. He is also director of the school's Center for Effective Organizations.

After receiving his Ph.D. from the University of California, Berkeley in 1964, Lawler joined the faculty of Yale University as assistant professor of industrial administration and psychology. Three years later he was promoted to associate professor.

Lawler moved to the University of Michigan in 1972, as professor of psychology and also became a program director in the Survey Research Center at the Institute for Social Research. He held a Fulbright Fellowship at the London Graduate School of Business. In 1978, he became a professor in the Marshall School of Business at the University of Southern California. During 1979, he founded and became the director of the university's Center for Effective Organizations. In 1982, he was named professor of research at the University of Southern California. In 1999, he was named distinguished professor of business.

Lawler has been honored as a major contributor to theory, research, and practice in the fields of human resource management, compensation, organizational development, and organizational effectiveness. He is the author and co-author of over 500 articles and 50 books. His books include *Rewarding Excellence* (Jossey-Bass), *Corporate Boards: New Strategies for Adding Value at the Top* (Jossey-Bass), *Organizing for High Performance* (Jossey-Bass), *Treat People Right* (Jossey-Bass), *Human Resources Business Process Outsourcing* (Jossey-Bass), *Built to Change* (Jossey-Bass), *The New American Workplace* (Palgrave-Macmillan), *America at Work* (Palgrave-Macmillan), *Talent: Making People Your Competitive Advantage* (Jossey-Bass), *Useful Research: Advancing Theory and Practice*

(Berrett-Koehler), *Management Reset: Organizing for Sustainable Effectiveness* (Jossey-Bass), *Effective Human Resource Management: A Global Analysis* (Stanford University Press), *The Agility Factor* (Jossey-Bass), and *Global Trends in Human Resource Management: A Twenty-Year Analysis* (Stanford University Press).

For more information, visit http://www.edwardlawler.com and http://ceo.usc.edu.

Anthony J. Nyberg is an associate professor at the Moore School of Business at the University of South Carolina, where he teaches courses in negotiations, compensation, and strategic human resources. Nyberg's research focuses on human capital, primarily within strategic human resource management with emphases on performance, compensation, employee movement, and international human resources.

Nyberg's work has been published in *The Academy of Management Journal, The Academy of Management Review, Journal of Applied Psychology, Journal of Management*, and *Harvard Business Review*, among others. He serves on the editorial board of *The Academy of Management Journal, The Journal of Applied Psychology*, and the *Journal of Management*. Nyberg has received numerous awards for his teaching and research, including awards for best dissertation and best published manuscript, and has been selected as a featured scholar and a Breakthrough Rising Star by the University of South Carolina. His research has been highlighted in major international media outlets, including *Business Week, Time*, National Public Radio, *US News & World Report, Harvard Business Review*, and CNBC.

Nyberg received his doctorate in management and human resources from the University of Wisconsin-Madison. Prior to that he received an MBA from Tulane University, where he focused on accounting and marketing and later earned his Certified Financial Analyst designation. He holds a Bachelor of Arts in philosophy and mathematics from St. John's College in Annapolis, Maryland. Prior to earning his Ph.D., Nyberg served for nine years as the managing partner for an international financial services firm based in Northern California, where he held Series 7, 24, 55, and 63 licenses. During that time he was also a licensed mediator and served as an arbitrator for the National Association of Securities Dealers.

Aki Onozuka-Evans, principal, AOSIS Consulting, LLC, is a management consultant with over 15 years of experience on national and international strategic planning and execution. She is deeply committed to identifying growth opportunities at both the corporate and business unit levels and facilitating the development and implementation of strategic plans to drive results. During her career at Monitor Group and BearingPoint, she managed various multidimensional project initiatives by promoting a holistic approach, with accurate and timely implementation to ensure meeting critical milestones.

Onozuka-Evans has participated in a broad range of industry engagements, including finance and banking, retail and distribution, and IT. She possesses an exceptional ability to analyze the industry structure and competitive landscapes to identify emerging trends and potential future challenges. She is also an expert in assessing business processes, identifying transformational opportunities, and leading change management processes. Her past clients include SunTrust, Oracle, H.E.B., Merck, Goldman Sachs, LG, Hitachi, and NTT Data. Key projects include corporate growth strategy, new market entry, organizational capability analysis, business process re-engineering (BRM), marketing management, data analytics/monetization, and change management.

Onozuka-Evans earned her MBA from the McDonough School of Business at Georgetown University and her BA in international relations and economics at American University.

Robert E. Ployhart is the Bank of America professor in business administration at the University of South Carolina's Darla Moore School of Business. He received his Ph.D. in industrial/organizational psychology from Michigan State University. He is an internationally known expert in human resources, with expertise relating to the acquisition, development, and maintenance of human capital. His more specific areas of focus are with recruitment, personnel selection, staffing-related legal issues, employee and leadership development, and organizational strategy.

Ployhart has published over 100 scientific articles and chapters. He holds two copyrights and has written two books (*Staffing Organizations* and *Situational Judgment Tests*). He has served as an associate editor on three leading scientific journals relating to human resources and organizational psychology. Ployhart has received many awards, and is a fellow of the American Psychological Association, the Association for Psychological Science, and the Society for Industrial and Organizational Psychology.

Ployhart has worked with private and public organizations ranging in size from a few employees to several hundred thousand. Representative organizations include Sonoco, URS/GMOS, Wells Fargo, Wachovia, Bank of America, Ford Motor Company, Rockwell-Collins, Kenexa, Skill-Survey, CPS, Grubb & Ellis, Denso Manufacturing, Time Warner Cable, the Equal Employment Opportunity Commission, the Army Research Institute, Walter Reed Army Institute of Research, and the Office of Personnel Management. With these organizations, Ployhart has developed job analyses, selection, and psychological assessments (for example, written and online tests, assessment and development centers, interview methods, simulations), recruiting strategies, culture and climate surveys, leadership programs, performance management processes, training programs, and statistical/legal support. He has also consulted and advised organizations on human resource policy and strategy.

Gina Qiao is senior vice president, human resources, Lenovo, and an author and speaker.

Known for her wit and humility, Qiao is a powerful role model for female executives striving for excellence in their respective fields. She is the eighth-highest-ranking female executive in China according to *Fortune China*, and, in many ways, her steady climb from secretary to C-suite of the largest personal computer-seller in the world reflects the extraordinary growth story of both China and Lenovo.

Qiao's recent book, *The Lenovo Way: Managing a Diverse Global Company for Optimal Performance*, provides a business guide for companies seeking to compete globally. It reveals the challenges behind the Lenovo strategy for going global and how the company overcame them during its acquisition of the IBM PC division and its iconic ThinkPad product line in 2005.

Qiao started her Lenovo career as a secretary in 1990 and rose steadily through the corporate ranks to her current position as senior vice president of human resources, which she has held since 2011. In

The Lenovo Way, Qiao and her co-author, Yolanda Conyers, share their stories. Together, the authors provide an engaging, insightful how-to guide for other companies looking to capture global markets by harnessing culture and diversity as core strengths. Lenovo has used this strategy to grow from a $3 billion China-based company to a $39 billion global technology powerhouse that sells PCs, tablets, smartphones, and other innovative devices in more than 100 countries around the world.

In her current position, Qiao is responsible for Lenovo's human resource strategy, including talent acquisition; building a diverse global culture; and ensuring the company has the required organizational structures, human resources, policies, practices, and programs to execute its business strategy and achieve its vision and aspirations. Previously, Qiao held various leadership roles in marketing, corporate strategy, and planning.

As leader of the computer giant's human resource function, Qiao directs the organizational development, global talent, compensation, and benefits of more than 60,000 employees across 60 countries. Her role involves nurturing a corporate culture that is so diverse that six different nationalities are represented on Lenovo's executive committee, and the company's top 100 executives include men and women from 20 nations.

Qiao holds a bachelor's degree in management science from Fudan University and an executive MBA from China Europe International Business School (CEIBS). She is also a 2012 graduate of the University of Michigan, where she completed advanced human resource executive training.

Qiao is married, has one daughter, and lives in Beijing.

Joe Ruocco is the former chief human resources officer for The Goodyear Tire and Rubber Company, a position he held for seven years following a long and successful career with GE. In 2015, Ruocco established Ruocco Consulting LLC, where he partners with and advises CEOs, CHROs and other business leaders in all aspects of human resources strategies and tactics to drive business success.

He serves as senior advisor to CamberView Partners, a leading source of independent, investor-led advice for management teams and boards of public companies on how to succeed with investors. He also is on the Advisory Board of Bright Funds, a venture-backed technology company that provides a cloud-based, intuitive platform for employees to execute high-impact charitable giving. Additionally, he is an advisor to principal investment firm Bay Grove Capital and to Lineage Logistics, a fast growing, industry leader in warehousing and logistics.

Ruocco spent 23 years at GE in progressively larger HR leadership positions. He was elected a GE Officer in 2002. His last role with GE was as the vice president of Human Resources for GE's Industrial Business.

In 2008, he was elected an officer and senior vice president of Human Resources for Goodyear, a position he held until 2015. Under his leadership at Goodyear, the percentage of "ready-now successors" for the top positions at the company more than tripled as a direct result of the implementation and execution of a world-class Global Talent Management and Leadership Development process leading to the recognition of Goodyear on AON Hewitt's 2014 list of Top Companies for Leaders. Additionally, Ruocco and the Goodyear team negotiated ground breaking and unprecedented labor agreements with the USW, which were game changers for the company.

Ruocco was elected a Fellow to the National Academy of Human Resources in 2011. He also served on the board of Cornell's Center for Advanced Human Resources Studies (CAHRS) and continues as an instructor at Cornell and at the University of South Carolina. He was a member of the HR Policy Association (HRPA) and continues as a special contributor to HRPA. He holds a BS degree from Cornell University's School of Industrial and Labor Relations and an MBA from Syracuse University.

Eva Sage-Gavin is a board director and senior advisor with broad experience in top human resources leadership roles at *Fortune* 500 global consumer, technology and retail corporations, including Gap Inc., Sun Microsystems, PepsiCo, Disney Consumer Products, and Xerox.

Sage-Gavin is a public board director for BroadSoft, a global unified communications software service provider, and for TalentSky, a private professional skills networking company. She was also the first female elected to the board of directors of Sapient Inc. in 2013, a digital and technology marketing firm, and served on its compensation committee through the firm's successful acquisition by Publicis in 2015.

Sage-Gavin currently serves as a BCG senior advisor focused on the consumer, technology and media, and public-sector practice areas. She also serves as a senior advisor for the G100 Network and Talent Consortium. Sage-Gavin is the former vice chair of the Aspen Institute's Skills for America's Future Advisory Board and member of the UpSkill America Coalition, working with public and private partnerships to build skilled workforces.

Previously, she was executive vice president, global human resources and corporate affairs, at Gap Inc., responsible for the company's internal and external communications, government and public affairs, social and environmental responsibility, and foundation, as well as for serving as chief people officer for over 136,000 employees worldwide. Sage-Gavin was an executive leadership team member at Gap Inc. for more than 10 years, reporting to three consecutive CEOs. Previously, she worked at Sun Microsystems and Disney Consumer Products as senior vice president, human resources. In addition, she has served in various senior human resource leadership positions for the PepsiCo Corporation, including its Taco Bell division, and for Xerox Corporation.

In 2012, Cornell University honored Sage-Gavin with the prestigious Groat Award for her accomplishments and outstanding service to the College of Industrial and Labor Relations. In 2005, *HR Executive* magazine recognized Sage-Gavin as one of the 25 most influential and prominent women leading human resource organizations. In 2006, she received the distinguished honor of Fellow from the National Academy of Human Resources in recognition of her lifelong professional achievements. In 2013 she became a member of Women Corporate Directors and in 2014 joined the International Women's Forum and serves on the membership committee.

Sage-Gavin served as past chairman of the Cornell Center for Advanced Human Resources Studies board and is an emeritus member of the President's Council of Cornell Women and the University of Southern California's Center for Effective Organizations. She previously served as an executive committee member of the HR Policy Association Board and chaired its Workforce Development Committee. She is the inaugural executive-in-residence at the Cornell Industrial and Labor Relations school and continues as a Cornell Silicon Valley Advisor. Sage-Gavin is also a guest lecturer at Stanford, the Massachusetts Institute of Technology, and the University of Southern California and is the newly appointed executive-in-residence for Santa Clara University's Initiative on Women's Economic Empowerment, partnering with the Leavey School of Business and the Miller Center for Social Entrepreneurship.

Sage-Gavin holds a bachelor's degree in industrial and labor relations from Cornell University.

Donald J. "DJ" Schepker is an assistant professor of strategic management in the Darla Moore School of Business at the University of South Carolina and is a faculty member in the Center for Executive Succession. His research has appeared in outlets such as the *Journal of Management* and the *Corporate Reputation Review* and focuses on corporate governance, executive succession and turnover, and board-level decision-making.

Schepker received his Ph.D. from the University of Kansas and B.S. from Babson College. Prior to completing his Ph.D., Schepker worked in the internal audit services advisory practice at PricewaterhouseCoopers based out of the Boston office, assisting a variety of publicly traded organizations and institutions of higher education.

Matthew W. Schuyler is chief human resources officer for Hilton Worldwide. Schuyler joined Hilton Worldwide in 2009 and leads the human resources, communications, corporate responsibility, and supply management organizations from the company's global headquarters in McLean, Virginia. As a member of the company's Executive Committee, Schuyler is responsible for all aspects of the company's human capital strategy globally.

Prior to Hilton Worldwide, Schuyler served as Chief Human Resources Officer at Capital One Financial Corporation. He has previously held prominent positions such as Senior Vice President of human resources at Cisco Systems, Inc., and as a Partner with PricewaterhouseCoopers.

Schuyler holds an MBA from the University of Michigan and a Bachelor's degree in business from Pennsylvania State University. He currently serves on the national board for the Make-A-Wish Foundation and is a member of the Board of Trustees at Penn State.

Jill B. Smart is president of the National Academy of Human Resources, a director at Alexander Man Solutions, EPAM Systems and the University of Illinois and an HR consultant. For the last 10 years of her 33-year career at Accenture, she was Accenture's chief human resources officer, with overall responsibility for the full employee lifecycle of all Accenture people globally—including resource planning, recruitment, onboarding, training and development, staffing and deployment, performance management, engagement and retention, succession planning, and transitions. Smart is a Fellow in the National Academy of HR and the HR Policy Institute, a member of the G100 Talent Consortium Advisory Board, a past director of the HR Policy Association, and a past member of the executive committee of the Personnel Roundtable.

Scott A. Snell is professor of business administration and senior associate dean for executive education at the University of Virginia's Darden Graduate School of Business. He teaches courses in leadership and strategic management and works with management teams on aligning their human resource investments to better enable strategy execution. Snell is the author of four books and was recently listed among the top 100 most-cited authors in scholarly journals of management. He has served on the boards of the Strategic Management Society's human capital group, the SHRM Foundation, the Academy of Management's human resource division, the *Academy of Management Journal*, and the *Academy of Management Review*.

Prior to joining the Darden faculty in 2007, Snell was professor and director of executive education at Cornell University's Center for Advanced Human Resource Studies and a professor of management in the Smeal College of Business at Pennsylvania State University. He received a B.A. from Miami University, as well as an M.B.A. and Ph.D. in business from Michigan State University.

Susan M. Suver is an experienced human resource and communications executive specializing in human capital strategy, CEO and executive succession, business transformation, organizational change, talent management, and corporate communications. Suver has more than 17 years' experience as a corporate communications executive and 18 years' experience in organizational development and human resource management in a variety of global sectors, including automotive, mining, manufacturing, supply chain management, and hospitality.

Currently, Suver serves as senior vice president and chief human resources officer for Delphi Automotive PLC. She previously held the roles of senior vice president—human resources and administration for United States Steel Corporation; vice president, global human resources for Arrow Electronics, Inc.; and vice president, organizational effectiveness and communications for Phelps Dodge Corporation. Earlier in her career, she served in a variety of public relations and communications management roles at Canadian Pacific/Doubletree Hotels, Ramada International Hotels & Resorts, and Best Western International, Inc.

Suver holds a bachelor's degree in communications from Arizona State University and attended the Global Executive Management Program at the Thunderbird Graduate School of International Management, and the Advanced Executive Human Resources Program at the University of Michigan.

Suver is a fellow in the National Academy of Human Resources and serves on the board of directors of the HR Policy Association. She speaks regularly on the topics of executive succession, organizational change, and talent strategy.

Mara Swan was appointed ManpowerGroup's executive vice president, global strategy and talent, in January 2009. In February 2014, Swan also assumed global brand leadership for the Right Management business. Since joining the company as senior vice president, global human resources, in 2005, Swan has had a significant impact shaping business strategy and talent development.

A recognized expert in human resources, Swan is regularly featured as a speaker at high-profile events, including the annual meeting of the World Economic Forum in Davos, and is vice chair of the World Economic Forum Global Agenda Council on Gender Parity. She sits on the executive committees of the Personnel Roundtable and the HR Policy Association, where she also currently leads the association's Talent Sustainability Initiative.

Swan is on the board of GOJO Industries Inc., and became a fellow of the National Academy of Human Resources (NAHR) in 2012. She is compensation committee chairman of the Boys & Girls Clubs of Greater Milwaukee and a member of the University at Buffalo School of Management Dean's Advisory Council, and she sits on the advisory board of the Alverno College School of Business. In recognition of her success, she was recently named one of the 15 Most Powerful Women in HR by *Human Resource Executive* magazine. The same publication named her HR Executive of the Year in 2012.

A veteran of the human resource profession, Swan joined ManpowerGroup from the Molson Coors Brewing Company, where she served as chief people officer for its global operations. Swan holds a bachelor's degree in business administration from the University at Buffalo and a master's degree in industrial relations from the University of Minnesota.

Michael Ulrich is co-director of the Human Resource Competency Study, the world's largest study of HR competencies. He is also a Ph.D. candidate at the University of South Carolina's Moore School of Business, where he studies international human resources. He has published in numerous journals and books, focusing on the strategic role of HR. Prior to starting his doctoral program, he was a research associate with the RBL Group. He holds a master's degree in statistics from Brigham Young University.

Judy Zagorski is senior vice president of human resources for BASF Corporation, where she is a member of the company's Executive Committee and is responsible for all HR functions in North America including performance management; compensation and benefits; talent management and succession planning; employee, leadership and organizational development; diversity and inclusion; and labor relations. Under her leadership, BASF Corporation has attained ranking on the *Forbes* list of America's Best Employers, been named to the *Workforce* 100 ranking of the world's top companies for human resources, and earned inclusion as one of the Top 50 Companies for Diversity by *DiversityInc*. She has extensive experience with HR strategy, business transformation and culture change in the consumer goods, industrial/commercial, and professional services industries.

Previously, Zagorski was vice president of human resources for Mars Inc. worldwide. Prior business experience includes global HR leadership roles at Mars, Honeywell, and the management consulting practice at KPMG. Zagorski's educational background includes a degree from Gettysburg College. She is a member of the board of directors of the BASF Foundation and is a member of the Hackett Advisory Council, the HR 50, HR People + Strategy, and the Society for Human Resource Management. She presents frequently at The Conference Board and other professional venues and is a guest lecturer at the University of Virginia's Darden School of Business Executive MBA program.

Additional SHRM-Published Books

The ACE Advantage:
How Smart Companies Unleash
Talent for Optimal Performance
William A. Schiemann

The Chief HR Officer:
Defining the New Role of
Human Resource Leaders
Edited by Patrick M. Wright,
John W. Boudreau, David A. Pace,
Elizabeth "Libby" Sartain,
Paul McKinnon, and
Richard L. Antoine

Employee Surveys That Work:
Improving Design, Use, and
Organizational Impact
Alec Levenson

Got a Solution? HR Approaches
to 5 Common and Persistent
Business Problems
Dale J. Dwyer and Sheri A. Caldwell

Hidden Drivers of Success:
Leveraging Employee Insights
for Strategic Advantage
William A. Schiemann,
Jerry H. Seibert, and Brian S. Morgan

HR's Greatest Challenge:
Driving the C-Suite to Improve
Employee Engagement and
Retention
Richard P. Finnegan

Investing in What Matters:
Linking Employees to Business
Outcomes
Scott P. Mondore and
Shane S. Douthitt

Point Counterpoint:
New Perspectives on
People & Strategy
Edited by Anna Tavis,
Richard Vosburgh, and Ed Gubman